D0846207

Randomized Controlled Trials

POCKET GUIDES TO
SOCIAL WORK RESEARCH METHODS

Series Editor
Tony Tripodi, DSW
Professor Emeritus, Ohio State University

Determining Sample Size
Balancing Power, Precision, and Practicality
Patrick Dattalo

Preparing Research Articles
Bruce A. Thyer

Systematic Reviews and Meta-Analysis
Julia H. Littell, Jacqueline Corcoran, and Vijayan Pillai

Historical Research
Elizabeth Ann Danto

Confirmatory Factor Analysis
Donna Harrington

Randomized Controlled Trials
Design and Implementation for
Community-Based Psychosocial Interventions
Phyllis Solomon, Mary M. Cavanaugh, and Jeffrey Draine

Needs Assessment
David Royse, Michele Staton-Tindall, Karen Badger,
and J. Matthew Webster

PHYLLIS SOLOMON
MARY M. CAVANAUGH
JEFFREY DRAINE

Randomized Controlled Trials

Design and Implementation for Community-Based Psychosocial Interventions

OXFORD
UNIVERSITY PRESS
2009

OXFORD
UNIVERSITY PRESS

Oxford University Press, Inc., publishes works that further
Oxford University's objective of excellence
in research, scholarship, and education.

Oxford   New York
Auckland   Cape Town   Dar es Salaam   Hong Kong   Karachi
Kuala Lumpur   Madrid   Melbourne   Mexico City   Nairobi
New Delhi   Shanghai   Taipei   Toronto

With offices in
Argentina   Austria   Brazil   Chile   Czech Republic   France   Greece
Guatemala   Hungary   Italy   Japan   Poland   Portugal   Singapore
South Korea   Switzerland   Thailand   Turkey   Ukraine   Vietnam

Copyright © 2009 by Oxford University Press, Inc.

Published by Oxford University Press, Inc.
198 Madison Avenue, New York, New York 10016
www.oup.com

Oxford is a registered trademark of Oxford University Press

All rights reserved. No part of this publication may be reproduced,
stored in a retrieval system, or transmitted, in any form or by any means,
electronic, mechanical, photocopying, recording, or otherwise,
without the prior permission of Oxford University Press.

Library of Congress Cataloging-in-Publication Data

Solomon, Phyllis L.
Randomized controlled trials : design and implementation for
community-based psychosocial interventions / Phyllis Solomon, Mary M.
Cavanaugh, and Jeffrey Draine.
p. cm.
Includes bibliographical references and index.
ISBN 978-0-19-533319-0
1. Social service—Research—Methodology. 2. Evidence-based social work.
I. Cavanaugh, Mary M. II. Draine, Jeffrey. III. Title.
HV11.S5946 2009
361.3'20724—dc22
2008029903

1 3 5 7 9 8 6 4 2
Printed in the United States of America
on acid-free paper

Acknowledgments

We would like to thank Mallory Jensen for her wonderful competence, responsiveness, and kind understanding. In addition, we want to acknowledge Leslie Alexander and Francis Barchi for their helpful comments on previous drafts of the manuscript. We express our gratitude to the reviewers for their thoughtful comments that served to strengthen the final manuscript. We also want to thank the agency administrators and providers who, in their pursuit of more effective interventions for the clients they so selflessly serve, allowed "outsiders" in to conduct our research. But most importantly, we thank the participants of our research interventions. Without these partners and collaborators sharing our belief in the value of sound research and its connection to more effective services, the many RCTs in which we have been involved would not have been a reality. We are forever indebted to far too many to name each individually, but without their support and participation we would not have learned the challenges and pitfalls of these deceptively simple designs and therefore, this book would not have been possible.

Contents

Acknowledgments   v

1   Introduction   3

2   Ethical Considerations of Randomized Controlled Trials   19

3   Planning the Randomized Controlled Trial   45

4   Developing Conceptual Foundations for Randomized
    Controlled Trials   80

5   Designing the Randomized Controlled Trial   96

6   Implementing the Randomized Controlled Trial   138

7   Generalizing Randomized Controlled Trial Outcomes
    to Community Practice Settings   170

Glossary   187

References   195

Index   209

1

Introduction

The primary objection raised about a randomized controlled trial (RCT) is related to its central feature: the randomness of the decision regarding an individual's treatment regimen. To some, it seems unethical to base such an important decision on mere chance. In order to examine this objection, it may prove useful to begin with a careful examination into the randomness and rationality in our health and social service systems as they typically operate. Adults and children experiencing acute challenges such as abuse, health crises, mental illness, substance abuse, and incarceration, to name a few, are sorted into varying categories, caseloads, service systems, and need levels, and placed onto wait lists every day throughout a wide variety of settings. How rational are these sorting mechanisms? How often is this sorting accomplished using validated procedures or reliable assessments? How often is this sorting driven by the relatively random availability of an open placement or funding streams? Quite often, the services individuals receive and/or are eligible for are dependent on layers of random decisions far beyond the control of individual practitioners, case managers, or program directors.

Moving the above discussion a step further, it would be useful to inquire to what extent these sorting mechanisms are *not* random, and rather are based on biases and choices that are more unfair than chance?

To what extent are behavioral health and social services offered to one individual and not another, dependent on differences in access to resources or disparities in care systems? How about personality traits? One parent whose child has a grave health need may be more persistent than another, who is more resigned to fate, but both children may be equally in need. In each of these circumstances, treatment access is sorted by social processes that are not principally a rational assessment of individual need.

At yet another level, what is the evidence base for interventions commonly offered to middle- and upper-class individuals versus those typically offered to poor and vulnerable populations? Socially and economically privileged individuals benefit from greater access to health and mental health care resting on a strong evidence base supported and generated by powerful economic interests. What is the extent of such an evidence base for interventions in prisons or homeless shelters? Social work provides some of this evidence base, but it does not compare with the evidence base offered at the other end of the economic ladder. Once we examine the extant randomness in service delivery systems, as well as the inherent disparities that shape these systems, the objection to the use of random assignment may be alleviated. In light of these considerations, would social workers *not* do more random assignment-based research? Why not control randomness to provide greater access to those who need care and improve the quality of care offered? Well-executed RCTs are a key weapon in social work's arsenal for accomplishing social justice for individuals who are particularly vulnerable to disparities in access to more effective service interventions.

RCTs encompass far more than merely providing an answer to the question: Does the intervention work? The full potential of RCTs lies deeper than what may be portrayed by the "X's" and "O's" in a research textbook. For example, the validity of a proposed study hinges on an in-depth rationale for "X" (the intervention proposed), which is grounded in theory or the clinical literature to which the RCT potentially contributes. The proposed alternative to which the intervention is compared generates a policy question for the allocation of resources. The process of how the intervention is accessed, delivered, and received is often steeped in questions relating to culture, social norms, and professional power relationships. Thus, the effectiveness of a single intervention idea encompasses nearly all aspects of professional social work practice. The promise of an RCT lies not only in answering the immediate effectiveness question, but in the extent to which it has the capacity to delve more deeply into the problem or question being investigated. This text encompasses both the method and the promise of RCTs to build social work practice through community-based psychosocial interventions. This chapter establishes the definition of an RCT within the context of real-world service delivery systems.

What Is a Randomized Controlled Trial?

An RCT is a true experiment whereby study participants are assigned by chance, following a pretest, to at least two conditions: An experimental treatment or intervention, and a control intervention used for purposes of comparison on outcomes. Research study participants are offered their assigned intervention and are expected to participate in their assigned treatments to at least a nominal extent, and then are compared by group on some outcome(s) theoretically linked to the interventions being compared. Random assignment enables direct, causal attribution of any difference in outcome to the intervention assignment and systematically rules out rival, plausible explanations other than the experimental versus control condition, thus enabling cause and effect determinations.

All the elements noted in the previous paragraph can be described with far more complexity. For example, there may be more than two alternative treatment or intervention conditions. The units for random assignment do not necessarily have to be people, but could be schools, families, or providers. Although study participants may be offered treatments or interventions, they may choose not to follow-up with their assigned intervention. From the service provider's perspective, the interventions may not be delivered as anticipated or expected. These problems develop into issues regarding the implementation of the intervention, which are discussed in more detail later in this text. This book is intended to provide an accessible guide to the basic method of RCTs and provides a framework regarding how to think through the various methodological issues in planning, designing, and implementing an RCT for settings in which social workers typically provide services.

Randomized Controlled Trials: A Gold Standard

RCTs are considered to be the "gold standard" of evidence when determining the effectiveness of policy and practice interventions. With increasing emphasis on providing empirical evidence on the effectiveness of psychosocial interventions by various professions, the use of RCTs is growing in prominence. Intervention science currently revolves around the RCT as *the* standard of evidence. Development studies are geared toward building a case for an intervention, its conceptualization, and its effectiveness in producing an outcome. These elements provide the structural basis for RCTs. Randomized trials establish evidence for particular populations and practice contexts. Although other research strategies may have some capacity to build an evidence base for an intervention, RCTs provide the strongest supporting evidence universally recognized to establish effectiveness.

Focus on Community-based Psychosocial Intervention

Social workers are diverse practitioners, covering health, educational, child welfare, behavioral health, and a myriad of other fields. In most of these fields, social workers contribute a unique point of view—and do so alongside other professional service providers who also engage in many of the same interventions. These interventions are sometimes considered clinical in nature, aiming for improvement in individual-level outcomes. In most situations, the changes sought are not merely in individual thinking, but also behaviorally based and embedded within the social context.

To provide a framework for social workers who may be planning the design of an RCT, this text focuses on interventions at the individual level. The term, *community-based psychosocial interventions*, will be utilized throughout the text. This term reflects the impact of the environmental context, in which interventions are embedded, on clients and providers and the transactions between both systems. A psychosocial intervention is any service, program, educational curriculum, or workshop whose goal is to produce positive outcomes for individuals confronted with social and/or behavioral issues and challenges. The term *psychosocial interventions* is not unique to the social work context but may also be used by other disciplines, including in a recent text that focuses on psychological interventions, particularly behavioral ones (Nezu & Nezu, 2008). However, community-based psychosocial interventions, in which social workers tend to be involved, are conducted in agency and social settings with individuals with multiple problems, as opposed to being confined to private, clinical offices or academic clinics. These factors increase the complexity of community-based, psychosocial RCTs, as the boundaries surrounding them may be more abstract and focus on processes and/or broader community settings. Social workers are not the only profession to engage in such psychosocial interventions: nursing, community psychologists, and rehabilitation counselors, to name a few, do so as well. Furthermore, the selection of this term also recognizes the fact that many of these interventions are not delivered solely by social workers but also by respected colleagues from other professions such as psychology, nursing, occupational therapy, and public health.

Distinctions from Program Evaluation

Textbooks on research methods and some government regulations make a distinction between *research* and *program evaluation*. Whereas research is the use of the scientific method to generate generalizable scientific knowledge, program evaluation is considered less generalizable and more focused on a practice or policy questions within a particular place or context. Randomized trials are used for both research and evaluation purposes, but within an evaluation context, the term used to describe an RCT is an *experimental study*, commonly referred to as a *randomized field trial* (rather than an RCT). Evaluation studies address particular program or policy issues; for example, whether an agency should continue to financially support a particular program intervention, or to evaluate an evidenced-based practice that the policy arena is currently promoting by comparing the outcomes of two interventions. Such questions still require a theoretical justification for comparing the two interventions on specified outcomes. Therefore, the findings of program evaluations also contribute to theoretical knowledge development and have broader application than solely the context in which the study was conducted. Consequently, the distinction between evaluations using experimental designs and RCTs may be a matter of semantics and historical considerations. RCTs were developed for medical treatments, such as testing new drugs, whereas evaluation research has been employed for testing the effectiveness of human service programs and policies. An examination of the evaluation research literature may prove useful to those designing community-based psychosocial RCTs within the social work practice context, as evaluation studies more closely resemble the interventions examined by social workers than those used in medicine and (often) psychology.

Distinctions from Quasi-experimental and Pre-experimental Designs

The primary distinction between RCTs and quasi- and pre-experimental designs is that the latter designs lack random assignment of participants to the different conditions, thus they are lacking the research design element that forges the gold standard of evidence. Quasi-experimental designs rely on comparisons among naturally occurring groups rather than chance assignment. For example, a research study in which providers asked their clients with a severe mental illness to sign a release-of-information form specifically developed for family members employed a quasi-experimental design, in which providers in one agency were trained to use the release form and providers in another were not (Marshall & Solomon, 2004). However, there was a possibility that providers, clients, and their family members differed by agency, especially in ways that may have interacted with the intervention. Therefore, any post-intervention differences between the two groups could have been the result of these differences and interactions, rather than solely the result of the experimental intervention itself.

Pre-experimental designs are weaker in terms of attributing change to an intervention as they involve only one group for which outcomes are often assessed before and after the intervention. Since the design does not control for other factors that could have occurred concurrently with the experimental intervention, it is difficult to attribute any differences between the pre- and post-intervention measures to the experimental intervention. A number of factors could have produced differences found in the outcomes, including the passage of time, repeated testing of outcome measures, and participating in other services, to name a few possibilities. Although change in the dependent variable can be determined, one cannot conclude that the intervention was the cause of the change. In contrast to RCTs, pre-experimental study designs are not adequate for causal attribution of change due to an intervention. However, findings from these studies can support the theoretical and empirical plausibility of change linked to an intervention, thus offering supporting evidence for conducting an RCT.

Efficacy versus Effectiveness Studies

Both efficacy and effectiveness studies employ randomized designs and are intended to establish a causal relationship between a novel or innovative intervention and its targeted outcomes. The major distinction between these two types of studies is that efficacy studies take place under ideal or optimum circumstances, whereas effectiveness studies occur in what is sometimes referred to as "real-world" settings. Thus, when compared to each other, efficacy studies have greater internal validity, and effectiveness studies have greater external validity. However, neither have extensive generalizability, as their primary emphasis is on controlling any potential threats to internal validity.

Ideal circumstances refer to the fact that efficacy studies are conducted in highly controlled research environments, such as the outpatient clinics of academic institutions with well-trained, experienced staff delivering a standardized intervention to restricted samples. These procedures are intended to control for environmental, provider, and participant effects on study outcomes. Standardized interventions are highly structured, with well-specified protocols guiding how the intervention is to be delivered. Efficacy study interventions are usually accompanied by a treatment manual that all providers who deliver the experimental intervention are trained to follow. In psychotherapy efficacy studies, treatment sessions may be audio- or videotaped to allow for even stronger assessment of treatment fidelity (that is, adherence to the standard treatment manual). Furthermore, in efficacy studies, sample eligibility is restricted to individuals who are "pure cases" by limiting the sample to a specific diagnostic group and eliminating any potential participants with other disorders or comorbidities, or eliminating those who have ever received any form of psychotherapy or similar intervention in the past for the presenting problem. These restrictive eligibility criteria reduce the possibility of study participant characteristics influencing the outcomes of the RCT.

Efficacy trials attempt to control for potential effects from the providers and the recipients of the interventions by blinding one or both as to whether a particular participant is receiving the experimental intervention or not. *Blinding* is an attempt to eliminate the reactions of either the provider and/or participants to the assigned treatment that may influence the outcomes, such as believing that an experimental drug is beneficial. All of these restrictions are also employed to increase the internal validity of the RCT and, therefore, to increase confidence that an intended outcome effect is solely the result of the experimental intervention and not due to participant, provider, or setting factors (Hohmann, 1999).

For effectiveness studies, criteria similar to those associated with efficacy studies are relaxed in order to achieve greater sample representativeness to treatment populations. The results may have greater relevance to the service settings in which the intervention is likely to be delivered. Effectiveness studies take place in community settings with sample eligibility criteria broadened to include participants who are representative of these settings. Similarly, intervention providers frequently are staff employed in the particular setting. Blinding generally is not feasible, as it is not possible to keep hidden to both providers and participants the nature of the services participants are receiving. As the prominence of effectiveness studies have grown, methodological rigor has been enhanced by attempting to incorporate more of the criteria from efficacy studies, resulting in a constant interplay between strong internal validity and generalizability (external validity).

Increasing Access to Child Mental Health Services for Urban Children and Their Caregivers

Objectives: The RCT was designed to evaluate the effects of two engagement interventions on the initial attendance and ongoing retention in child mental health services. Numerous studies documented the barriers to accessing child mental health services in urban areas. A prior study demonstrated that highly focused telephone intake procedures produced an increase in first clinic appointments as well as service attendance subsequent to intake for adolescent substance abusers and their families.

Methods: Consecutive requests for services at a mental health agency were randomly assigned to three conditions: telephone intervention alone ($n = 35$), combined engagement intervention (telephone plus critical engagement procedures in the first interview) ($n = 35$), and usual intake procedure ($n = 39$). One hundred nine children of caregivers who were biological parents or foster care parents were accepted for child mental health services. The telephone intervention was implemented by two master's level clinicians and six master's level social work interns were trained for the intake interview. Both interventions had specified protocols. The research included monitoring 15% of the telephone calls and videotaping 25% of the first interviews to ensure integrity to the interventions, i.e., that the protocols were implemented as designed. Data on first scheduled appointment for study participants were obtained from agency therapists, and the number of sessions attended was extracted from the agency's computerized tracking system.

Results: Both the telephone (86%) and combined telephone and first interview (89%) resulted in increased attendance at the initial intake appointments, as compared to the usual intake procedure (44%). Only the combined intervention resulted in increased continued use of services during the 18-week follow-up period.

Intervention manuals are more frequently used to support standardization of effectiveness RCTs. Effectiveness intervention manuals are more likely guidelines than the step-by-step procedures that are utilized in efficacy studies. Experimental interventions tend to consist of complex services, such as case management, as opposed to highly structured interventions. Services such as case management are not highly specified treatments delivered in an office for a set amount of time, but rather delivered in the community, with all the vagaries that entails, for an indeterminate amount of time.

"What works best" types of questions of importance to social work and other psychosocial service professions best fit the effectiveness RCT paradigm rather than the efficacy RCT. McKay and colleagues' (1998) RCT study of innovative engagement approaches for low-income, "hard-to-reach" youth who received services in an inner-city outpatient child mental health clinic emerged from her social work practice observations of the extraordinarily high rates (approaching 50%) of "no-shows" (McKay, 2006). McKay designed an intervention to be delivered by social work interns. The intervention was based on her previous experience with a delinquency prevention trial in which a similar service population faced comparable barriers to service engagement. Barriers to the use of mental health or other social services are not an uncommon problem for social workers who frequently work with low-income clients of color.

The Importance of RCTs to Evidence-based Practice

Growing interest in evidence-based practice (EBP) by the social work profession is reflected in emerging journals devoted to the topic, such as *Journal of Evidence-based Social Work*, with its first issue appearing in 2004; recent books entitled *Foundations of Evidence-based Social Work Practice* (Roberts & Yeager, 2006); *Using Evidence in Social Work Practice: Behavioral Perspectives* (Briggs & Rzepnicki, 2004); and, *Evidence-based Practice and Social Work: International Research and Policy Perspectives* (Bilson, 2004). For example, *Research on Social Work Practice* has allocated extensive space to invited articles discussing the issue of EBP. Schools of social work are reorienting their curriculums to teach the necessary skills for using EBPs (Howard, McMillen, & Pollio, 2003) or developing institutes on evidence-based social work (Regehr, Stern, & Shlonsky, 2007). This movement is not unique to social work, but has pervaded every practice discipline since its initiation in evidence-based medicine more than a decade ago (Chambless & Ollendick, 2001; Sackett, Richardson, Rosenberg, & Haynes, 1997).

The EBP movement has precipitated an increasing interest in RCTs, as they provide the foundation of EBPs. A rather explicit and well-accepted hierarchy of research designs and methods are considered to have the ability to produce credible evidence for designating a practice as an EBP or empirically supported treatment or intervention (Chambless & Ollendick, 2001; Fox, Martin, & Green, 2007; McNeece & Thyer, 2004; USDHHS, 2006). At the top of the hierarchy are systematic reviews/meta-analyses, which generally include RCTs for determining an EBP (Table 1.1). *Systematic reviews* are designed to answer a specified research question, based

Table 1.1. Hierarchy of Evidence for Establishing Evidence-based Practices

Strength of available evidence increases in this direction		Number of available studies increases in this direction
	Systematic reviews/meta-analyses, frequently include RCTs	
	Multiple RCTs, some by independent investigators	
	Narrative reviews; may include RCTs	
	Single RCTs, multiple quasi-experimental studies, large scale multi-site single group designs	
	Quasi-experimental	
	Case-control and cohort studies	
	Single group pre-/post-test studies; pre-experimental group studies	
	Pilot and case studies	
	Correlational and descriptive studies	
	Qualitative studies: Observational, interviews, focus groups	

on a planned strategy for identifying specific studies to be included in the review, in order to synthesize the results from a multiplicity of research studies. Related to systematic reviews are *meta-analyses*, which are statistical procedures used to synthesize the findings from the corpus of research studies included in the review. Littell, Corcoran, and Pillai (2008) assert that systematic reviews do not require the inclusion of RCTs. However, generally, reviews designed to answer questions of effectiveness do include RCTs, and may in some cases restrict their inclusion criteria to RCTs. The strength of the available evidence increases as you move up the hierarchy, while the quantity of research available increases at the bottom levels of the hierarchy.

Social work has not reached the point of designating specific social work practices as EBPs. One of the primary reasons is the shortage of available evidence, particularly empirical evidence from RCTs. The caution here is that if social work researchers do not engage in RCT investigations, EBPs may not be developed for social work interventions, nor will social workers contribute to the broader arena of EBPs for psychosocial interventions. The challenge faced in social work is the complexity inherent in the conducting, designing, and implementing of RCTs for its practice interventions. Practice decisions in social work, as in other community-based professions, is grounded in the particular circumstances that confront the practitioner. It is not a simple application of population-level evidence to individuals (Groopman, 2007). This does not mean that the meta-analytic or population-level evidence is irrelevant. It means that there is a greater complexity as to how the process is applied than a simple step-by-step algorithm. Evidence needs to be examined in-depth for the differences in populations, in intervention strategy, and in service context to understand what variations in these factors mean regarding effectiveness. Therefore, a true evidence base provides sufficient evidence at all levels of a hierarchy, with enough randomized trial evidence to develop this knowledge base. This text is therefore designed to exemplify the importance of RCTs and to increase the comfort and skill level of social workers in designing and conducting RCTs.

Purpose and Utility of RCTs for Social Work

Social workers have a professional and ethical responsibility to ensure that the services they provide to their clients are effective. The National Association of Social Workers (NASW) code of ethics clearly specifies the need for social workers to evaluate their own practices. Furthermore, social work values require that service provision to clients produce the greatest benefits and the least risk of harm. The highest level of confidence in the value of practice interventions can be attained through subjecting those interventions to the most rigorous of research designs, which are considered by many to be RCTs. Strong, empirical evidence guides effective social work practice. With the increasing emphasis on EBPs and the growing acceptance of a hierarchy of scientific evidence, the use of RCTs to determine the effectiveness of social work interventions is becoming an inevitable requirement in the field of practice. In addition, social work has an obligation to determine EBPs for the profession and, in order to achieve this requirement, RCTs are considered to be the present gold standard. Funders of services in the current resource-restricted environment are increasingly requiring evidence of service effectiveness. Consequently, to ensure that social work interventions are not diminished, eliminated, or replaced in this environment, RCTs for social work interventions, which are implemented through an understanding of social work practice, are an ethical and practice imperative.

The rationale for conducting RCTs in social work need not be merely a defensive stance. It is also an opportunity for social workers to develop a body of RCT research that accurately reflects social work practice and values. Yet, competence in the design and execution of RCTs has not been adequately developed in social work. By utilizing more rigorous research methods, social work practitioners can claim their role as experts regarding service interventions, and social work researchers can contribute even further to the evaluation of program effectiveness. A residual benefit to these foci may be an increase in the status of the profession-at-large.

Overview of the Text

One of the major goals of this text is to provide an accessible and practical guide to planning, designing, and implementing RCTs. Scientific rigor in conducting RCTs takes into consideration the complex realities of community settings, sample availability, and relevant ethical issues. Carefully considering these multiple, intersecting factors assures the proper implementation of RCT studies. An RCT that cannot successfully be executed cannot provide empirical evidence for making accurate and ethical practice decisions.

A word of caution: RCTs are not appropriate for every effectiveness question of importance to social work. In some cases, the use of randomization may not be ethical and/or feasible. For example, developing an ethically innovative service alternative with incarcerated or involuntarily hospitalized populations may prove difficult without extensive cooperation and commitment from a variety of governmental entities—at times, possibly requiring a legislative act. Such arrangements are necessary in order to assure community safety and thus reduce risk for study participants and others. In other cases, the researcher may be able to randomly assign participants, but clients may not be motivated to participate in the experimental intervention. Kaufman and colleagues' (1994) RCT of a mental health self-help group unraveled to the point at which the study was aborted, as only 17% of those assigned to join the self-help group complied. To further complicate the study, 17% of the control participants chose to attend the self-help group.

Alternate research designs may be more appropriate when addressing some effectiveness questions. The examples mentioned earlier exemplify issues raised by those who are concerned with an overreliance on RCTs for establishing EBPs. It is not within the scope of this text to debate the role of RCTs in EBP, but to advocate that social workers become familiar with RCT methodology, so that it may be a viable option to utilize in investigating appropriate questions under feasible circumstances.

This text focuses on community-based psychosocial service interventions for three primary reasons: (1) practice-level RCTs are more feasible to design and implement than macro-level interventions and thus are the most frequently implemented, (2) RCTs have been commonly used with service interventions; consequently, this enables drawing on them for illustrative purposes, and (3) the authors' knowledge and experience with RCTs is derived from service interventions. However, as McNeece and Thyer (2004) noted, RCTs are valuable and possible in the macro practice arena and have been undertaken there, although social workers have rarely conducted such studies. This text will also be of interest to those planning to design macro-level interventions that address policy, community, and administrative practice questions. It may prove useful, however, to also refer to texts such as *Randomized Experiments for Planning and Evaluation* (Boruch, 1997).

The following chapters offer practical guidance in designing, planning, and conducting RCTs for social work practice, using case examples to illustrate the material presented. For example, Chapter 2, Ethical Considerations of RCTs, deals with ethical issues relevant to RCTs that must be considered as one begins to plan and design the RCT. The ethics of RCT are inextricably intertwined in the design of the study; therefore, the discussion on ethics provides the foundation for the remaining chapters. Specifically, the researcher needs to consider the ethical appropriateness of the services the control condition will receive, because social work populations often are vulnerable and the use of a no-service placebo, as may be utilized in many efficacy RCTs, may not be ethical in social work. Further, since RCTs have a service component, in which agency staff frequently is asked to deliver the experimental intervention, the researcher must assess whether agency providers are also research participants and what this means for human subject protection procedures.

Chapter 3, Planning the RCT, deals with preliminary studies and tasks that are essential prerequisites in designing an RCT. The first step is clarifying the research question underlying the RCT. This incorporates an understanding of the current state of empirical evidence in the specific practice areas and the logical next steps in developing interventions for an RCT. After these tasks are addressed, the researcher moves to the pragmatic aspects of implementing the RCT in the practice environment. For instance, the researcher needs to assess whether sufficient, available, and eligible participants are willing and motivated to attend the experimental service intervention. Ultimately, a decision needs to be made whether to move forward with an RCT or not.

After completing the preliminary work of obtaining requisite data and information, such as conducting pilot studies and developing intervention manuals, Chapters 4 and 5 provide specific information for designing an RCT. These chapters present the various aspects of the research study, ranging from the theoretical framework (Chapter 4) through research design, data collection, and statistical analysis (Chapter 5).

Chapter 6, Implementing the RCT, presents the necessary procedures to be considered for actually implementing the RCT in the service environment. This chapter emphasizes the importance of utilizing qualitative methods in assessing the implementation process. This discussion includes suggested procedures for monitoring the experimental intervention to ensure that the proposed experimental service was implemented as intended. Finally, Chapter 7, Considerations for Generalizing RCTs, discusses the tendency to neglect external validity in RCTs. It examines procedures for achieving external validity as well as how external validity relates to EBP.

The authors' hope that this text provides an accessible guide to understanding the basic principles and tenets of an RCT and how, if properly planned, designed, and executed, it can inform and strengthen both service delivery and research in social work. RCTs need not remain primarily within the purview of the biomedical sciences. For scientific, investigative purposes, RCTs can be readily applied to the myriad of current social work practice interventions. Indeed, some factors inherent in their design may make the choice of utilizing an RCT more challenging than other available research methods; however, the weight of the scientific evidence produced from an RCT is well worth the effort.

For Further Reading

Littell, J., Corcoran, J., & Pillai, V. (2008). *Systematic review and meta-analysis.* New York: Oxford University Press.

Nezu, A., & Nezu, C. (2008). *Evidence-based outcome research.* New York: Oxford University Press.

Roberts, A., & Yeager, K. (Eds.). (2006). *Foundations of evidence-based social work practice.* New York: Oxford University Press.

2

Ethical Considerations of Randomized Controlled Trials

Careful attention to ethical concerns strengthens the overall design of a research study. The development of well-executed randomized controlled trials (RCTs) as ethical research protocols involves thoughtful consideration of such factors as the most appropriate questions to ask, who may be ethically eligible to be randomized, what the most ethical comparisons are to make, and how and when individuals should be randomized. Research ethics (i.e., the proper conduct of scientific investigation based on cultural norms as well as professional ethics) must be taken into account in planning and designing an RCT. The intention of this chapter is not to review general research ethics, but rather to examine ethical issues particularly relevant to RCTs. The ethical justification for RCTs from the perspectives of both social work ethics and research ethics will be explored, as well as the overall ethical issues of designing RCTs.

Ethical Concerns Regarding Randomization

Social work professional ethics endorse the conduct of RCTs to test the effectiveness of social work practice interventions. The National

Association of Social Work (NASW) Code of Ethics states that "social workers should base practice on recognized knowledge, including empirically based knowledge, relevant to social work and social work ethics." However, a wide array of social work practices has not been subjected to rigorous scientific evaluation. Consequently, many generally accepted social work practices are considered, by scientific standards, to have little to no empirical support, and therefore require further research before they can be accepted as effective. The ethical imperative is that RCTs *should* be conducted on social work practices in order to provide estimates of their effectiveness.

It is not uncommon for social work practitioners to raise ethical concerns about the process of randomization, which may result in denying service to highly vulnerable clients. Indeed, from a practice perspective, an RCTs use of a control condition in which service may be withheld from clients who are in need of and otherwise eligible for the service seems ethically unjustifiable. In studies that do not utilize a "no-service" control condition, social work professionals may resist random assignment if they perceive that clients are being denied a more beneficial service intervention. This problem is compounded when innovative, experimental service interventions with limited evidence are promoted as effective solutions to challenging issues and problems or difficult client populations. Declarations of program effectiveness are about four times more likely to occur when based on poorly designed studies than on adequate ones (Boruch, 1997). However, when the advertising hype for an experimental intervention is based on weak or limited evidence (as, for example, when evidence is based on only one RCT with low power that was conducted by the developer of the intervention), ethical justification for an RCT can easily be argued. Social work researchers have a professional obligation to thoroughly review the relevant empirical evidence for an experimental intervention, in order to situate any overstated claims or beliefs regarding the benefits of an intervention in line with the existing empirical evidence. Otherwise, the RCT would not be justified. Often, practitioners believe that researchers are conducting a study to prove what is already known. To some extent this may be true—but there are also gaps in the knowledge base regarding what we know about service effectiveness. The social work researcher has an ethical responsibility to satisfactorily demonstrate that an RCT is warranted and to make a convincing argument that no client is being denied a known beneficial service. Without adequate scientific evidence, claims of benefits cannot be made.

An ethically acceptable justification for randomization to an experimental service arm of an RCT is that, despite a lack of adequate evidence for the effectiveness of the intervention being studied, there is sufficient reason to believe that the experimental intervention has the potential to benefit the target population. If there were no uncertainty with regard to the effectiveness of the experimental intervention, then there would be no scientific reason for the study itself and, consequently, no ethical basis for randomization. However, an ethical justification for randomization may be made in circumstances in which an intervention of proven effectiveness is to be employed in a novel situation or for a different client population than is implied by the evidence. In such a case, the defense for randomization is that further research will improve the external validity of the evidence for the intervention. In efficacy trials, the absence of evidence for the experimental intervention ethically justifies randomization; this is referred to as the *principle of equipoise.* This principle dictates that randomization is only ethically justified when a substantial degree of uncertainty exists as to which of the treatments would benefit the study participants the most. In such instances, if there is any ambiguity with regard to the evidence, including the evidence for particular populations or circumstances, then randomization to generate this evidence is ethically justified.

Ethical Principles That Frame Randomized Controlled Trials: Respect, Beneficence, and Justice

The Belmont Report (National Commission for the Protection of Human Subjects [NCPHS], 1979), which was the product of The National Commission for the Protection of Human Subjects of Biomedical and Behavioral Research, recognized three ethical principles: respect, beneficence, and justice. *Respect* refers to the right of autonomous individuals to make their own decisions regarding their treatment and participation in research, and to the obligations of clinicians and researchers to protect those individuals with diminished autonomy. *Beneficence* has to do with maximizing possible benefits while minimizing any potential risks of harm. Lastly, the principle of *justice* requires that those undertaking the burden of risk ought to receive the benefits derived from the research being conducted (that is, those participating in the research must be representative of the group that will benefit from possible positive outcomes). For example, Nazi concentration camp experiments and the Tuskegee syphilis study used vulnerable individuals as research participants, and these samples were not representative of the population that was intended to accrue the potential benefits from the study results.

The aforementioned ethical principles do permit RCTs to be conducted, assuming that the experimental and control conditions are appropriately justified. Those individuals with autonomous capacity can self-determine whether or not to participate in RCTs, although, in so doing, they are giving up some autonomy in the selection of a service, because they will be randomly assigned. Temporarily giving up autonomy is not unique to RCTs, but occurs in other medical care situations (Piantadosi, 1997) and in social services as well. As reviewed previously, clients seeking services from an agency are rarely in a position to freely choose their service, but rather the providers make choices based on assessment and available service.

An RCT also "makes it possible to avoid the harm that may result from the application of previously accepted routine practices that on closer investigation turn out to be dangerous" (NCPHS/Belmont Report, 1979). One notorious example of this situation was the evaluation of the Scared Straight intervention, in which prison inmates with life sentences were employed to scream at juveniles about the "degradation, fear, and violent homosexual behavior" that they commonly encounter in prison in order to turn these juvenile delinquents away from crime. Although about 30 states had implemented the program, later evaluation found that fewer control condition participants had committed delinquent acts than actual program participants (Gibbs, 1991, p. 10). Psychosocial RCTs comply more readily with the justice principle than do efficacy RCTs that restrict the sample to pure cases, because an effectiveness study tries to ensure that the sample is representative of the population for which that service is intended.

The Integration of Practice and Research Ethics

The Belmont Report (1979) notes that the distinction between practice and research is frequently blurred, as both often occur concomitantly. This is inherently the case with RCTs, as one is investigating the effectiveness of practice. *Practice*, as defined in this report, "refers to interventions that are designed solely to enhance the well-being of an individual patient or client and that have a reasonable expectation of success" (NCPHS/ Belmont Report, 1979, p. 3). In contrast, *research* is designated as activities "designed to test a hypothesis, permit conclusions to be drawn, and thereby to develop or contribute to generalizable knowledge" (NCPHS/ Belmont Report, 1979, p. 3). Thus, in the context of RCTs, the service interventions being offered are considered research, not just practice to enhance the well-being or alleviate the suffering of specific individuals being served.

One of the ethical dilemmas that surround an RCT is that of the artificial distinction between research and practice. Practice interventions are implemented in the best interest of the client, whereas activities in the realm of research are undertaken for the collective or societal good or for acquiring knowledge (Piantadosi, 1997). However, as is well-articulated by the NASW Code of Ethics, great overlap exists between practice and research, as practitioners have a responsibility to engage in research. Certainly, in conducting RCTs, social workers are engaged in both domains, and their activities are nearly inseparable. Nonetheless, the ethics of both research and practice generally are not in conflict. If a research participant is deteriorating under the experimental intervention, then both for the protection of other human subjects participating in research and in the best clinical interest of that participant, she should be removed from that condition. Research ethics mandate that study participants be removed from the experimental intervention if they are deteriorating more than those in the control condition. Similarly, if participation in the experimental intervention is likely to be detrimental to certain participants, they should be excluded from the research for clinical reasons. For example, Witte and colleagues (2004) excluded severe domestic abuse victims from their human immunodeficiency virus (HIV)/sexually transmitted infection (STI) prevention RCT, since evidence indicates that participation in couples-based interventions by such victims may well increase their risk of injury. In Solomon and Draine's (1996, 1997) family education RCT, family members whose relative with a severe psychiatric disorder was diagnosed less than six months prior to recruitment were excluded on the clinical assumption that being in a group with families who had been dealing with the illness for many years would be discouraging and possibly harmful.

In an RCT, both practice and research ethics of the profession are of paramount importance. Thus, the ethics of research may, in some cases, be in conflict with scientific design issues, but less so with the ethics of practice. For example, adhering to ethical responsibilities may, in some instances, result in biased study attrition; however, it is a necessary price to pay to keep participants safe from harm.

Ethics of Using Scientifically Untested Service Interventions

The ethics of research clearly demand, at a minimum, that theoretical justification exists for expecting that the proposed experimental intervention is likely to produce effective outcomes. This minimal expectation can be supported by evidence from prior related research that indicates potential effectiveness. Ethically, the case needs to be made that the experimental service intervention is at least as effective as generally acceptable social work practice and that any potential risks are either no greater than those of the acceptable service, or are reasonably accepted by the informed client in anticipation of the proposed benefit. Both research ethics and social work professional values dictate that social work RCTs do not cause harm to participants (even if they voluntarily consent) or to others with whom participants may come into contact. Risks are to be assessed not only for study participants, but also for the safety of others and the community-at-large.

Ethical Concerns in Selecting a Control Condition

Social work practitioners are frequently concerned that vulnerable clients will be denied needed services. Although efficacy RCTs frequently employ a no-service control or placebo condition, such conditions are definitely an ethical concern for at-risk or distressed clients who may want and need services. For this reason, conventionally offered social work services (sometimes referred to as treatment as usual [TAU] or standard of care) are commonly used as the basis of comparison in effectiveness RCTs. Furthermore, it is questionable whether a comparison to receiving no services is an ethically valid test of an experimental service intervention. Such comparisons raise the concern of whether it is an ethically valid question to test if the experimental service is more effective than no service or than standard social work practice. The former question seems to be scientifically and ethically indefensible in many social work situations.

One author [PS] is reminded of an instance when she was on a grant review panel where a reviewer likened the no-service control condition to comparing a car with gas to one with no gas; if the outcome was merely to see if the car ran, there was no contest. The reviewer declared that this RCT was unethical as it was not a worthy test of the innovative intervention. The investigator has an obligation to justify a no-service condition in an RCT both ethically and scientifically. In some circumstances, a no-service condition may be justified by the virtual absence of any services in the setting in which the intervention will be tested. Thus, the experimental service will be compared as an alternative to what is conventionally offered. This may raise other ethical issues, as in certain environments, such as a prison, assignment to usual care may reinforce a sense of deprivation.

Some RCTs use a waiting list control in lieu of a no-treatment control. This option may be ethically considered for situations in which clients are willing to wait for treatment until after they complete their research purpose, and they are not likely to deteriorate during the delay (Kazdin, 2003). Using a waiting list control in crisis situations such as those involving persons attempting suicide or victims of abuse will likely place these individuals at further risk and would therefore not be ethically valid. Waiting list controls, however, may be appropriate in situations in which an agency normally has a wait time for receiving services. However, if the wait time is increased for control condition clients, but research participants assigned to the experimental intervention receive services faster than under usual circumstances, then potential participants need to be informed of this situation and only those agreeing should be randomly assigned (Kazdin, 2003).

A waiting list control is also not ethically problematic under circumstances in which the participant would not receive the services at all, except as a participant in the RCT. In such a case, the research is not denying a service to which the individual would otherwise be entitled. For example, in an RCT of family education interventions for family members with relatives with a severe mental illness, a waiting list was an ethically acceptable control condition because, without the study, the family members were not likely to receive any service, given their absence in community mental health agencies. However, since families were clearly expressing a need for the service by freely consenting to a possible waiting list condition, investigators felt that the service ought to be offered to the waiting list families upon their termination of study involvement (Solomon, Draine, Mannion, & Miesel, 1996, 1997). Ethically, the researchers believed that even if the experimental intervention was not found to be effective, it was unlikely to cause any harm.

In some situations, such as prevention intervention RCTs in which the target population is not service recipients, but research volunteers, then a dummy or inert intervention (one that is expected to provide no benefit, but serves to control for attention) can be an ethically viable alternative. Under such circumstances, a waiting list or no-service intervention is also ethical, particularly if all participants could not be accommodated at one time. Similarly, participants in prevention interventions would not normally receive prevention educational service and therefore are not at risk of being deprived of a service or delayed in receiving a service to which they normally would be entitled.

Informed Consent

Consent Forms

As in any research, a study participant must be informed of the purpose of the research, the expected duration of participation, the nature of the procedures to be undertaken, identification of which procedures are experimental, the potential risks and benefits of participation, the right to refuse or withdraw from the proposed study, and the availability of alternative treatments or therapies (Part 46, Protection of Human Subjects, Code of Federal Regulations). The procedural aspects of the consent form for RCTs need to specify clearly that participants will be randomly assigned either to an experimental or a control condition. Random assignment must be explained in the consent form in such a way that it can be understood by a nonscientist. Usually, it is stated that the specific intervention (i.e., the experimental or control condition) a study participant receives will be determined by chance, such as flipping a coin. Also, the probability of receiving either intervention needs to be specified, such as indicating that a participant has an equal chance of receiving either of the interventions. However, if an RCT's allocation is not done equally, then a participant must be informed of the chance of receiving a particular intervention—for example, "a one out of three chance of receiving intervention x." Research has found that individuals grasp the meaning of natural frequencies better than probabilities (Hoffrage, Lindsey, Herwig, & Gigenzer, 2000).

Potential study participants should be informed of what is involved in the experimental and control interventions. Each of the study interventions must be described in sufficient detail, such that the potential participant can make an informed decision of whether or not to participate in the RCT. This information includes describing all experimental interventions (if more than one), as well as the control condition. Merely saying that they will receive standard social work service or service as usual is not helpful to a potential participant in making a decision. If it is a placebo service, inert service, no service, or a waiting list, the condition has to be identified and clearly described. In addition, measurement procedures, including specifying the content of interviews or questionnaires and at what points they will be administered, need to be discussed.

As part of the consent process, and in the consent form itself, individuals must be advised of the potential risks and benefits regarding their participation in the RCT. Risks may include physical or psychological harm or discomfort, as well as damage from a breach of confidentiality. Researchers must articulate the areas of risk at the same time that they identify steps that will be taken to protect study participants from these risks occurring. Researchers must be equally clear about the likelihood of no benefits from participation in an RCT. Although some participants will be receiving an intervention that the researcher reasonably believes will have a benefit, it would be dishonest to promise any benefits to participants from the intervention, given that the justification for the study is that the effectiveness of the intervention is not certain.

Clients may feel that their standard treatment or service is contingent upon their participation in the study, particularly when the proposed RCT will take place within service environments or concurrent with service delivery. In such settings, the consent process (and the consent form itself) must underscore the right of individuals to refuse to participate in the RCT, or to withdraw from the RCT once enrolled, without fear of jeopardizing their access to such treatments and services.

Excerpts from two consent forms for RCTs are provided as illustrative examples of how to inform potential participants of assignment to service conditions and how to describe each of these service conditions. Note that all study information is presented in a form appropriate to the educational level, culture, and age of the potential participants, and every effort is made to ensure that the content can be easily understood by the target population.

Excerpts From a Consent Form for Family Education and Family Consultation: A Randomized Trial

Purpose of the Research. You have been asked to participate in a research project that has the following purpose and length of involvement: Its purpose is to examine whether educational programs that provide information to family members about their relative's psychiatric illness and how to cope with it are helpful. You have been asked to work with this research project for about nine months to help answer this question because you have a relative who has been diagnosed with a mental illness.

Procedure and Duration. You have been told the following things will be done: You will be assigned by chance, like flipping a coin, to one of two types of educational programs that will start soon after you are assigned to a program or to wait nine months and then choose one or both educational programs. One educational program will be ten weekly group sessions of two hours that will provide information about mental illness and strategies for dealing with your relative's psychiatric illness. The other group participants will be family members who also have a psychiatrically disabled relative. The other educational program to which you may be assigned by chance is at least six hours with a mental health expert who will provide you information and help in coping with your relative's psychiatric illness based on your needs. At least four hours will be in person and up to 15 hours may be either in person or by telephone, depending on your choice. These will take place over the course of three months. You may also be assigned by chance to waiting nine months before you can choose to receive either one or both these programs. If you are assigned to wait nine months, you will be given a directory of mental health resources in your area. You understand that you have an equal chance of receiving any one of these.

Regardless of which program you receive, you will be asked to answer a number of questions about the impact that your relative's illness has had upon your life and how you deal with your relative. If you are assigned to enter either the group or individual educational program, you will be asked these questions at entrance and termination of the program and again six months later. If you are assigned to wait nine months at the time you will be assigned to waiting for these educational programs, then at three and nine months from assignment you will be asked these questions; and you will be paid $20 for each of these three interviews.

Excerpts From a Consent Form for an RCT Regarding Case Management for Jailed Homeless Adults with Severe Mental Illness

Purpose of the Research. You are being asked to participate in a research project that has the following purpose and length of involvement: to see whether a team approach to case management is more helpful than the usual case management service that you would receive or a referral to a community mental health service. Normally, you are referred to either an intensive case manager or to a community mental health agency whereas we are offering a team approach to case management as well. We are asking you to work with us for about a year and a half to help answer this question.

Procedures and Duration. You have been told the following things will be done: You will be assigned to either one of two kinds of case management services or a referral to the community mental health agency by a process that is like flipping a coin. You will be assigned to a service purely by chance. All three kinds of services are thought to be helpful for people with your type of problem. (1) One kind of service is provided by a team in which a primary worker will teach you skills where you live, work, shop, etc., will assist you in getting to needed services; and a psychiatrist will provide medication management. (2) The other kind of case management service will be the usual type given to people after they leave the jail, in which an individual will assist you in getting needed services and making referrals for outpatient counseling, medication management, and/or day treatment. (3) Or, you may receive a referral to a community mental health agency, which may include outpatient counseling, medication management, day treatment, and/or case management. You have a 1 in 4 chance of receiving either the team case management or the usual case management and a 2 in 4 chance of receiving a referral to a community mental health agency. No matter what kind of service you receive, we will be asking you to answer a number of questions about your life, your mental state, your history of drugs and alcohol use, and the type of offenses that you previously committed for which you were arrested and/or convicted. We will also need to get information about you and your problems from your treatment records. We will ask you questions and look at your records when you start the project, during the project, and up to six months after the project. We will pay you $20 for answering these questions at program entrance, at 6 and 12 months in the program, and at 6 month follow-up. If you are in the community team service, the team will work with you for one year. After that time, you will receive the usual service to help you.

When to Gain Consent from Participants

Consent from RCT participants must be obtained *before* random assignment to the study condition occurs. If the researcher assigns a participant prior to consent, there may be biased attrition to one particular condition rather than balanced attrition to all conditions. Those not wanting the control condition will likely not consent to the study, thereby reducing the condition enrollment and resulting in an imbalanced design. In addition, if prospective participants are assigned to a specific condition of the RCT in advance of seeking their consent, this approach requires two separate consent processes and forms. In such a situation, each prospective participant would be asked to agree to a specific role in the study as a recipient of the experimental intervention or as a recipient of the control. It is dishonest to inform potential study participants that they may be assigned to either study condition based on a chance procedure, when they have, in fact, already been assigned.

Use of Multiple Consent Forms

It is important to note that, in some RCTs, more than one category of consent forms may be necessary. For example, in instances requiring prescreening to determine eligibility, the participation of minors (for whom surrogate decision making is necessary) or information about intervention processes or impact as perceived by others who are not study participants, may necessitate more than one consent form. Should a researcher need to engage in an initial screening procedure to determine if potential participants meet the eligibility requirements for entrance into the study, then there may be a need for a separate consent form. If potential participants will be asked questions of a sensitive nature, or an investigator will extract private information from medical or other records to ascertain their eligibility for inclusion in the RCT, a consent form for this purpose is necessary. If eligibility questions are not of a sensitive nature (e.g., asking a potential participant if she is interested in increasing her participation in community activities), eligibility consent is probably not warranted. The consent form for eligibility assessment also needs to indicate that, if the participant is determined to have certain problems or characteristics, they may be asked to participate in a study of services for people like themselves (that is, participate in the RCT).

Also, RCTs that are conducted with children, such as McKay and colleagues' RCT (1998) discussed in the previous chapter, require a signed consent form from the parent or guardian of the child (which may be an agency in some instances), as well as an assent form (i.e., a child's agreement to participate in the study). Under the current U.S. Federal regulations, children are protected as a vulnerable population in research. As a result, additional standards for consent apply if the study is assessed to be at greater than minimal risk (i.e., the probability and magnitude of harm or discomfort anticipated in the research is not greater than ordinarily encountered in daily life or during the performance of routine physical or psychological examinations). Also, state laws concerning the emancipation of minors and the capacity of minors to consent to treatment may apply to research.

If RCTs also conduct process assessments of the intervention, in which views about the service are sought from individuals other than the primary study participants, an additional consent for this purpose may be required. These assessments may include interviewing family members of clients about their perceptions regarding the benefits of the intervention for their relative. This situation would require additional consent from family members, even though they are not primary recipients of the experimental intervention.

Consenting Providers of Randomized Controlled Trials

Providers of the service intervention in the RCT may also be considered participants in the research in those instances when they are asked to engage in activities that are not part of their normal job requirements of service provision. If, for example, the investigator is collecting specific data from providers that are not part of their usual practice documentation, or if providers are being asked about their opinions and attitudes, then they should be duly informed about the research study and what will be asked of them, as well as asked for their voluntary consent to participate. The same practice is required when providers are asked to be active study participants. For example, in an RCT in which the first author is involved, case managers were randomly assigned to deliver or not to deliver the experimental intervention to all of their consenting clients. Consequently, the nature of the service that their clients received was determined by their random assignment. Case managers were asked to agree to participate in the study and thus to be randomly assigned. The clients of these experimental case managers still were required to consent to receive the prevention intervention. Therefore, not all clients assigned to experimental case managers received the services, only those voluntarily consenting. Those clients served by control case managers were not eligible to receive the service during the study. However, they were required to voluntarily agree to participate in the study, which consisted of their responding to periodic interviews, and to sign a written consent form. Should the intervention be effective, control condition case managers will be trained in the intervention, and they can then provide the intervention to former control participants. Furthermore, if a research investigator interviews RCT intervention providers about their views regarding the challenges of implementing the experimental intervention, obtaining consent from the providers is ethically necessary, as their private views are being sought.

In many community-based psychosocial RCTs, agencies agree to have their staff engage in the RCT (i.e., deliver the experimental service), but agency administrators cannot agree on behalf of their staff to provide private information for purposes of research. If, on the other hand, agency staff is being asked to deliver an innovative service that their agency administration has agreed to provide in place of the usual service, and no data about their personal thoughts are being collected only data pertaining to their clients, then voluntary consent from the provider would likely not be required.

In other instances, providers of the experimental intervention are specifically hired for the RCT. On the basis of a job description that includes such job responsibilities as the completion of specific data collection forms about the actual delivery of the service, consent would not usually be required. However, once service providers are asked for private information about themselves or their personal thoughts, their rights as a research participant must be protected, and consent needs to be obtained. Also, in those instances requiring informed consent from providers, these providers need to be informed that their participation or nonparticipation in the study will not impact their employment status or performance evaluations.

When Providers of Randomized Controlled Trials Are Research Personnel

Providers of service interventions in RCTs may, at times, be considered as research personnel. Consequently, for federally funded RCTs, providers may be required to complete the human subject protection training required of research personnel and obtain certification that they have completed this training before delivering the RCT service intervention. If providers are employed by an academic institution, the service intervention falls within purview of the Institutional Review Board (IRB) assurance of the university, and they can take the university/college's human subject training courses.

However, in federally funded RCTs, in which the service interventions are being delivered at a community agency by service providers employed by the agency, this host agency may be asked to apply for a Federal-wide Assurance (FWA) from the federal Office for Human Research Protections (OHRP). The agency can apply for the assurance online under the Department of Health and Human Services. This application can be completed by mail as well, but the online process may be timelier. The host agency must indicate why the FWA is being sought. Once being awarded an FWA number, the host agency can either use an existing committee or develop a new committee to oversee the protection of study participants, or they can use the IRB of the academic institution that is primarily responsible for the RCT. This latter option is preferable, as the research study must be monitored by the sponsoring IRB.

Once the host agency receives an FWA approval number, the agency can complete an IRB authorization agreement with the researchers' institution and come under the auspice of the IRB of the researchers' institution for the specific RCT. The FWA is valid for three years, and additional agreements for other RCTs can be developed between the agency and the IRB of the academic institution under the same FWA. However, if the agency and academic institution have a contractual agreement for collaborative research that already delineates the responsibilities of each party for the protection of subjects, then the agency does not need to seek an FWA, because the host agency is covered by the academic institution's IRB.

Protecting Confidentiality of Study Participants

In psychosocial RCTs, the major risks are violations of confidentiality (i.e., protecting a study participant's personal information by ensuring under what specific circumstances this information will be disclosed). Issues of confidentiality must not be treated lightly, as if they were "research risk lite," because violation of confidentiality can impact the course of a participant's life. For example, in a current trial of an HIV prevention educational intervention for adults with severe mental illness and substance abuse disorders, in which the first author is involved, one of the research assistants inadvertently left her backpack with identifiable data from a participant interview on the bus when returning to the office. A protocol was immediately put in place for the handling of field data. Although this event may be a seemingly innocuous oversight by the research worker, consider that these data included an individual's name with other private information about that individual, left on public transit that possibly travels through the participant's own neighborhood. Treating such an incident as a serious risk to confidentiality, even if classified as minimal risk, is an ethical obligation.

Protecting Health and Behavioral Health Information

When an RCT requires the collection of health or behavioral health information from health records, in certain circumstances, adherence to the Health Insurance Portability and Accountability Act (HIPAA) will be required. To meet HIPAA requirements, informed consent must include specific descriptions of what type of information will be shared and among what organizations. At times, separate forms are required for HIPAA as part of the consent procedure. For example, an HIV prevention education RCT, with which the first author is involved, required additional HIPAA forms as part of the consent process. Protected health information includes identifying information for individuals (e.g., actual date of birth, as well as information about health conditions and treatments that are being collected from the records of institutions covered by HIPAA). In some ways, HIPAA increases the complexity of the consent process by requiring additional steps. However, in other ways, the process is eased through federally standardized procedures that are accepted across institutions. HIPAA does not apply to data collected from outside the United States, unless it is processed or maintained at a covered entity within the United States.

Certificates of Confidentiality

A number of social work target populations, particularly criminal offenders and substance abusers, engage in illegal activities. In order not to jeopardize participants' willingness to share their private information with researchers, certificates of confidentiality were developed to protect sensitive information that is revealed in the course of conducting research. These certificates are issued by the National Institutes of Health to protect identifiable research data from forced release to other parties, regardless of whether the research is funded by the federal government. These certificates allow researchers to refuse the release of information about the identification of participants, even under court subpoena, in any federal, state, or local, civil, criminal, administrative, legislative, or other proceedings, with a few exceptions. However, these certificates do not take precedent over the requirements that social workers report instances of child abuse, nor do they absolve researchers from taking appropriate action in situations in which there is a reason to believe that research participants may harm themselves or someone else. In addition, investigators cannot resist a demand for information from the IRB or personnel of the U.S. government when that information is to be used to audit or evaluate federally funded projects. Potential study participants need to be informed of these circumstances.

Coercion and Participant Payments

In effectiveness RCTs, payments are commonly offered as an incentive for participating in the research procedures of the study, but usually not for participation in the intervention. There are instances when incentive payments may be part of the intervention. For example, funds may be provided for travel costs to the intervention, which may enhance attendance among low-income participants who may not otherwise be able to attend services. The amount of an incentive payment needs to be enough to serve as an incentive, but not be of such a magnitude as to be coercive. Payments should not entice potential participants to agree to participate in the RCT against their better judgment or their initial desire. If the incentive seems excessive, it may appear/be that participation in the study was due largely, if not solely, because of the compensation amount.

Ethical concerns regarding cash payments to individuals who may engage in substance abuse are often raised as a concern by providers. In place of cash payments, gift cards for restaurants or stores are often regarded as less of a concern, although these may well be sold for cash. With those who have representative payees, agencies and/or providers may require the incentive payment to be placed in the participant's account. As one provider noted, "I have to deal with the repercussions of the incentive if he uses it to purchase drugs." To test concerns regarding amount and type of incentive payments to clients who are in drug abuse treatment, Festinger and colleagues (2005) conducted an RCT of payments of $10, $40, or $70 in cash or gift certificates for attending a six-month research follow-up assessment. They found that neither the amount of cash nor the type of incentive had a significant effect on new rates of drug use or perceptions regarding coercion. However, higher payments and cash payments did result in increased rates of follow-up. The researchers concluded that higher payments may be more cost-effective as the intensity of follow-up efforts is reduced, and that there may be an ethical obligation to pay cash, since the higher payments assure greater validity of the data while not increasing risk of harm. It is important to note that providers assuming a harmful outcome for cash payment to study participants is regarded, by some, as a paternalistic stance and antithetical to the ethical principle of respect for study participants.

Responsibilities at Termination of Randomized Controlled Trials

Both research and practice ethics permeate the RCT during the intervention phase of the study, but practice ethics remain in place at the termination of the intervention as well. Given that RCTs have a set timeframe for the duration of the service intervention, providers need to work with clients on termination issues well in advance of the defined completion of the research intervention, for both ethical and practice reasons. Many social work clients have chronic and long-term problems that will likely not be resolved with a short-term intervention, even if the intervention is determined to be effective. Consequently, providers participating in an RCT, who are serving participants with continuing problems, have a professional responsibility to make provisions for uninterrupted service at the conclusion of the intervention. RCT providers need to make appropriate referrals and provide assistance in connecting participants to the new service, and ensure that they are accepted for services and can access them in a timely manner. In an RCT for adults with severe mental illness leaving jail (Solomon & Draine, 1995), participants were not easily accepted as clients by community mental health agencies, even though the agencies were required to serve these clients. It took extensive effort on the part of the experimental intervention providers to make appropriate arrangements once experimental participants completed the intervention.

Diversity of Sample Selection

For purposes of both the ethics of social work practice and research ethics, the sample of a community-based psychosocial RCT must be representative of the target population regarding issues of diversity such as ethnicity, race, orientation, class, and gender, unless it is scientifically justifiable to limit the sample in terms of specified characteristics. However, a number of barriers have been documented regarding the recruitment of minorities into RCTs, including past research abuses, the most notorious of these being the Tuskegee Syphilis experiment (Witte et al., 2004). It is appropriate, at times, for a gender-specific intervention to be limited to the target population for whom it was designed. But it is difficult to make ethically and scientifically defensible arguments for restricting a social work intervention by race and ethnicity, even though it may require concerted effort to recruit a more diverse group of participants who are representative of the target population.

Data Safety and Monitoring

In June 1998, the National Institutes of Health (NIH) issued a policy regarding a system for "the appropriate oversight and monitoring of the conduct of clinical trials to ensure the safety of participants and the validity and integrity of the data for NIH-supported and conducted trials." Initially, these regulations were applicable only to biomedical trials, most commonly, drug trials. This policy now includes psychological and behavioral treatments, as well as psychosocial service RCTs.

Procedures for monitoring require an oversight committee—a data safety and monitoring board (DSMB)—with members who have expertise "in all scientific disciplines needed to interpret the data and ensure patient safety," including biostatisticians, bioethicists, and clinicians knowledgeable about the disease and treatment, but not otherwise associated with the trial (i.e., project personnel cannot be included; NIH, June 10, 1998). The level of monitoring must be commensurate with potential risks. Given the nature of psychosocial RCTs, DSMBs usually comprise three or four members who meet quarterly either in person or via telephone conference call. These members are provided with summary material on the status of the RCT, the collection and management of data, and subject recruitment and retention. They are also advised of any adverse events (i.e., any untoward or undesirable event experienced by a research participant), whether the event was expected or related to the participant's involvement with the research study. This oversight monitoring is part of the ongoing examination of the basic research question of the study: the effectiveness of innovative or new interventions. If an experimental service intervention seems to be consistently showing a less desirable effect than hypothesized, or less desirable than the control condition, the investigators may consider stopping the trial.

Approval from Institutional Review Boards and Agency Research Committees

Researchers affiliated with academic institutions are required to submit protocols as well as recruitment letters and advertisements regarding the RCT to their IRB for approval. But, since community-based psychosocial RCTs are frequently conducted in community agencies, these studies may be required to be submitted to other IRBs and to agency research committees. For example, RCTs conducted in health and mental health agencies in the city of Philadelphia are required to seek approval from the city's health department IRB, as well as the IRB of the host academic institution of the research study. Community agencies usually do not have an IRB per se, but rely upon a research committee or some other committee that reviews research to be conducted at the agency. Often, these committees are concerned not only with human subject protection, but also with the extent to which the research may interfere with the operations of the agency, as well as with the policy implications of the research for the agency itself.

Special Consideration for Internet Randomized Controlled Trials

RCTs can be conducted entirely over the Internet. The same ethical principles apply, but they must be considered in interaction with the technology. One aspect of the Internet, as with telephone conversations, is that consent can be implied by continued engagement in the communication, and refusal is as simple as hanging up or signing off a Web page. In the case of RCTs, one must be certain that the individual understands into what Web page they are entering. Internet randomized trials may include testing of different modes of Internet support, psychosocial treatments, or educational interventions. For example, a researcher at the University of Pennsylvania is currently completing an RCT of Internet peer support for people with mental illness. An individual may encounter a promotion of this study on any number of Web sites across the United States that target individuals with mental illness. If someone believes she is eligible, she can follow a link to an e-mail address for more information. Once the project is contacted, the individual is screened for eligibility by the research team. Consent forms for this study are handled by postal mail, but in some studies consent is completed through the Internet.

The randomized conditions for the study include access to support through a Web site bulletin board, support through a listserv, and a no-service control condition. The content of the bulletin boards and the listserv are not monitored as part of the research. Internet studies may be monitored or unmonitored. However, the postings may be analyzed as part of the research. An ethical concern here is the extent to which participants understand that their support conversations may become content for research analyses. To manage this risk, a number of options are available for masking identity on the Internet, but not all may be available to everyone, and not every participant will be savvy in the use of these options.

Although entries from participants may not be routinely monitored, the research investigators may become aware that a study participant may be at risk of harming herself. Such a situation has occurred with the above-mentioned Internet study on a few occasions. In one case, a new research specialist familiarizing herself with the study was reviewing recent entries to the bulletin board and came across an entry that was of concern. The participant talked about cutting herself, which is not unexpected behavior, given the population. However, the research coordinator for the RCT contacted the participant and followed the prescribed protocol in place at the research center to assess the risk of suicide. It was

Case Example: Consent Form Content for
Internet RCTs Procedures

You may be removed from the Listserv or Bulletin Board if you send notes to others that are harmful, threatening, or damaging in any way. The Listserv and Bulletin Board are only available to people enrolled in this study. If assigned to the Control Condition, you are being asked to refrain from using Internet support groups for a period of twelve months.

Regardless of which group you are assigned, you will be asked to refrain from participating in any other Internet support groups for the duration of this study. However, if you are experiencing a crisis, you may pursue any means of online or face-to-face support that is available to you . . . .

We will also be analyzing the content of all messages that are sent on the Listserv and posted on the Bulletin Board in order to gain a better understanding of the types of communications that occur. Any publications or presentations that include direct quotes from the Listserv or Bulletin Board will not include any information that identify you. . . .

Risks. If assigned to the Experimental Condition Listserv, there is a risk that you may receive a high volume of e-mails, and that the content of these e-mails may potentially include information that may be upsetting. If assigned to the Experimental Condition Bulletin Board, there is a chance that you will open a message that could include information that may be upsetting. . . . Your risk will be lessened if you reserve sending personal information to others, including your full name, address, and phone number. You may also find the Listserv or the Bulletin Board communications to be unhelpful or upsetting. You can limit this by not reading the postings or withdrawing from the Listserv or the Bulletin Board at any point just by contacting the research team.

There is a remote possibility that your individual computer and e-mail settings (e.g., Web browser, spam filters, e-mail program, etc.) will limit our ability to consistently mask your individual e-mail address. Your risk will be lessened as a result of our restricting the list to only those people involved in this study and by your option to reserve sending personal information to others, including your full name, address, and phone number. For example, we strongly advise you to disable your signature setting when sending e-mails to listserv.

Cost and Financial Risks. You are responsible for any costs associated with accessing your e-mail in order to participate on the Listserv or Bulletin Board (i.e., computer costs, Internet access costs). The researchers will not reimburse you for these costs.

(*continued*)

> **Confidentiality.** No one from the University of Pennsylvania School of Medicine is routinely monitoring the content of the Internet communications. If it comes to our attention, based on your Listserv messages, Bulletin Board messages, or other communications, that you have plans to harm yourself or others, we may be required to take certain actions (e.g., contact local authorities, family members) that will involve the loss of confidentiality.

determined that the participant was not suicidal and did not have a plan to commit suicide. In another situation, another study participant contacted the researchers about postings by another participant regarding death and wanting to die. This incident resulted in trying to personally contact the participant by telephone and e-mail to ensure that the participant was all right. Being unable to reach the participant, the researchers reviewed recent postings in which she noted that she was going to check herself into a hospital. This situation was brought to the attention of the DSMB, which determined that the participant's collateral contacts (son and therapist) should be contacted. Unsuccessful in reaching either, the researchers left messages for the therapist. Subsequently, the study participant made contact using a new phone number, and the researcher conducted a risk assessment that determined the individual was not at risk and was seeking clinical treatment. The IRB was also notified of these adverse events.

The consent form (shown here) for this study contains specific content related to Internet technology.

Although a good deal of research is being conducted over the Internet, much of it consists of one or two data collection episodes that are easily handled ethically without including any identifying information. However, in the case of RCTs, the need to randomize and follow often-vulnerable individuals through the duration of the interventions raises new risks for the disclosure of sensitive information. Internet technology offers new challenges for assuring protection from these types of risks that are yet to be fully resolved.

Conclusion

Ethical issues are integral to both the practice and research aspects of RCTs. These ethical issues need to be carefully considered when beginning to plan an RCT, and this consideration must continue through to design and implementation. Thought must be given to ethically justifying the experimental intervention and to the selection of an appropriate control condition. The consent process is of special significance when designing an RCT. It involves thoughtful consideration of such areas as the scope of necessary information of which the study participant must be made aware, how such information is made available, when and how consent should occur, whether more than one consent form is required, and if providers must be consented. Procedures for protecting confidential information and consent from potential study participants must also be taken into account.

Because RCTs are specifically investigating practice interventions, professional social work practice ethics provide the framework for the design and implementation of RCTs. Determining whether providers involved with the RCT are research personnel and how that affects the overall study, deciding when participants should be terminated from the study interventions, as well as what the researchers' responsibilities are at study termination are all essential practice and research issues in conducting RCTs. Research and social work practice ethics must take precedence over issues of scientific integrity in the design and implementation of RCTs.

For Further Reading

Beauchamp, T., Childress, J. (2001). *Principles of biomedical ethics.* New York: Oxford University Press.

Kazdin, A. (2003). *Research design in clinical psychology.* Boston, MA: Allyn and Bacon.

Piantadosi, S. (1997). *Clinical trials: Methodological perspective.* New York: John Wiley & Sons, Inc.

3

Planning the Randomized
Controlled Trial

With the recent focus on evidence-based practice (EBP), it may seem to some that the only valued research method is the randomized controlled (or clinical) trial (RCT). This is far from true, even among the most ardent randomized trial intervention researchers (count these authors among those who do not believe that RCTs are the only valued research). The strongest RCTs build upon research conducted both by RCT investigators and other investigators in their field. Initial research defines a need, a social problem, or an emerging gap in clinical services; this research begins to focus interest on an area of intervention. In addition, such research intersects with theoretical work that builds a conceptual foundation for what types of interventions may reliably lead to a change in behavior or social conditions, especially as the interventions apply to the identified problem. Development of a specific model of intervention is built upon this research.

As the research and conceptual literature develop and expand, core ideas about the intervention area emerge. This iterative process develops scientific and theoretical knowledge on which an RCT builds. The RCT provides one context for learning more about an area of social work practice. Furthermore, research offers an opportunity to examine your practice from multiple perspectives, not simply from the perspective of "does it work—or not." Therefore, although this text focuses on RCTs, it presupposes that the RCT typically follows other preliminary research, and, in fact, rests upon the quality of that work.

This chapter discusses the requisite research necessary for designing and conducting a full-scale RCT. Preliminary efforts include assessing and negotiating with possible settings, assessing the likelihood of agency/provider cooperation and level of engagement, gauging the capability of providers in executing the interventions, determining the availability of potential study participants, and tracking the flow of participants in and out of a preliminary (pilot) research study. Other topics include developing recruitment procedures and ways to plan for the engagement and retention of study participants, with a particular emphasis on culturally competent procedures. Consideration is given to the identification, modification, and development of intervention manuals, workbooks, and educational curriculum. Particular attention is focused on planning for the design of the RCT, as well as on the importance of ensuring the feasibility of the RCT through essential pilot work.

Determining Whether to Undertake a Randomized Controlled Trial

The question of whether to conduct an RCT contains several elements. The intervention must be adequately developed, so that researchers can discern clearly into what type of intervention participants will be randomized and who will be randomized. Community-based psychosocial interventions are set within a service context. Defining what is being addressed by the intervention, for whom, and under what context requires conceptual clarity and theoretical insight, based on sound, existing empirical research. Conducting a community-based psychosocial RCT is also a question of finding a policy moment when a field of practice may be ripe for this level of development.

An example of the intersection of policy and research is the introduction of supported employment and supported housing. Several generations of programs for people with psychiatric disabilities focused on complex, laborious interventions that were specifically designed to prepare individuals for work and housing. Recently, ground-breaking randomized trials in employment (Drake, McHugo, Becker, et al., 1996; Drake, McHugo, Bebout, et al., 1999) and housing (Goldfinger, Schutt, Tolomiczenko, et al., 1999; Tsemberis, Gulcur, & Nakae, 2004) have demonstrated that having housing or employment goals as the primary focus may be more effective than a long-term period of preparation for those goals. These RCTs broke new ground by providing rigorous empirical evidence that individuals with mental illness were better served by these seemingly radical intervention approaches. These trials moved the field toward new questions and challenged the perceived wisdom of existing policies. Unresolved questions still exist regarding these interventions; therefore, research is continuing through RCTs and other types of research. Widespread implementation of these interventions has still not occurred. However, RCTs were instrumental in moving these programs forward, arguably achieving a higher quality of life for those with a psychiatric disability.

The driving force behind the plausibility of an RCT is a compelling research question and a substantive experimental intervention/condition. The experimental condition should respond to a relevant policy and/or service design question. For example, what may be more effective than the status quo, and in what ways? For research to be compelling, the experimental intervention needs to be adequately developed to the point at which fidelity can be assessed by manualized standards. The argument for the experimental intervention must be set in comparison to treatment-as-usual (TAU), in a way that is grounded in *equipoise* (a stance in which one genuinely does not know the answer to the research question) and that has the potential to move a field forward, through improving the lives of vulnerable populations or in solving difficult service delivery problems. If a theoretical argument cannot be made for the experimental intervention demonstrating a high probability for effectiveness, then there is no compelling reason for an RCT.

Selecting a Site

Following from a compelling research question, a service context needs to offer a reasonable and ethical opportunity for the trial. Sometimes a researcher starts a planning process for an RCT by collaborating with a setting in which he has a connection, so that the "selection" of a setting may not appear to be an issue. However, even in these cases, a variety of unknowns must be assessed. The investigator needs to assess the motivation of the site for instituting the intervention and for assisting in subject recruitment and maintaining clients in the RCT. The onus of explaining the realities of conducting an RCT is the responsibility of the researcher, who then makes a determination of the willingness and ability of the site to undertake the effort. It is better to decide not to go forward with an RCT in a particular setting than to have to withdraw later after numerous resources have been invested. At the same time, the investigator must be open-minded and collaborative with agency personnel in designing the RCT, as they understand best how their setting operates.

The research setting must have a pipeline of potential clients available (and willing) for services. If the setting's pipeline does not yield sufficient clients to be randomized adequately, questions must be explored as to how that system will adopt an additional intervention with a limited client population.

In addition, the setting must be committed and prepared to support the research intervention, including any medical and legal coverage that may be necessitated by the particular intervention. Providers need to be capable of delivering the interventions. If they are not qualified to execute the interventions, the researcher will have to consider implications regarding hiring of qualified staff. The setting has to be prepared to allocate appropriate space for the interventions; in some instances, separate locations are necessary to ensure no interaction between providers and recipients in the various RCT conditions. Furthermore, investigators must make sure that agencies understand the financial commitment involved in the experimental intervention. Will there be sufficient resources to support the intervention, not only in terms of direct cost, but also considering administrative costs, space, and clinical supervision? If not, where else might one seek financing for the RCT? Are local or state governmental entities willing to invest in the RCT? If the intervention proves to be effective, will the agency or organization have the capacity to sustain the intervention over time (e.g., financially)? In one study by the authors, a consumer case management program was continued beyond the study period because the host agency could mount an effort to build the administrative infrastructure to bill for the intervention service. Other agencies may have the capacity to tap financial resources, as well as have the political capital to assure the continuity of an effective service beyond the RCT. Some funding sources may require such an assessment as part of the criteria for financially supporting the proposed RCT. This requires carefully considering the cost involved in delivering the intervention.

The decision to move forward with designing an RCT is a complex process involving concerns about the state of science, policy, and services in a particular area of expertise, as well as pragmatic and feasibility issues. Resolving these matters will further shape the intervention in interaction with the service context. Before moving forward with the design of the RCT, one must have the necessary commitments from those who have a realistic understanding of what is involved in undertaking an RCT.

Negotiating with Settings

Since many community-based psychosocial RCTs frequently occur within an agency context, which has responsibilities to funding sources, clients, and to the public, this situation requires negotiation at a number of administrative levels. One of the first considerations in negotiating with research settings is determining whether the researcher begins in a service setting with the top administrators or closer to the front-line workers. Frequently, the location of researcher's connections determines where to start. For example, if the researcher knows the Commissioner of the Department of Human Services well enough to ask her out for lunch, then that connection should certainly be kept in mind. If a researcher begins with such a top system administrator, the weight of this administrator's approval for the RCT can be effective in gaining cooperation throughout the entire service system, as this endorsement is an implied directive to cooperate with the researcher (Solomon & Draine, 2006).

However, if the researcher is not careful, this "insider-advantage" can be a double-edged sword that can cause difficulty further down the planning and implementation path. Many service systems have levels of expertise and authority. These levels of authority are both formal and informal. Often, the informal lines of authority are the most helpful— and the most formidable. Although the executive is empowered to hire, fire, begin, and end programs, there is also the authority of the seasoned veteran social worker at the front lines, who can tell you "how things are really done" and, even more to the point, whether the RCT has a chance of being implemented at all. The most likely thing one may be told are the numerous reasons why the RCT is not feasible, and some of those reasons may likely be quite valid—and ones that no one "higher up" was in a position to discern.

In the authors' experience, a far more effective strategy has been to begin the process from the "bottom-up," gaining and building support for the RCT idea up through the ranks of an organization, while respecting the authority of administrators. In actuality, the most feasible approach is the combination of a "top-down/bottom-up" approach. Respect for administrators requires that you seek their permission to become involved with their staff. The best first step is not to go in with "I want to do a randomized trial. Can I do it here?" A more effective first step is, "I have some ideas about studying the most effective ways to serve your client population. But first, I'd like to talk with you about my idea, and then spend some time with your service providers and program directors and find out more about how they do their job." Of course, one can only accomplish this with integrity if one actually intends to include input from the front-line staff in developing the intervention. Any intervention must fit within the service context. In the process of exploring these top- ics with the agency staff, the researcher will gather essential information about who are the most informative and cooperative staff members, the way the services are delivered, the pipeline of clients, and the likely ways an intervention will (or will not) fit into the agency. Thus, designing the RCT and negotiating with the potential host setting is an iterative process that interacts with various service elements.

In working with any agency setting, the researcher must be honest about how the RCT will likely impact the agency. Researchers are often tempted to negotiate with a setting by claiming that "we will do all the work, and you won't have to do anything. You'll hardly know we're here."

This is partially motivated by a sense of guilt for imposing on busy agency staff, who are perceived as already overburdened. The problem with this approach is twofold: (1) It is not accurate. The RCT will impact agency time and resources in ways a researcher is not in a position to understand because the researcher is not aware of all the administrative and service demands of the organization. There will almost certainly be demands on the agency in terms of its internal requirements for record keeping, in medical and legal responsibility and liability, and staff resources. And: (2) It is important to draw the agency in as a collaborative partner, rather than to promise that no burden will be placed on them. Taking a collaborative partner stance, a researcher will gain from the agency an investment in the success of the project, and hopefully, flexibility in making the changes and adjustments as the RCT goes forward that may be needed to assure research rigor, as well as clinically appropriate service provision. This negotiating process is made easier when the funding for the RCT is adequate to cover the experimental service. However, even in cases where relationships are not fostered with the promise of compensation, it is to the benefit of all parties involved to understand the demands that will be made. Therefore, buy-in and honesty about work demands are far more important than promises of little or no impact on day-to-day operations.

The importance of establishing clear expectations also applies to understanding the different roles of the researcher and the agency. The researcher is responsible for the science of the RCT. The agency is assuming medical and legal authority, as well as liability risk for the intervention and to the clients, and thus agency staff has responsibility for the integrity of these services. Consequently, there may be varying expectations that can result in conflict. It is usually helpful to begin the negotiation process with a short concept paper that delineates the scope of the study, the importance of the study, what is being asked of the agency, and what the advantages are for the agency, specifically articulating the benefits in ways that best match the agency's interests/mission. The concept paper should be brief (one or two pages) and in outline form. Eventually, a letter of agreement needs to be negotiated, so that all parties know what is expected of them in terms of both the intervention and the research

Table 3.1. Principles for Working with Providers and Consumers
in Designing and Conducting Intervention Research: "REAL SCORE"

- Respect for providers and consumers
- Establish credibility
- Acknowledge strengths
- Low burden
- Shared ownership—reciprocity
- Collaborative relationship
- Offer incentives—be responsive and appreciative of providers
- Recognize environmental constraints—be flexible
- Ensure trust—be sure providers feel heard

being implemented. A draft agreement documented by memos or e-mails will at least enable the researcher to proceed in designing the RCT. Principles of working with agencies to negotiate, design, and conduct the RCT form the acronym "REAL SCORE" (Table 3.1). If these principles are not adhered to, it is likely that negotiations will fall apart before or during the design of the RCT, or worse yet, in the conduct of the RCT.

Pilot Studies

Conducting pilot studies that are well-conceived with clear aims and objectives will lead to higher-quality RCTs (Lancaster, Dodd, & Williamson, 2004). Generally, external pilot studies are stand-alone pieces of research planned and carried out prior to the design of the RCT, as opposed to internal pilot studies, which are part of the primary RCT (Lancaster, et al., 2004, p. 307). Pilot studies enable the researcher to assess the worthiness, practicality, feasibility, and acceptability of the intervention, recruitment, retention, and data collection procedures. In addition, pilot studies may help to determine what the most appropriate outcome measures are. One of the main reasons for conducting a pilot study is to obtain initial data for calculating the primary/future study's sample size. Although data for estimating sample size is the reason promoted by many researchers and funding sources for pilot work, Kraemer and colleagues

(2006) caution against using the effect size from an inadequately powered pilot study to make decisions for a larger study. However, other researchers and statisticians believe that some data are better than no data. Analyses of data from pilot studies largely use descriptive statistics, as the sample size is usually too small for hypothesis testing (Lancaster, et al., 2004). If hypotheses are tested using pilot data, it should be interpreted with caution. Generally, there is a need for some positive, empirical evidence from pilot work to warrant proceeding with a full-scale RCT. Pilot work is an essential component of specifying those elements of the experimental intervention necessary for developing manuals and fidelity assessments.

Pipeline Assessment of Sample Recruitment

Frequently, investigators of RCTs begin with optimistic estimates of the number of potentially eligible participants and the subsequent number who will likely voluntarily agree to consent. These optimistic estimates often do not consider the reduction in numbers that will come from the interaction of eligibility criteria and the operational details of the referral source. Thus, a problem in achieving a proposed sample size in efficacy trials is a commonly reported downfall in implementation.

Inadequate sample sizes may also result from practitioners' treatment preferences in making referrals and potential participants' decisions to refuse to consent (McDonald, Knight, Campbell, et al., 2006; Rendell & Licht, 2007). McDonald and her associates (2006) found that efficacy trials that conducted a pilot study generally made changes in recruitment strategies, design, inclusion criteria, number of sites, and written trial material. However, these investigators were unable to determine what specific features of the trial resulted in successful recruitment. Another recent review of recruitment plans identified a few effective strategies that appeared promising. Those that are most relevant to effectiveness RCTs were monetary incentives and employing culturally responsive strategies in recruitment and retention (Watson & Torgerson, 2006).

Recruitment problems are not unique to efficacy trials. These problems are endemic to all research using primary data collection. It is therefore important to undertake certain activities prior to designing the RCT in order to address issues of sample availability and recruitment. First, it is essential to be familiar with the recruitment site and to determine where and how potential participants can be recruited. Boruch (1997) refers to this as "scouting research." Spending time in the service environment and interacting with the providers, in order to understand exactly how the setting operates, is key to being able to design a successful recruitment process. Time allocation provides an opportunity for the researcher to observe how clients enter services (that is, complete the intake process; wait for service appointments) and how programs actually function. Depending on the nature of the proposed RCT, this information determines where and how recruitment should be considered.

Specifically, undertaking a pipeline study that "directs attention to how, why, and when individuals may be included in the experiment or excluded, and to the number of individuals who may enter or exit the study at any given point" will be helpful in determining whether the study can feasibly be conducted at the proposed site, or whether other sites need to be considered, or perhaps abandoning the project. Once a site is assessed as feasible, the process of designing how to enroll eligible individuals into the trial begins (Boruch, 1997, p. 88). Most helpful pipeline studies include qualitative observations of the processing of clients into the service program (Boruch, 1997). In addition to spending time observing at the recruitment site, it is useful to conduct initial pilot work, to try to recruit a small number of the target population to determine how many of the potential target population actually meet the study eligibility criteria and how many of those who are eligible are actually willing to enroll in the RCT. Questioning those who refuse as to why they are unwilling to participate offers important information in designing the recruitment process, intervention, and research protocols, as well as site selection. Pilot work can provide some estimate of how large a sample pool is available and willing to participate in the study. Furthermore, it will produce estimates of how much time may be needed to recruit the RCT sample.

What may seem like a large pool from which to draw a sample may in reality not be very large at all in terms of numbers of individuals who are both eligible *and* willing to participate in the research. An excellent example of delineating the size of the target population and the final number of enrollees for an RCT is the human immunodeficiency virus (HIV)/sexually transmitted infections (STI) prevention trial for African American and Latino heterosexual couples undertaken by a team from the Social Intervention Group at Columbia University School of Social Work. For this study, the investigators screened 2,416 women and found only 16% ($N = 388$) who were eligible and just over half of eligible women enrolled with their male partners ($N = 217$) (Witte, El-Bassel, Gilbert, et al., 2004). To recruit such a population is not an easy task, especially given the complexity of the issue being studied and the recruitment of dyads. Part of Witte and colleagues' success can be linked to the research team working in the host setting for a number of years; therefore, having familiarity with the operations of the clinic and its staff. But more to their credit, they employed carefully constructed culturally competent recruitment strategies developed from their initial pilot work.

Developing Culturally Competent Recruitment Strategies

Investigators often justify the use of homogeneous research samples in RCTs to reduce possible confounds and for practical reasons, such as lack of literacy or English language proficiency, as well as the complexity of including individuals with varying cultural backgrounds. However, for community-based psychosocial RCTs, minority populations are often the target populations of interest or certainly a major portion of them. Given the characteristics of community-based RCT samples, there is a need to conduct pilot work to ensure that the final sample, in the larger/ future RCT, is not biased and unrepresentative of the target populations

Four primary recruitment barriers to minority participation in RCTs have been documented: (1) Individual barriers—that is, believing study procedures are invasive, or being fearful of research; (2) research barriers, including being aware of past research abuses; (3) sociocultural barriers, including racial and ethnic discrimination, and suspicions of the intentions of health care and other systems where research is conducted; and

(4) economic barriers, including the ability to access health care or lacking available funds for transportation to/from the research site (Witte et al., 2004). Limited formal evaluations of recruitment strategies have resulted in no empirically supported approaches (Oakley, Wiggins, Turner, et al., 2003). However, based on a recent review of minority RCT recruitment procedures, four strategic targets have been suggested (Swanson & Ward, 1995 as cited in Witte et al., 2004). The Columbia Social Work investigators, mentioned previously, incorporated these suggestions in their recruitment protocol for their RCT. Their approach is an excellent example of a thoughtfully crafted culturally competent recruitment process that resulted in successfully achieving an adequate sample. The development of their recruitment strategy began with qualitative pilot work that included input from individuals who represented potential participants (see Case Example below). This case example has a number of suggested approaches that are relevant to many RCTs that may be conducted by social workers.

Pilot Testing for Retention of Participants

When planning an RCT, investigators commonly pilot recruitment strategies, but frequently neglect piloting for retention of participants (that is, the continuing involvement of participants through the duration of the study; Davis, Broome, & Cox, 2002). In the planning stages of an RCT, procedures for retaining participants in both the service intervention and the outcome data collection need to be developed. Attrition is frequently a challenge in RCTs, as outcomes are collected during the intervention, at termination, and at the various follow-up points. RCTs conducted by social workers are further complicated by the nature of the target populations, who tend to have unstable housing arrangements and/or (for a myriad of complex reasons) involvement in activities that may result in not wanting to be located.

Pilot work regarding the intervention is crucial, involving feedback on the receptivity to the experimental and control intervention. Clients liking the intervention, seeing it as beneficial, and believing that it is the most desirable service are all essential ingredients to treatment retention

Case Example: Recruitment of Minority Women and Their Main Sexual
Partners in an HIV/STI Prevention Trial

To develop a culturally competent recruitment protocol for their HIV/STI
RCT, Witte and colleagues (2004) initially reviewed the relevant literature.
Their search revealed two primary domains in the literature: (1) minority RCT recruitment strategies, and (2) marital and family therapy studies'
couple recruitment strategies.
  The minority recruitment literature yielded four categories of recruitment strategies:

  1. Individual Strategies:
     • Incorporating an understanding of cultural beliefs, practices, and
       lifestyle into promotional materials
     • Offering compensation
     • Providing child care, and transportation
  2. Researcher Strategies:
     • Demonstrating sensitivity to participants' safety concerns
     • Demonstrating usefulness of the project
     • Using ethnically and racially matched recruitment staff
  3. Study Site Strategies:
     • Including site staff in design and procedure development
     • Clearly defining the role of site staff
  4. Community Strategies:
     • Involving community members and organizations in developing
       recruitment procedures and protocols
     • Demonstrating study benefit to the community

Witte and colleagues (2004) report that much of the existing literature on
minority recruitment pertained to African Americans; however, there was
some literature on barriers to the recruitment of Latinos. These barriers
were translated into the following recruitment strategies:

  • Including the importance of strong and traditional family values
    (*familismo*)
  • Demonstrating respect toward male figures (*personismo*), particu-
    larly the role of the father (*machismo*) in family decision making

(*continued*)

- Employing Spanish-speaking research staff
- Using Spanish-language research materials

A review of the marital therapy literature was limited regarding RCT recruitment strategies for couples, but a qualitative study of families of Mexican immigrants offered direction. The strategies suggested were:

- Standard approach, in which one partner is contacted in person and the researcher followed up with both partners by phone
- On-the-spot approach, in which both partners are present at clinic recruitment setting and recruited together
- Co-recruitment strategy, in which a woman is first recruited in person, then asked to approach the topic with her partner
- Brokering strategy, in which a woman is first recruited in person, then she independently recruits her male partner with support from the research team

Given the sensitive nature of the subject matter and the potential to threaten the stability of the subjects' interpersonal relationships, special caution was required regarding protecting partner safety and respecting the confidentiality of the partner enrolled first. Issues of negotiating with couple participants require consideration of gender-based issues of power, control, and dominance in sexual relationships.

Methods
Based on the prior literature, Witte and colleagues (2004) developed a recruitment protocol that ensured the cultural relevance, utility, and safety of the couple recruitment process on three levels: research staff, study site staff, and participant couples. In addition, they conducted pilot work that included focus groups and materials from debriefings with research staff and pilot study participants. This preliminary work also resulted in the following strategies:
Preparing the research staff:

- The most experienced research staff conducted project enrollment.
- Recruiters were full-time positions who became well-known and familiar to community.

(continued)

- Twenty hours of training was given, employing the latest recruitment technology for HIV prevention trials.
- Skill-building approaches, modeling best-practice recruitment technology and role-playing recruitment with representative members of the target population, was used.
- Relationship between project staff and participants was emphasized, demonstrating respect for participants through appropriate attire, body language, etc.
- Weekly research team meetings during the trial provided encouragement, oversight, accountability, and assistance in troubleshooting effective interactions with potential participants.

Although Witte and colleagues (2004) had the advantage of being familiar with the host site, the investigators still conducted site staff preparation:

- At luncheon meetings with site staff, the study was presented and discussed, and site staff was engaged in defining the study process and encouraged to buy-in to the importance of the study.
- Research staff clarified that no additional responsibilities fell to site staff.
- Research staff highlighted benefits to study participants.
- Research staff clarified human subject process regarding safety and confidentiality protections.

(Good & Schuler, 1997). Using pilot testing to improve control conditions have been shown to result in higher retention (Davis, Broome, & Cox, 2002). Also, involving host site providers in the intervention development assists in staff buy-in, which may translate into their encouraging participants to stay involved in the intervention. To prevent biased attrition, emphasis must be given to research tracking strategies employed to retain participants in the data collection efforts (to be discussed in Chapter 6). Unfortunately, what is known regarding recruitment and retention strategies of community-based, in-person studies cannot easily be translated to the new venue of online RCTs (Bull, Lloyd, Rietmeijer, & McFarlane, 2004). Consequently, pilot work in this area is even more imperative.

Defining, Identifying, and Developing Community-based Psychosocial Intervention Manuals

Definition and Use of Manuals

The expectation with RCTs is that the interventions will be delivered in a standardized manner (that is, essentially all providers of the interventions will be engaging in the same processes and practices with each of the subjects). The method for achieving this uniformity and repeatability of the intervention in efficacy RCTs is through the treatment manual. A treatment manual details specifically the experimental treatment and provides careful guidelines for treatment implementation (Carroll & Nuro, 1997; Carroll & Rounsaville, 2008). The treatment manual specifies the intervention, provides standards for evaluating adherence to the intervention, offers guidance for training, provides quality assurance and monitoring standards, facilitates replication, and stimulates dissemination and transfer of effective interventions (Carroll & Rounsaville, 2008). Treatment manuals have become a virtual requirement of all efficacy trials, as they are the means to the operationalization of the independent variable. They are increasingly expected in effectiveness RCTs as well. However, in some instances, the community-based psychosocial interventions may entail services or programs as opposed to psychotherapies. A program manual delineates the core elements and structures of the program, as well as the various roles of the different providers.

Traditionally, treatment manuals describe a single program and often include brief literature reviews, general guidelines for establishing a therapeutic relationship (e.g., tips for working with groups), descriptions of specific techniques and content (sometimes in the form of a curriculum), suggestions for structurally sequencing activities and strategies for dealing with special problems, implementation issues, and termination (Fraser, 2003). Manuals outline specific details regarding the core intervention: the when and how of delivering the intervention, and elements that are not parts of the prescribed treatment intervention (Miklowitz & Hooley, 1998).

Program or practice manuals deal not only with practitioner behaviors, "but also structural aspects of a program (e.g., caseload size and staff qualifications), location of services (e.g., in community settings) and 'behind the scenes' activities (e.g., integration of treatment and rehabilitation)." Bond and colleagues (2000) assert that practice manuals are conceptualized at a more macro level. Many community-based psychosocial interventions are difficult to manualize because they occur in multiple settings, with a diversity of providers and recipients, and involve a range of activities that go beyond one-to-one psychotherapy or counseling (Bond, et al., 2000).

The literature contains guidance on the development of treatment manuals; however, the information is not geared to community-based psychosocial interventions. Adapting the work of Carroll and colleagues (Carroll & Nuro, 1997; Carroll & Rousaville, 2008), the outline below provides a framework for a service or program manual. In some cases, the intervention may have an operation manual, as with an educational curriculum.

1. **Overview and description of the intervention—Service, program, curriculum, and rationale.** Description of approach, theoretical rationale for the intervention; review of the empirical research underpinning and supporting the effectiveness of the intervention.

2. **Conception of the problem or condition.** Forces or factors that led to the development of the condition; research and/or theory indicating factors or processes leading to change or improvement; what is/are hypothesized to be the agent(s) of change; conceptual framework for understanding the problem or condition; procedures for assessing the problem or condition, including any standardized measures.

3. **Defining the target population.** Delineate characteristics and criteria for those whom the intervention is (and is not) designed.

4. **Intervention—Service, program, and curriculum goals.** Specification of primary goals of the interventions; procedures and strategies for determining specific goals for clients.

5. **Contrast to other approaches.** Indications of how the service/ program differs from other similar approaches; specification of approaches for the problem or condition that are most dissimilar to this approach.

6. **Defining and specifying the intervention.** Specify unique and essential elements; specify recommended processes and strategies; which processes and strategies are prohibited and which may be harmful or counterproductive.

7. **Client–provider relationship.** Define role of various providers; delineate importance of provider–client relationship to outcomes; specify strategies to be used in developing desired relationship; specify strategies to address weak relationship.

8. **Format/structure of the intervention.** Specification of structural elements— frequency of meetings of providers, hours of operations of service, staff-to-client ratios; delineate number, types, and qualifications of providers—individual, group, or mixed format(s); if group is open or closed format; length of intervention; frequency and intensity of contact(s); specify content and sequencing of content, as well as degree of flexibility of presentation; specify content for educational sessions, including a mix of didactic material and experiential exercises; delineate any relevant behavioral exercises and homework assignments; may include forms to guide the work of providers and clients and informational handouts. The information for this domain may vary greatly contingent on the nature of the intervention.

9. **Standards of care.** Guidelines and procedures for assessing progress; strategies and procedures for responding to lack of progress or deterioration; procedures for resolving contradictions of progress and problems from perspectives of clients, families, and providers; assessing and responding to crises.

10. **Strategies for dealing with special problems.** Guidelines for dealing with common issues of motivation; missed appointments; relapses; crises; suicidal threats and/or attempts; violent acts. This section will vary according to the nature of the intervention.

11. **Relationship with other formal and informal supports/
    resources**. Relationship and role of natural supports; necessary
    adjunctive services and treatments; referral processes for other
    services, treatments, programs, etc.; procedures for integrating
    and monitoring other needed services; administrative
    arrangements with agency and governmental entities.
12. **Process for managing transitions and terminations.** Criteria
    and guidelines for transitions to other services, treatments,
    programs; procedures for termination and referrals, guidelines
    for working with clients, natural supports, and formal supports
    and resources.
13. **Selection of providers.** Specific educational, training credentials,
    and experience requirements for the various intervention
    provider positions.
14. **Training of providers.** Goals of training; training components
    and approaches to training, including didactic and experiential;
    troubleshooting; booster sessions; training delineated by varying
    positions of providers.
15. **Supervision of providers:** Recommendations for frequency,
    type, goals, and intensity of supervision of various providers;
    strategies and methods for assuring adherence; preventing and
    correcting service or program drift (that is, fidelity monitoring
    forms and approaches to assessing implementation of the
    intended intervention).

Criticisms of Treatment Manuals

Although the use of treatment manuals offers a number of advantages,
including ensuring the standardization of treatment, a number of criticisms have been directed toward them. These criticism include: (a) limited application to clinical practice with diversified populations who
often have complex problems; (b) overemphasis on specific techniques
as opposed to competency of positive relationship formation; (c) a focus
on technique rather than theory; (d) restrictive use of clinical expertise
and judgment; (e) reduction of provider competence due to focus on

adherence to technique; (f) lack of applicability to diverse providers with varied training, experience, and expertise (Carroll & Rousaville, 2008); and (g) designed for highly motivated and single-problem clients (Havik & VandenBos, 1996). Some of these concerns, such as a lack of applicability to settings and populations, are inherent in the design of these manuals, as they were developed for efficacy RCTs, as opposed to community-based psychosocial RCTs. Other criticisms are an advantage for community-based settings, such as being highly focused on technique. With providers who have limited training and/or experience, a well-structured blueprint provides clear directions in an area in which they may not otherwise have knowledge and/or skill. Well-designed manuals allow for flexibility, recognizing that clinical judgment regarding when clients can progress to the next stage is essential to good treatment.

Identifying Treatment Manuals

Given that community-based psychosocial RCTs take place in actual clinical settings or agencies, these existing manuals, if appropriate to the specific intended intervention, will need to be modified in order to fit the environmental context as well as the diversity of the population to be served. Existing manuals are a good starting point, as they offer direction and a model as to how to proceed in developing one. Numerous manuals are available in the psychotherapy arena, particularly for cognitive behavioral interventions.

Treatment manuals can vary extensively. Some are detailed texts on a given approach such as, *Assertive Outreach in Mental Health: A Manual for Practitioners* (Burns & Firn, 2003); however, this work does not offer clear direction for implementing an intervention. A number of federal agencies, such as the National Institute of Drug Abuse (NIDA), National Institute of Alcohol Abuse and Alcoholism (NIAAA), and the Substance Abuse and Mental Health Services Administration (SAMHSA), provide manuals and other types of material that functionally serve as manuals. For example, SAMHSA has issued draft implementation resource kits for six EBPs for adults with severe mental illness. At the beginning of each kit, it is noted that "an implementation resource kit is a set of material-written documents, videotapes, PowerPoint presentations, and a website that support implementation of a particular treatment practice." The materials are written for each of the relevant stakeholder groups: consumers of mental health services, family members and other supporters, practitioners and supervisors, program leaders of mental health programs, and public mental health authorities. The resource kit materials are designed to address three stages of change: engaging and motivating for change (i.e., why do it), developing skills and supports to implement change (i.e., how to do it), and sustaining the change (i.e., how to maintain and extend the gains). These toolkits are directed to structured programs that require input from state and local mental health authorities to administratively and financially support the intervention programs. All of these psychosocial intervention kits are for programs on which a number of effectiveness RCTs have been conducted. They are a useful source for potential RCT interventions adapted for new or specialized populations/settings or for determining how a practice manual or resource kit is devised.

A literature search conducted for conceptualizing and developing the RCT will likely be a source for locating relevant manuals or comparable materials. Furthermore, a number of educational curricula may serve as a starting place for educational-type interventions. Many of these resources may be found by conducting relevant Web searches. Inquiring of experts in a specified topic area may likely produce relevant materials as well.

Adapting Existing Treatment Manuals

Researchers have noted the importance of utilizing ethnography in adapting existing treatment manuals (Wingood & DiClemente, 2008). Currently, a few models offer guidance for accommodating evidence-based interventions (EBIs) to different settings and cultural groups. One such model is ADAPT-ITT, which has eight phases:

1. **Assessment**. Conducting focus groups, elicitation interviews, or needs assessment.
2. **Decision**. Reviewing interventions, deciding on interventions and whether to adopt or adapt

3. **Adaptation**. Using innovative pretesting methods
4. **Production**. A draft of the adapted EBI
5. **Topical experts**. Offering their input
6. **Integration**. Integrating content provided by topical experts
7. **Training**. Training those involved in testing the adapted intervention
8. **Testing**. Conducting pilot testing (Wingood & DiClemente, 2008)

Cavanaugh (2007) developed and tested a brief, targeted, psychoeducational intervention for the prevention of intimate partner violence, employing some of the aspects of Dialectical Behavior Therapy (DBT) for borderline personality disorders and utilizing specific exercises and hand-outs from Linehan's (1993) DBT skills-training manual. In certain instances, the desired intervention may be a combination of more than one intervention manual. In a study in which the first author is currently involved, two validated interventions were combined: RESPECT, a program developed by the Centers for Disease Control (CDC) as an HIV prevention program that utilizes one-on-one counseling to reduce at-risk sexual behavior in a multisite demonstration, and the Community-Based Outreach Model (CBOM), which was designed to reduce the risk of HIV and other blood-borne infections in drug users. Both are highly structured and manualized practices with demonstrated effectiveness.

Preventing AIDS Through Health (PATH) was developed by revising the above-mentioned interventions. PATH was designed to be delivered by case managers to adults with severe mental illness and substance abuse problems. To aid in the delivery of PATH, a set of cards placed on rings were constructed along with an operational manual. The cards contained the content of the intervention and were written at a level of literacy appropriate to its client population, along with illustrations to help clarify the material presented. The intervention is designed so that a case manager reviews the cards with the clients. This structured approach was necessitated by the fact that case managers were not highly trained in this content area. Furthermore, the cards are easy to manipulate and are transportable, which is advantageous, as many of the services are delivered in community settings (e.g., clients' homes, homeless shelters, or residential facilities).

Practice guidelines are broader than manuals, but are also a helpful way to begin planning and developing an intervention for a community-based psychosocial RCT, particularly when designing the intervention from the ground up. Similar to manuals, practice guidelines indicate what services to deliver, to whom, and how. However, guidelines are not as program-specific as manuals and are targeted for services directed at specific populations across a range of services (Bond, et al., 2000). Rosen and Proctor (2003) defined practice guidelines as "a set of systematically compiled and organized statements of empirically tested knowledge and procedures to help practitioners select and implement interventions that are most effective and appropriate for attaining the desired outcomes" (p. 1). Practice guidelines differ in their degree of specificity (Bond et al., 2000). Although numerous guidelines have been developed, most are not specifically designed for social work issues, populations, or practice methods (Howard & Jenson, 2003). However, some may be relevant to social work type interventions.

Focus groups and in-depth interviews with providers, service recipients, supervisors, and administrators may assist in defining the parameters of an intervention. In the development of a Social Enhancement Workbook to increase participation in community resources by adults with severe mental illness, the first author (working with another social worker) conducted process groups with supervisors and providers of case management services in order to receive their input on a draft outline of the workbook. Interestingly, it was discovered that the term "teaching skills" could not be used, as "teaching" was not a Medicaid-reimbursable service. The workbook used terms such as "helping to access resources in the community," as this was a fundable service (and perhaps more descriptive of what was being implemented, anyway). Also, individual input was sought from service recipients who were potential users of the workbook. Suggestions from these sources helped to determine some of the content and structure of the workbook. For example, the workbook was designed with "tips" on the sides of the pages, one side was for supporters and the other was for the users. "Tips" for supporters included: "Be prepared to help the person practice . . ."; and "If you can show the person examples . . . ," etc. Also, a worksheet was included in the booklet, so that clients could do a self-assessment, identify their goals, and develop a plan for achieving their goals.

In the development of their couple HIV prevention intervention, the researchers from Columbia School of Social Work mentioned previously used input from focus groups as a means to developing their intervention (Sormanti, Pereira, El-Bassel, Witte, & Gilbert, 2001). Based on the results of the focus group, the investigators incorporated specific elements into the intervention. For example, they discovered that "both men and women report that poor communication was a critical issue in their relationships and were eager to learn new ways to enhance their communication skills" (Sormanti, et al., 2001, p. 319). In response to this concern, the investigators incorporated the Speaker-Listener Technique, a tested method for improving couples communication. Participants also voiced concerns about condom use interfering with love-making, which resulted in a session being devoted to eroticizing condom use. These examples illustrate how focus groups with potential participants can help to delineate some of the service elements of the intervention that are necessary prerequisites to developing community-based psychosocial intervention manuals.

In addition to focus groups, other, more structured approaches may serve to define and refine an existing program. These approaches are the nominal group process, Delphi method, and concept mapping. These methods are more controlled procedures for obtaining consensus on the specific service elements and processes of a service program. The *Delphi method* is a structured procedure for generating ideas from a group of individuals and, through rounds of controlled feedback, to come to a consensus on the topic (or, in this instance, a service program). This method was employed "to identify a valid and reliable set of categories to describe the clinical work practices of intensive case management" (Flander & Burns, 2000). The researchers categorized service activities that matched everyday practices of the clinicians. *Concept mapping* employs a group process to brainstorming about a topic, procedures for sorting and rating the emerged items, and multivariate techniques to develop clusters regarding the items, with the final output being a concept map (that is, a visual display of the categories in relation to each other) that the group then interprets. This procedure has been used to outline program activities and their sequences, as well as the contextual elements that impact the program for supported employment for individuals with severe mental illness (Trochim, Cook, & Setze, 1994). These methods offer approaches to operationally define the activities of a service/program into categories and procedures, in order to structure and standardize the intervention.

The next case example of Building Practice-Based Evidence offers a review of existing manuals that includes input from experts to develop a standardized intervention. This process can be used to define and delineate an intervention for an RCT. A similar process of using experts has been employed in developing the elements of the Assertive Community Treatment (ACT; McGrew & Bond, 1995). ACT's clearly defined program and structural elements have enabled a number of RCTs to be conducted, with the result that ACT has become an EBP for adults with severe mental illness.

This case example of practice-based evidence demonstrates the nature of the work that needs to be undertaken to outline the structures and processes of an existing service program that is well-regarded, but not clearly defined. Such efforts serve to provide focus and clarity to support the development of a rigorous RCT that is capable of informing practice, as well as moving the field forward from practice-based evidence towards EBP. It is not uncommon to be interested in conducting an RCT on an existing service model that is variably implemented or that is ill-defined, but considered by many to be a promising practice with limited supporting empirical evidence.

The development of a treatment manual is an iterative process that requires pilot implementation of the intervention. Based on results of the pilot work, the manual is revised and reimplemented. Eventually, the manual is piloted with providers who are trained in the intervention, and the implementation is evaluated using both quantitative approaches (e.g., fidelity assessment) and qualitative approaches (e.g., in-depth interviews, focus groups, ethnographic methods). The treatment manual is then revised and/or refined and is sufficiently ready to be tested by an RCT. If

Case Example of Building on Practice-Based Evidence

Walker and Bruns (2006) report using experts to define wraparound services for children and adolescents with serious emotional and behavioral problems. They note that relying on traditional manuals may hinder implementation in community-based programs because of a lack of transportability to usual care settings, where service populations are ethically and socioeconomically diverse, and problems are severe and heterogeneous. Such efficacy-based interventions "may be difficult to implement given available community resources, may not be acceptable to clinicians, and/ or may fail to promote engagement or adherence among service recipients" (Walker & Bruns, 2006, p. 1,579).

One means to compensate for these limitations is to "capitalize on accumulated practical experience." Walker and Bruns (2006) held a three-day meeting with stakeholders that produced a consensus document of the philosophy that guides wraparound practice. This document was a useful beginning, but did not result in comprehensive guidelines for carrying out wraparound practices. Subsequently, an advisory group comprised of experienced practitioners, trainers, administrators, family members, and researchers were brought together to develop a strategy for standardizing and testing the wraparound process. These experts prioritized a need for developing a set of standards for activities to be defined in a manner that was precise enough to be measurable for fidelity purposes, but flexible enough to allow for diversity in implementation.

A core group of eight experts reviewed existing manuals and training materials from which to develop a draft of a practice model. Manuals were obtained from national-level trainers and from well-regarded programs. To identify programs, the opinions of national-level trainers were sought. A second source for manual identification was derived from programs considered to be promising practices by the Center for Mental Health Services at SAMHSA.

The first draft of the model organized wraparound activities into four phases: engagement, initial plan development, plan implementation, and transition. This draft was sent out for review and comment by administrators of wraparound programs who were widely recognized, in addition to these well-regarded programs. The resultant feedback was then incorporated into a new draft. This draft was reviewed by the core group, and consensus approval was obtained. The core group then decided to seek

(*continued*)

feedback from an advisory group. Each member was asked to rate the proposed practice model: "First, to indicate whether an activity like the one described was essential, optional, or inadvisable for wraparound; second, whether, as written, the description of the activity was fine, acceptable with minor revisions, or unacceptable" (p. 1581). They were also asked to provide a rationale for their ratings or to give general comments about each of the activities delineated. In addition, they were asked for feedback on each phase and each of the procedures, including whether essential activities were covered. The core group reviewed and accepted the document by consensus, which is now publicly available at: www.rtc.pdx.edu/nwi/Phase Activ/WAProcess.pdf.

Examples of Major Task Activities:

> Phase 1: Engagement and Team Preparation
> Orient the Family and Youth
> Orient family and youth to wraparound
> Address legal and ethical issues
> Stabilize Crises
> Ask the family and youth about immediate crisis concerns
> Elicit information from agency representatives and potential team
>   members about potential crises (Walker & Bruns, 2006).

the manualized intervention is not feasible and acceptable to providers in the settings for which it is intended, it is unlikely to be implemented. However, if the intervention is appealing and practical, it has a greater likelihood of being implemented (Carroll & Nuro, 2002).

Developing and Piloting Fidelity Assessment

The elements detailed in the treatment manual provide the basis for assessing the fidelity of the intervention (i.e., whether the intervention was conducted as planned and is consistent with service or program elements delineated in the manual, including structures and goals). Frequently monitoring forms (e.g., a fidelity scale) are included in the treatment manual. A fidelity assessment is essential to evaluating the extent to which the planned intervention is actually implemented as intended (Orwin, 2000). Otherwise, researchers may incorrectly conclude that the intervention did not produce its intended objectives, when the real culprit was deviation from the planned intervention. Or, the conclusion may be that the effective outcome was a result of the intervention, when in fact, providers enhanced or changed the service program from what the investigator intended. Thus, at the point of development of the intervention, it is necessary to craft the procedures for monitoring the integrity of the intervention and then to test the fidelity measure to ensure that it is valid and reliable. Fidelity measures are scales or tools that assess the adequacy of implementation of a service or program, or provide a means to quantify the degree to which the service elements in a program or service are implemented (Bond, et al., 2000). Basically, the question of implementation of the intervention is not answered by a simple yes or no response, but rather to what degree. The purpose of these measures is to verify that the intervention is being implemented in a manner consistent with the service or program, as it is delineated in the treatment manual, workbook, or educational curriculum. Successful implementation has to do not only with whether the service program was delivered by the providers as intended, but also whether the program was received by the recipients (Orwin, 2000). Consequently, multiple approaches are needed to obtain both the provider and the recipients' perspective. Furthermore, treatment differentiation (ensuring that the intervention differs from other similar services) must be assessed (Bellg, Borrelli, Resnick, & Hecht, et al., 2004). Therefore, some components of the fidelity measure may need to capture the service elements of other interventions as well.

In conducting an RCT, one must assess the extent of contamination between conditions. Orwin (2000) refers to this type of assessment measure as a *leakage scale*, one that captures the degree to which participants in the control condition received services planned only for the experimental intervention. Frequently, the fidelity measure may serve this purpose as well by having providers in the control condition complete the same scale as the experimental providers.

The key to developing a sound fidelity measure is to have a well-defined service or practice model for the intervention. The treatment manual needs to define the structural elements and behaviors that are measurable in order to create a quantifiable scale that can be used in future analyses of the RCT's effectiveness. However, developing a fidelity measure for community-based psychosocial interventions is more difficult than for psychotherapy, which is the context for which these measures were originally developed. As Bruns and colleagues (2004) noted, "When considered for complex, individualized, or multimodal treatments, such as community-based treatments for youth and families fidelity assessment becomes particularly difficult" (p. 80). This is due to the complex structural and administrative characteristics of the programs and systems within which they are embedded.

Frequently used methods for assessing fidelity are self-report forms completed by either or both providers and participants, but more multimethod approaches are encouraged (Bond et al., 2000). These methods may include chart reviews, observation of elements of the service, data extraction from service billing forms, service logs, or videotaping with ratings by observers (as used by McKay in the case example in Chapter 1).

Mowbray and colleagues (2003) delineated a three-step process for developing a fidelity assessment instrument: identifying and specifying fidelity criteria, measuring fidelity, and assessing the reliability and validity of fidelity criteria. Fidelity criteria are comprised of two aspects of the program or service: the structure or the framework of service delivery, and the process or manner in which the service is delivered. The criteria generally include the following: "specification of length, intensity, and duration of the service (or dosage); content, procedures, and activities over the length of the service; roles, qualifications, and activities of staff; and inclusion/exclusion characteristics for the target service population" (Mowbray, et al., 2003, p. 318). Bond and his colleagues (2000) detailed a process for developing fidelity assessments employing a 14-step process (Table 3.2).

Bond and colleagues (2000) note that if the purpose of the scale is for an RCT, then the fidelity measure must be comprehensive, identifying both those aspects of the program/service that are unique and those that distinguish it from the control condition. Thus, it is apparent that

Table 3.2. Steps for Developing a Fidelity Measure

- Define the purpose of the fidelity scale.
- Assess the degree of model development.
- Identify model dimensions.
- Determine if appropriate fidelity scales already exist.
- Formulate fidelity scale plan.
- Develop items.
- Develop response scale points.
- Choose data collection sources and methods.
- Determine item order.
- Develop data collection protocol.
- Train interviewers/raters.
- Pilot the scale.
- Assess psychometric properties.
- Determine scoring and weighting of items.

Source: Bond et al. (Nov. 2000). Psychiatric Rehabilitation Fidelity Toolkit.

the construction of a fidelity assessment measure is closely intertwined with treatment manual development. A lack of specificity of the program model led Carol Mowbray to develop a fidelity rating instrument for consumer-run drop-in centers (CRDIs; Holter, Mowbray, Bellamy, MacFarlane, & Dukarski, 2004; Mowbray, Holter, Stark, Pfeffer, & Bybee, 2005a). When Mowbray consulted with the first author about designing an RCT on CRDIs, she was advised to first determine what the critical elements were and how they differed from the control condition before she proceeded with the RCT (Mowbray, Holter, Mowbray, & Bybee, 2005b). Without this preliminary work, it would have been less likely that the RCT would contribute to the evidence for consumer-operated drop-in centers, because the results of any difference could not be interpreted given that the control condition shared a number of service elements with CRDI centers. Mowbray received National Institute of Mental Health (NIMH) funding for the development of a fidelity measure of CRDI centers (see Case Example). Her initial research included the use of both quantitative and qualitative methods. Developing a fidelity measure often requires a mixed-method approach.

Case Example: Development of a Fidelity Rating Instrument for
Consumer-run Drop-in Centers (FRI-CRDI)

Mowbray and associates (Holter et al., 2004) note that effectiveness research
has made black-box outcome studies unacceptable. RCTs require that there
be a valid service model, based on a program theory that results in valid and
reliable criteria for fidelity to the model, and which also has discriminant
validity between the target model and other program models, and that the
program model is assessed on these criteria. Although effectiveness research
of consumer-run services is sorely needed to build an evidence base for both
advocacy and policy, there is a need to describe the model and to develop a
fidelity instrument.

These researchers conducted a review of published and unpublished
literature produced by consumer-run organizations and advocacy groups
on the activities, values, and goals of consumer drop-in centers. From this
review, they produced a comprehensive description of CRDI centers, which
included their primary objectives and essential activities. From this narrative description, they constructed a preliminary list of the essential ingredients of CRDI centers that were then grouped into conceptual domains
of structure and process using Donabedian's classic framework for health
services research. Because the process encompassed the values and activities of CRDI centers, these processes were further refined based on another
conceptual framework. To validate the criteria, a modified Delphi method
was employed, with two waves of data collection from a panel of national
experts on consumer-run services. Experts were identified through a search
of consumer newsletters, professional journal articles, and book chapters.
Experts included consumers, advocates, service providers, and researchers,
as well as individuals involved in a national multisite study on consumer-
operated services funded by SAMHSA.

Procedures

Wave I experts were mailed a survey that asked them to indicate whether
each criterion that was listed was critical to a CRDI program, using
response categories of agree, disagree, or neither. An open-ended question
was employed to elicit additional criteria. Mailed surveys were followed by
e-mail and telephone reminders.

Based on the results of Wave I, Wave II used a Web-based survey. Respondents were asked to choose 10 items that were the most essential and 10
items that were the least essential to a CRDI center (assigning a neutral value

(*continued*)

to the remaining 11 items). From the two lists of ten, respondents were then asked to choose four items from each list that were most essential and least essential. In this manner, items were given ratings as most essential (with a value of 2), essential (1), neutral (0), less essential (–1), and least essential (–2). This method was chosen to force respondents to distinguish critical ingredients from important but noncritical components of consumer-run programs. Respondents were also asked about their own characteristics (Holter, et al., 2004, p. 54).

Results and Discussion

Experts tend to rate structural components, which are most visible, as most essential. Process domains are rated as less important, although research has found that adhering to process criteria may be more significant to maintaining a program model as intended. "Structured measures have the advantage of being less subjective and can often be obtained through existing documentation. Process criteria may be more difficult to reliably measure, but more significant in terms of program effects, that is, process criteria include measures of program style, staff–client interactions, client–client interactions, individualization of treatment, and emotional climate, which require subjective judgments, often based on observations, interviews, etc. Process measures require more time and effort to obtain, and are likely to be more costly and less reliable" (Holter, et al., 2004, pp. 59-60).

Based on this preliminary work, Mowbray and colleagues (2005a) developed the Fidelity Rating Instrument for Consumer-Run Drop-In Centers (FRI-CRDI). (Two additional studies were conducted to produce the measure.) Developing the instrument and the resulting ratings were based on two-day site visits to 31 consumer-run drop-in centers in Michigan that met specific sample selection criteria. A field research team of three conducted the site visits. All consumers in attendance were asked to complete a questionnaire or were interviewed by the researchers. The director at each site was also interviewed. An Instrument for Site Observations (ISO) was constructed, and the team engaged in qualitative observations "from conversations directly with consumers, observing interactions between staff and consumers and of consumers with each other, and observing the physical environment of the interior and exterior of the center . . . " (Mowbray, et al., 2005a, p. 282). Following all site visits, the researchers constructed the measure, using a benchmark process to operationalize each criterion. The fidelity instrument was subsequently used by the researchers to rate several of the programs, employing the information from the ISO. The results of

(continued)

this second study assessed four programs that were not included in the first study. The researchers found that inter-rater agreement was very good, with 18 of the 21 fidelity criteria showing excellent agreement and with three criteria needing additional work. The investigators undertook another set of analyses on 31 programs to assess the convergent validity of the measure. They found good validity for the measure, with only four of the 14 fidelity variables not being validated (Mowbray, et al., 2006).

Mowbray and colleagues (2005b) assessed the differences between CRDI centers and the control programs. The two models shared similar aspects, but differed structurally and programmatically. They conducted two-day site visits matched by geographical area. Both groups of programs were funded by the local public mental health system. As expected, investigators found greater member control and involvement in CRDIs, whereas the control programs offered more instrumental services and activities (Mowbray et al., 2005a, 2005b, 2006).

If interventions are straightforward, such as educational interventions, a checklist can be created with the elements of the intervention. For the previously discussed HIV educational prevention intervention for those with severe mental illness, a form that mimics the service document that the case managers complete for billing purposes was developed. The case managers indicated on this form the card numbers that they discussed for the particular session. This process demonstrated whether all the cards were reviewed with each study participant or exactly which cards were reviewed with each client, the number of sessions of the intervention, and how much time was spent at each session.

Observation checklist may be developed and then researchers may observe the providers delivering the intervention. For example, in the first author's RCT of HIV prevention intervention, experimental interventionists were periodically observed via a one-way mirror to determine whether they were delivering the intervention as intended. Observers recorded their observations on a checklist that was based on the intervention and were provided praise and critical feedback as well as offered booster session on delivering the intervention, if necessary.

In the social participation workbook intervention, a checklist was developed delineating in which activities the providers may engage with the participants. These forms were collected from both the experimental and control condition providers to assess fidelity and leakage (i.e., control condition providers delivering any of the activities of the experimental intervention). In the outcome interviews conducted at six-month intervals, participants were asked about the extent to which they engaged in these intervention activities, in order to assess fidelity and leakage from the participants' perspectives.

The importance of fidelity assessment is essential, as it has significant implications for internal, external, and construct validity, and statistical power (Moncher & Prinz, 1991). Fidelity is necessary to maintain internal validity and to be assured of a fair comparison between conditions. Fidelity assessment is an efficient way to know if contamination has occurred, and to specify the nature of the contamination. Structured manuals are the key to the reproducibility of the intervention in other settings.

Conclusion

Planning a community-based psychosocial RCT requires both time and effort. Initially, one must assess whether the knowledge base is developed sufficiently to warrant designing an RCT and whether the social political timing is opportune for such an endeavor. Once deciding to move forward, the process of selecting and negotiating with a setting may precipitate the rethinking of one's innovative idea, because the real world of services may not be receptive. Collaborative processes will require more than a knowledge of science, and will include social work practice, advocacy, and collaborative skills as well. The planning of an RCT is an iterative process of acquiring data, reconceptualizing, obtaining more data, and returning to the drawing board. Furthermore, one must have confidence in the selected site being able and capable of delivering the intended service interventions. A valid RCT that will contribute to EBP necessitates the assurance of high-quality practice as well as good science.

This chapter demonstrated that the planning of an RCT encompasses a number of small-scale research studies. Extensive consideration based on empirical data must be given to whether enough eligible and willing clients/volunteers can be recruited for randomization to all of the study conditions and be retained through the duration of the study. It is incumbent upon all those involved to be particularly mindful of the importance of a diverse sample that accurately represents the target population.

To meet the criteria of competently provided interventions delivered in a standardized and reproducible manner, a practice intervention manual must be utilized. Given that many treatment manuals were developed for efficacy trials rather than effectiveness studies, these manuals may entail a good deal of work to adapt them to environments more common to social work settings. In some instances, the researcher will need to undertake additional preliminary work to create a treatment manual in an area in which there is little from which to build upon. As previously outlined, strategies and methods for adapting and developing manuals require a variety of pilot studies involving both qualitative and quantitative approaches. Along with the development of the service or program manual is the construction of a fidelity assessment. As was made evident, these two major preliminary activities are intertwined and, in some instances, may be conducted concurrently rather than sequentially. Having successfully completed the necessary pilot work, one can proceed with confidence in having a solid foundation on which to begin conceptualizing and designing an RCT.

For Further Reading

Bond, G., Williams, J., Evans, L., Salyers, M., Kim, H.W., Sharpe, H., Leff, S. (Nov. 2000). *Psychiatric Rehabilitation Fidelity Toolkit*, Cambridge, MA: Human Services Research Institute.

Carroll, K. (Ed.). *Improving compliance with alcoholism treatment*. Bethesda, MD: National Institute of Alcohol Abuse and Alcoholism.

Nezu, A. & Nezu, C. (Eds.). *Evidence-based outcome research*. New York: Oxford University Press.

4

Developing Conceptual Foundations for Randomized Controlled Trials

Service providers are skeptical about the impact of research on community-based psychosocial interventions and social work practice. Some differentiate the "real world" from a mythical world of ivory-tower theories that are removed from practical action. However, without theory, most research would be merely a cacophony of numbers, Greek letters, and funny charts with X's and O's (see Chapter 5). Theory provides the foundation for the conceptualization of methods for randomized controlled trials (RCTs) in the "real world." Its constructs enable the researcher to interpret findings and generalize these finding to other service settings.

A conceptual framework for an RCT is a system of ideas for understanding how an intervention is believed to lead to its outcomes. The conceptual framework defines the potential effectiveness of the intervention in terms of activities that are thought to produce change, in what context, and toward what outcome. Through the judicious application of theory, RCT conceptualization and research design *operationalizes* the effectiveness of an intervention within its service context. A well-developed conceptual framework shapes the basic RCT design, provides an understanding of the pipeline of clients that feed into an intervention, grounds the sample and sampling strategy, and offers direction as to how the interventions are implemented, as well as determining what is measured and how the study is analyzed.

Conceptual work is iterative. Throughout the design process, researchers revisit and revise decisions made earlier based on conceptual, logistical, or political stumbling blocks that may be encountered later. A strong conceptualization will provide a plumb line, a guide for decision-making that will strengthen the overall research design.

The Role of Theory in Randomized Controlled Trials

RCTs are grounded in theory-driven deductive hypotheses. The challenges faced by clients and social workers' are presumed to be real phenomena that can be measured, quantified, and studied over time to produce generalizable results. A quantitative approach presumes that a researcher is an objective observer, even while the work is motivated by the researcher's values, grounded in social work ethics. These assumptions provide the structural underpinnings of the intervention.

Therefore, the most effective theories for RCTs are those that support explanatory models of process and outcome. These theoretical models should have the following characteristics:

- A grounding in empirical, quantitatively-driven social science
- Theoretical and empirical support that provides direction for operationalizing both process and outcome(s)
- A conceptual framework that delineates the role of the intervention in affecting change
- An empirical base that justifies change over time, as well as the expected timeframe for specific levels of change

In addition, *stronger* theoretical models are those that can support the following:

- Proposed mediators that allow for operationalizing mechanisms of change in outcomes that are associated with the intervention and precede the outcome
- Proposed moderators that are associated with the service context and/or service population

A discussion of the full range of theories that can be applied to RCTs employing psychosocial interventions is beyond the scope of this text. The scientific literature available for this work is virtually limitless. For illustrative purposes, the following enumerates selected theoretical traditions commonly utilized in designing conceptual frameworks in RCTs for psychosocial interventions:

- Cognitive Behavioral Theory (Blagys & Hilsenroth, 2002; Babcock, Green, & Robie, 2004; Vaughn & Howard, 2004)
- Social Learning Theory (Cohen, Gottlieb, & Underwood, 2000; Kanter, 1996; Sarason, Sarason, & Gurung, 2001; Strauss & Carpenter, 1972, 1977)
- Stress, Coping, and Adaptation (Folkman & Moskowitz, 2004), including mastery (Pearlin & Schooler, 1978; DeVillis & DeVellis, 2000)
- Social Support (Lazarus, DeLongis, Folkman, & Gruen, 1985; Sarason, Sarason, & Gurung, 2001)
- Social Capital (Bourdieu, 1986; Coleman, 1988; Draine & Herman, 2007; Portes, 1998; Putnam, 2000; Van Der Gaag & Snijders, 2005)
- Health Beliefs (Rosenstock, Strecher, & Becker, 1988)
- The Theory of Reasoned Action (Ajzen & Fishbein, 1980; Fishbein & Ajzen, 1975)
- Theory of Planned Behavior (Armitage & Conner, 2001; Godin & Kok, 1996)
- Transtheoretical Model of Change (DiClemente & Hughes, 1990; Pollio, Spitznagel, North, Thompson, & Foster, 2000; Sutton, 2001)

Developing Conceptual Frameworks

In some instances, it may prove problematic to identify an adaptable and relevant theory in justifying a proposed intervention leading to targeted outcomes. An integration of a number of smaller theories, along with prior empirical research to provide a rationale for linking the intervention to specific outcomes may be utilized. For example, in designing the RCT of Assertive Community Treatment (ACT) for clients leaving jail, researchers could not apply a specific theory that justified the study outcomes. Instead, a clinical case for integration and coordination of services and resources, along with a number of research studies employing this intervention, provided the framework for justifying the outcomes. Similarly, in RCTs of consumers and nonconsumer case managers, research on the working/professional alliance supplied the conceptual grounding. Furthermore, supportive relationships assist in developing positive adjustments to life stressors. In addition, other relevant literature demonstrates that through helping others, individuals help themselves, or what is called the "helper therapy principle" (Solomon, 2004). Consequently, expecting that clients of consumer case managers will have more positive psychosocial and service outcomes than those of their nonconsumer counterparts was justified by prior research studies, as well by a variety of small theories (Schmidt, Gill, Solomon, & Pratt, 2008). In circumstances in which there is not a single, theoretical tradition shaping an intervention, a clear conceptual framework that links the intervention to each of the specified outcomes is necessary to provide sufficient guidance for the intervention. The RCT may serve to build new theory for future interventions. In summary, a clear theoretical and empirical foundation must be established to justify the anticipated causal relationship between the intervention and each hypothesized outcome.

Mediators and Moderators

Theoretical models that include mediators and moderators serve two important functions for RCT research. First, these conceptualizations allow for explanations of what was changed (mediators) and for whom (moderators) in delivering an intervention. The mediator allows for testing mechanisms for change in specified outcomes. Moderators, on the other hand, enable one to test factors that may interact with the intervention in such a way that the interaction of the moderator variable with the intervention has different effects (or strengths of effect) on outcomes. An RCT with a framework that includes mediator and/or moderator effects has the potential to increase the theoretical understanding of the process of change in outcomes.

Specifically, mediators are variables that are hypothesized to help make change happen (Baron & Kenny, 1986). They are a conceptual link in the middle of a cause-and-effect argument. Thus, in intervention studies, the mediator concept measured needs to be one that occurs after the intervention, but before the outcome. Some may think of the intervention itself as a mediator between baseline and outcome. Although this may be statistically accurate, considering the intervention as the mediator does not conceptually provide the most substantial contribution. In an RCT, the hypothesis is not that baseline status caused the outcome—this is likely already supported by the preponderance of evidence in almost any field—but rather that an intervention causes a *change* in outcome(s) greater than what is otherwise expected without the intervention. The mechanism of change is an interaction of both the intervention and the immediate change that is expected to induce the proposed outcomes. For example, in cognitive behavioral therapy, the homework and skill-building used in therapy (intervention) acts to reframe thinking about a stressful problem (mediator), which leads to reduced anxiety or depression (outcome). Therefore, to understand if the intervention works as intended, both the effect of the intervention on outcomes and the mediating role of the intervention's impact on change in thinking must be examined.

The benefits of a theoretical grounding for a psychosocial intervention are exemplified in a recent article by Herbst and colleagues (2007). They assert that research in human immunodeficiency virus (HIV) prevention for gay men had moved to a point at which specification of mediators is to be expected in any proposed intervention study, in order to adequately enhance the effectiveness literature in this area. Herbst and colleagues

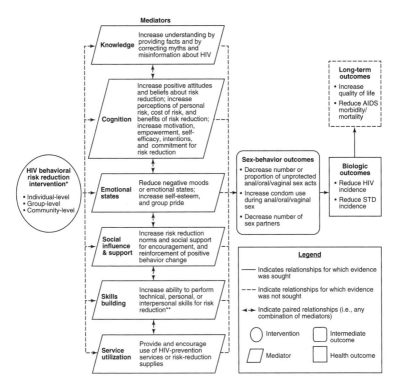

Figure 4.1. Mediators model for human immunodeficiency virus (HIV) risk reduction

delineated the mediation process as depicted in Figure 4.1. This figure reviews the empirical research in HIV and acquired immune deficiency syndrome (AIDS) intervention, as well as the potential mediators for change supported by the literature to date. Note that the mediators proposed explicitly cover several areas of theory. In addition, the conceptual framework includes immediate, intermediate, and long-term outcomes.

Figure 4.2 proposes a mediation model for an RCT of Critical Time Intervention (CTI) for men with mental illness leaving prison in New Jersey. In this study, CTI is thought to be associated with a number of positive changes in men returning to the community—such as stable housing, fewer symptoms, and increased social functioning. Using an

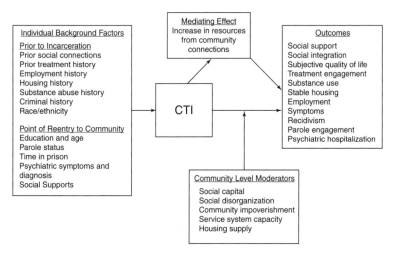

Figure 4.2. Mediator and moderators for effectiveness of Critical Time Intervention (CTI)

individual-level social capital conceptualization, Van Der Gaag and Snijders (2003) propose that an intervention such as CTI functions as a means to increase resources associated with social connections (people who can help obtain jobs, lead to pro-social activities, solve problems, etc.), and that the outcomes of CTI are likely to be mediated through this effect. Therefore, a measure of individual-level social capital (Van Der Gaag & Snijders, 2005) is included as a mediator in the outcome model of this intervention (Draine & Herman, 2007).

Furthermore, the model includes an exploratory set of questions that operationalize poverty as a moderating factor. This moderating factor is also based on a social capital formulation, as the social and economic resources that are accessible to individuals are likely shaped by the social and economic resources available in the neighborhood where an individual resides. Therefore, the moderating influence of the neighborhood is proposed to impact the outcomes of CTI. Conclusions based on the theoretical framework can thus be drawn at both the neighborhood level and the individual level. Such analyses will contribute to our knowledge of how CTI works in community re-entry in general. It will also enhance the theoretical literature on how the construct of social capital can increase our understanding of re-entry for people leaving prison with mental illness in particular.

Research Question and Control Condition

The essence of the research question for an RCT is the response to the query: "Compared to what?" Integral to operationalizing the experimental intervention is operationalizing what it is not. Chapter 6 details the process of implementing these conditions. Chapter 5 will discuss how to incorporate them into the research design. The following discussion examines the research question and conceptualization as it relates to the control condition.

A beginning point is to understand what the usual course of care or service may be for the population under study. If the population is a group that is expected to be receiving some treatment or service for the condition or circumstances, then the most relevant control condition is that accepted standard of care. Thus, the comparison for the experimental intervention is made more rigorous by a comparison to what would usually be provided (i.e., treatment as usual; TAU). In some cases, the experimental intervention is sufficiently novel, or addresses a problem that is not within the usual realm of care, such that a no-treatment control can be justified. Examples might be an educational group intervention, creative arts therapies, or any service for a group that traditionally receives little formal treatment or service. Therefore, the relevant comparison is no special intervention as the usual is not receiving care.

However, in other cases, the researcher may be compelled to set up a control condition service that is considered benign in its impact. These are often supportive interventions that are not expected to have a deep or lasting impact on outcome measures. The reason for these control interventions/conditions is that the very fact of paying attention to those in the experimental condition may have an impact on them, independent of the nature of the specific intervention. Therefore, in some RCTs, a control intervention is offered to control for the attention or placebo effects. *Placebo effects* refer to the effect of attention to the participant on the participant's outcome. For example, supportive talk interventions without detailed protocols or general skill-building activities are known to have low to no impact on health and social welfare outcomes (Crepaz et al., 2006; Herbst et al., 2007; McFarlane, Dixon, Lukens, & Lucksted, 2003). Such models of intervention can therefore be considered relatively benign in terms of substantive outcomes for most populations of interest to social workers. Consequently, a control group intervention that may be a supportive discussion group, operating for an equivalent duration and intensity to the experimental intervention, can provide a design control for an experimental intervention that is expected to yield greater effects. In RCTs in which interventions are time-limited (e.g., with educational groups or time-limited therapy), the control condition could be a wait list control. In these instances, the control group is assigned to wait a period of time and is then offered the experimental intervention if they desire. However, with particular populations, some type of intervention may need to be offered to keep participants involved in the research.

In deciding on a control condition, ask: What question is being answered by the comparison? (see research question examples below). Is this the relevant question? Answering these questions thoroughly is worth extra consideration up front, as there are few chances for a "do-over" once data collection has begun. For example, in Solomon and Draine's (1995) study of consumer case management, two case management teams provided services to clients of a public mental health system. One team was composed of case managers who identified as consumers, and the control team was a team typical of the case management teams (community treatment teams, or CTTs) operating in the system at the time and consisting mostly of bachelor's-level mental health workers. The study hypotheses were that outcomes would be essentially the same between the teams, which would support the belief that consumer-run teams could do the core work of case management, as opposed to being limited to supportive, adjunctive roles. As hypothesized, results demonstrated similar outcomes between teams (Solomon & Draine,

1995). However, as the study was presented and reviewed, some pointed out that the teams could have been equally ineffective. Because there was no control group without a case management team, this possibility could not be ruled out. The study has since been replicated with the same measures and data points by other investigators—and with a third condition (a no case management control group). This subsequent study essentially showed the two case management conditions as being equally effective when compared to the control condition, with some differences in how the teams operated and only a few positive outcomes for the consumer team clients compared to the nonconsumer team clients (Clarke et al., 2000; Herinckx, Kinney, Clarke, & Paulson, 1997; Paulson et al., 1999).

In a pilot study of a problem-solving educational intervention for older adults with depressive symptoms who were in home care, with a comparison of standard acute home health care for their medical problems with depression education materials and referral for antidepression medication, Gellis and colleagues (2007) noted that standard care alone was not an appropriate control condition. Although the comparison employed limits on the generalizability of study findings, it is a stronger

---

Examples of RCT Research Questions

For adults with severe mental illness, is Assertive Community Treatment more effective than the prevailing intensive case management approach in terms of social skills and functioning, symptomatology, medication compliance, employment, degree of independence in housing, number of emergency services and hospitalizations, and arrests?

Is Preventing AIDS Through Health (PATH) effective in reducing high-risk sexual behaviors among persons with severe mental illness and substance abuse problems compared to no educational control condition?

Is group family education and/or individual family consultation for families of severely mentally ill relatives more effective in reducing family burden, stress, and increasing social support, self-efficacy, and coping with their relatives' illness than those families on a wait list?

comparison for testing the effectiveness of the experimental intervention. Given that the Problem-Solving Therapy-Home Care includes many of the nonspecific therapeutic factors typical of psychotherapies, it was expected that there would be an improvement in depression.

Formulating Hypotheses

A testable hypothesis poses a relationship between two concepts that are operationalized as the independent and dependent variables. In an RCT, the intervention (versus control) is the independent variable. The outcome is the dependent variable. Incorporating a brief description of the population, the hypothesis for an RCT may be: "Among children who are hospitalized, those who receive play therapy while hospitalized are more likely to be discharged earlier than those who receive only unstructured play time while hospitalized." The independent variable is operationalized as an intervention of play therapy versus a control condition of unstructured play time. The outcome is a shorter hospitalization, under the assumption that this represents a positive outcome, all things being equal due to randomization. As noted in the previous discussion about research questions, the control condition shapes the question as much as the experimental intervention, and thus also shapes the hypothesis.

The hypothesis encapsulates the conceptualization of the RCT in an empirically testable statement of a relationship of the intervention to specific theorized outcomes. The direction of the relationship is explicit. Ultimately, the test of this hypothesis is only an approximation of the abstract concepts in the study, as each variable (length of hospitalization, play therapy versus unstructured play) is only a close approximation of the abstract phenomena of interest (play therapy, health status). However, given these limitations, empirically supported hypotheses can provide strong evidence for the effectiveness of an intervention as play therapy or any other theoretical relationship of an intervention to specific outcomes.

Because community-based psychosocial interventions incorporate the social environment as a key element of the intervention, the context for any psychosocial intervention is complex. Researchers often seek to control for potential confounds (i.e., alternative explanations for variables) that may affect the results of their study. Age, gender, and racial identity are only the initial confounds frequently assessed. Depending on the field of interest, any number of risk factors, protective factors, or background characteristics may be critical confounds. These confounding variables need to be reflected in the hypotheses, with qualifying clauses, such as "controlling for length and severity of illness, insurance status, and age, children who are hospitalized" (adding to the hypothesis stated previously). One must have a full conceptualization of the intervention and outcome(s) reflected in the hypotheses, with all abstract concepts in the hypotheses clearly operationalized with appropriate measures and complete tests of the hypotheses delineated in advance. In this way, a well-crafted hypothesis synthesizes all the various elements of the proposed RCT. Thus, whereas the best hypotheses are often elegantly simple, the stated hypothesis includes both complexity and logic.

Examples of Hypotheses

Among family members with a relative with a severe mental illness, group family education and individual family consultation will decrease family burden and stress and increase social support, self-efficacy and coping behaviors at termination of the interventions and at six-month follow-up as compared to a wait list control.

Individuals with a severe mental illness who employ the social participation workbook will increase their use of community resources, increase their social support, and increase their degree of community integration than those who do not use the workbook.

Participants with severe mental illness and a substance use problem who receive PATH (Preventing AIDS Through Health) will have fewer high-risk sexual behaviors than controls at three, six, and 12 months.

If mediators and/or moderators have been theoretically established, hypotheses need to reflect these relationships. A specific logic exists to testing these relationships in terms of hypotheses that build on one another, and which then support mediating or moderating relationships among variables. For example, in the randomized trial of CTI, the testing of the mediating relationship illustrated in Figure 4.2 consists of testing three hypotheses:

1. **First, it is hypothesized that CTI is associated with a greater growth in individual-level social capital than the control condition.** This relationship is represented by the arrow from CTI to the "Mediating Effect" of an increase in resources from community connections.

2. **Second, it is hypothesized that CTI is associated with stronger positive outcomes than the control condition.** This relationship is represented by the arrow from CTI directly to outcomes.

3. **If both these hypotheses are supported, then it is further hypothesized that when the mediator from hypothesis one is included as a control variable in the model that measures the effect from CTI to the outcome, the direct effect of CTI on the outcomes will be reduced or eliminated,** with the effect of increased social capital (the arrow from the mediating effect to outcome) significantly explaining the outcomes.

Thus, this interactive system of all three hypotheses is tested to determine support for a mediating relationship (Baron & Kenny, 1986). The hypotheses and the statistical analysis plan for the CTI RCT study reflect this logic, and every outcome in the model corresponds to data collected in the study and a potential test of a mediated effect of CTI on each of the outcomes.

Strategies are available for testing a moderating relationship as well. In the CTI model, an exploratory question concerns the extent to which community-level characteristics may moderate the effect of CTI. For illustrative purposes, setting aside issues relating to the geographically situated nature of these concepts, let us assume that one can measure for each CTI study participant a "poverty" variable based on their living situation upon release. Following from the Baron and Kenny method (Baron & Kenny, 1986), this relationship may be more directly portrayed as a moderating effect, as shown in Figure 4.3. To determine a moderating relationship involves testing the direct effects of both CTI and poverty on outcome. If there is an effect for CTI on outcome, and poverty on outcome, the effect of CTI on outcome may be linked to the poverty level of the individual participant, and thus warrants a test of the interaction as well.

Moderating relationships can be complicated by the nature of the effect, as the relationship between the moderating variable and the intervention may be curvilinear, rather than linear. For example, there may be a level of poverty at which CTI is most effective; where those impacted by a greater or lesser degree of poverty have less benefit from CTI services. Further reading of any reliable text on testing such relationships is needed for more detail. For our purposes, the take-home message is that to pose these relationships requires clear, conceptual reasoning grounded in a theoretical framework. Otherwise, the analysis phase can dissolve into the proverbial "fishing expedition," in which a researcher is searching for statistically significant relationships, may find one by chance (and/or error), and thus feel compelled to dream up an ad hoc theory to explain the significant findings. What is far more likely to contribute to the psychosocial and social work intervention evidence base is a clear

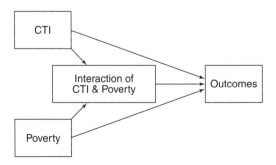

Figure 4.3. Example of moderating relationship for Critical Time Intervention (CTI) study

conceptualization developed at the very beginning of RCT design, one that is thoroughly testable and eventually is tested employing hypotheses derived from the conceptual model.

Many studies fail to explore fully the study hypotheses so as to test the change process relationships. Hypotheses based on the proposed relationships between intervention and outcome provide the guide to what concepts will be measured, and what outcomes and processes (change concepts, moderators, and mediators) are expected to be included in statistical models. Building a hypothesis may not be as simple as it seems. Like other aspects of RCT design, the process is iterative. As a preliminary set of hypotheses are conceptualized, the investigator assesses the extent to which they are testable, using measurable concepts and statistically testable interrelationships. In this iterative process, measurement strategies can be reformulated, conceptualizations refined, and even a rethinking of basic elements, such as the experimental and control conditions, may occur. Only after the conceptual work is completed, where hypotheses summarize precisely the question to be explored, does the research being designed have sufficient guidance for developing the detailed mechanics of an RCT.

Conclusion

In reviewing the role of theory, this chapter does not delve into the myriad of theoretical frameworks. Rather, it reviews how theory drives a defensible conceptualization of an RCT design. Therefore, a conceptual framework becomes a structure on which to hang focused research questions and hypotheses. The research question is shaped in interaction with the service context and also in reviewing the relevant research literature. After deriving a clearly defined and measurable research question, a testable hypothesis is drawn. This hypothesis (or hypotheses) should incorporate all elements of the research design (as reviewed in the Chapter 5).

Mediating and moderating frameworks are tools in conceptualizing community-based psychosocial interventions, including those delivered by social workers. Using these tools, researchers can operationalize and test mechanisms for change and differential effects for the intervention based on theory, client characteristics, or varied organizational and community contexts. These enhanced frameworks enable further development of theory grounded-in community-based service settings, as well as test the effectiveness of the psychosocial intervention.

For Further Reading

Frazier, P., Tix, A., & Barron, K. (2004). Testing moderator and mediator effects in counseling psychology. *Journal of Counseling Psychology, 51,* 115–133.

Reynolds, P. (2007). *A primer in theory construction.* Boston: Pearson Allyn and Bacon.

Becker, H. (1998). *Tricks of the trade: How to think about research while you are doing it.* Chicago: University of Chicago Press.

5

Designing the Randomized Controlled Trial

The research design represents the core science of the randomized controlled trial (RCT). The design itself can be deceptively simple—deceptively, because the "devil is in the details" when specifying a design, and it often represents some of the most vexing problems in conducting RCTs. A researcher's response to these challenges can demonstrate a great deal of creativity and intellectual prowess. Alternatively, some resolutions to thorny design issues may insert a fatal flaw into the validity of the RCT. This chapter provides a guide to avoid possible pitfalls in crafting a sound RCT for community-based psychosocial interventions.

In many cases, design is a constant exchange between issues of research validity and the realities of the service environment. This chapter reviews the basics of RCT design elements, complete with the familiar "X" and "O" design illustrations. This, however, is only the starting point, as an important consideration in design is careful attention to potential confounds. Following discussion on the issues of confounds is a description of the design elements of sampling and operationalization of interventions and outcomes, as well as a discussion on determining the details of follow-up data collection points and data analysis. The chapter concludes with a brief summary of the emerging literature on alternatives to basic RCT design strategies.

The Influence of Service Context on Design

As discussed in Chapter 3, the answers to two questions raised during the negotiation process with the service environment are integral to an RCT's design: What intervention is being manipulated? And, to what intervention may clients be randomized? As in many elements of RCT design, randomization is not a process that simply gets dropped into a service setting; it is proposed and negotiated with the service context. Therefore, the researcher's relationship with providers in an agency becomes the key to shaping important design elements of an RCT. Across the many realms of social work practice, many administrators understand the value of RCTs in developing an evidence base for service interventions. Currently, agency administrators are far more likely to agree to participate in a randomized trial, as opposed to a research study with less internal validity, because the expectation for evidence-based practice (EBP) among agency leaders, funding sources, and advocates has increased in recent years.

Part of the argument for the feasibility of randomization is often the numbers of individuals who are already in line for service and who could benefit from more intensive or potentially more effective intervention models that are not currently available to them. In negotiating with a service setting about the availability of clients, a researcher needs to get reliable information on the numbers of individuals in line for service who would meet the criteria for an RCT. Then the researcher needs to make a realistic assessment of how many individuals may actually be available over a given period of time to enroll in an RCT. This number of potential clients will interact with statistical power considerations (discussed later).

An RCT can be considered as a circumstance in which a new and necessary service will be provided. The randomization procedure allows for a scientific comparison to be made about the effectiveness of the new intervention. Randomization is thus a rational way of allocating a limited resource, especially when the default alternative is to the conventional method of service assignment. The caseload for the new service can be filled up immediately, and new clients can wait for the occasional opening in that caseload. For example, one comparison of a new service model to the existing system of care compared Assertive Community

Treatment (ACT)-based case management to individual intensive case management and usual referral to community mental health services for homeless individuals with mental illness leaving jail (Solomon & Draine, 1995). In this RCT, three conditions were examined. The base condition was usual referral, which was a passive referral of people leaving jail to a community mental health agency. The usual referral to community mental health agencies was not a very effective means of reentry planning for people leaving jail; but it was the modal service offered to individuals in this circumstance, and thus the logical base comparison. The two experimental conditions allowed a comparison of intensive case management and an ACT team model against this base of services offered. Unfortunately, in most jail systems, little has changed since then, so even today, this is likely to be the legitimate comparison of interest.

To which intervention a researcher will randomize clients and to what service intervention clients can be randomized is often shaped by an interaction of multiple factors. (Many of these factors are discussed in other chapters of the text.) One factor is the available evidence of which open, unanswered questions may ethically be supported to justify a randomized trial (as discussed in Chapter 2). Another factor is the political environment of the service setting and system for accepting a trial as feasible and justified—which may include legal constraints on what service elements can be controlled. Finally, one of the most essential factors is the number of individuals in a service system who are in a position to benefit from an experimental service. These factors are discussed in Chapter 3, and to some extent in Chapter 6, where the design process interacts with the implementation in the service context. The number of individuals available and not being served by effective interventions provides the base for sampling, as well as a justification for offering new service models to test.

Design Components

So, finally, we have arrived at the X's and O's, basing our discussion on the preliminary material covered in earlier chapters that gives meaning to these figures. The classic randomized pre-test/post-test experimental control group design is typically represented as such:

$$R \quad O \quad X \quad O$$
$$R \quad O \quad\quad O$$

in which "R" indicates that membership in groups is determined by random assignment. Each line across is a group. The progression of time is from left to right. Each "O" is an observation point of the outcome(s), and the "X" is the experimental intervention. To researchers, both novice and experienced, this diagram is the picture of elegance in simple logic. There are almost inexhaustible possible variations on this design. Consider that one can have more than one experimental condition:

$$R \quad O \quad X_1 \quad O$$
$$R \quad O \quad X_2 \quad O$$
$$R \quad O \quad\quad\ O$$

This design was employed in two of the authors' research studies. One is the example described earlier, in which the control condition of usual referral to a mental health center after jail was compared to two intensive case management models, one being individual intensive case management, and the other being to an ACT team. Therefore, the analysis compared intensive follow-up with usual follow-up—and also compared individual case management to a full-fledged ACT Team (Solomon & Draine, 1995). Another example was an examination of family education for family members with a relative who had a mental illness. In this case, a wait list control was compared with group family education or an individual family consultation model. Using this approach, researchers were able to determine the relative effectiveness of each model to a control, and even within subgroups of the population served, including those who were involved in support groups, for example (Solomon, Draine, Mannion, & Meisel, 1996, 1997). Conceivably, a researcher could place the ultimate trust in randomization by not even making observations before the intervention is delivered—a randomized post-test only design:

R   X   O
R   O

Going to the other extreme in the number of observations, multiple observations could be made both before and after an experimental intervention to incorporate a time series analysis into the RCT. This design is most feasible when outcomes are measured using administrative data sets:

R   O   O   O   X   O   O   O
R   O   O   O   O   O   O

Other well-known variations can be seen in similar displays in almost any introductory research text used in social work (Monette, Sullivan, & DeJong, 2005; Rubin & Babbie, 2007). The purpose of this book is not to review a comprehensive list of these designs, but rather to introduce some of the major issues that are faced in designing community-based psychosocial RCTs; issues that may not be adequately described in a basic research methods text. As experience with experimental design increases, researchers gain an appreciation for the extent to which each of these elements is infused with a number of design considerations that interact with conceptualization, feasibility issues in a setting, and analysis to produce valid, reliable, and generalizable results. Therefore, this section addresses a number of issues and how they intersect with these basic randomized trial designs. These considerations include the selection of a control condition, potential confounds (a variable other than the intervention variable that produces a change in the outcome), potential problems related to attrition, and design issues related to sampling, data collection, measurement, and analysis.

Complex Interventions

Another issue that arises, which may be of particular concern to social workers, is the complexity of community-based psychosocial interventions. Many of the populations served by social workers are defined by having multiple, interrelated problems. Therefore, intervention models are complex and are often examined as a complete package of interlocking services. Surveying multiple service elements of psychosocial interventions will create problems in interpreting the results from an RCT and may result in misleading interpretations of effectiveness. An example of this comes from the literature on mental health courts, an intervention model that provides for a specialized, less adversarial court to supervise individuals with a mental illness who come in contact with the law. Cosden and colleagues (2003, 2005) conducted a randomized trial in which individuals facing criminal charges were randomly assigned to mental health court or the usual adversarial court processing. Those assigned to the mental health court also received ACT and supported housing. This study has provided some of the most positive results to date in favor of mental health courts, including reduced criminal recidivism and reduced drug use. However, the question arises: Was this result due to the mental health court? Or ACT? Or supported housing? Or perhaps the positive outcomes were due to some combination or interaction of these service programs? We cannot definitively know from this one study. To conduct RCTs of all the iterations of comparisons in this case would be far more time-consuming and expensive than would likely be tolerated by funders of research or service setting providers. Therefore, it is important to carefully select the most informative comparison for experimental and control conditions. In this case, a more policy-relevant design would be to test the relative effectiveness of the intensive interventions (ACT plus supportive housing) and the mental health court, as well as the interaction of the mental health court and the intensive intervention together. An option for doing this would have been a 2×2 multifactorial design. Multifactorial designs provide an opportunity to examine the main effect of the interventions alone, as compared to the interaction of the different interventions. Such a design may be portrayed as follows:

		ACT Plus Supportive Housing	Usual MH Services
MH Court		A	B
Usual Court		C	Control

In this design, each cell represents a different iteration of two experimental comparisons. One axis represents the two court conditions; the other axis represents the two mental health service options. Individuals in this study would need to be randomized across all four cells. If positive effects for a particular condition were produced by such a design, it would provide a more direct answer to questions regarding the extent to which desired outcomes are attributable to the mental health court, intensive mental health services, or the interaction of the two. Substantial feasibility questions are implied by such a design. At an operational level, a researcher would need to have sufficient collaboration with courts and mental health service providers to validly provide all four intervention options. At the design level, a large enough sample size is needed to randomize enough participants to each of the four cells, to provide sufficient statistical power. Using the charting system we have employed before, the design would look like this:

$$
\begin{array}{cccc}
R & O & X_A & O \\
R & O & X_B & O \\
R & O & X_C & \\
R & O & & O \\
\end{array}
$$

In designing the study, selection of the proposed control condition is integral to defining the basic question answered by an RCT. Taking the time to understand the current standard of care and determining how an experimental intervention may build on that standard is likely the most policy-relevant way to conceptualize a control condition. Other options may provide more in-depth information about the relative effectiveness of different intervention strategies.

Potential Confounds

The previous section reviewed one way in which RCT results can be confounded in the initial design stage. That is, interpretation of cause and effect is limited by the extent to which more than one service intervention factor could be the cause of the outcome. One cannot separate the impact of these service factors in analysis. In the example of mental health courts, the confound in the original RCT design by Cosden and colleagues (2003, 2005) was the inability to separate the impact of the court arrangement from the intensive mental health service intervention in explaining the outcome.

This section will examine potential confounds that may arise in the implementation of an RCT. They are worth considering in the design phase, because steps can be taken in planning and designing the RCT to reduce the likelihood that these confounds will become a problem in implementation, and consequently, in analyzing results. Confounds have to do with the threats to internal validity, testing, and instrumentation, and how these may interact with the conditions of a randomized trial. To review, *testing* refers to the impact of measurement (taking a test) as a potential learning mechanism for individuals. For example, if one takes a test with provocative, memorable questions about sexual behavior, this memorable event may have the impact of raising awareness and thus result in new thinking about these behaviors. Consequently, one rationale for employing post-test-only designs is when there is a plausible argument that the pre-test measures will be highly reactive with the intervention (that is, testing may sensitize individuals in an experimental condition to be more receptive to learning skills or information that are integral to the outcome measure). Therefore, the pre-testing becomes potentially part of what explains the effectiveness of the intervention. If there is a concern about this possible reactivity, a Solomon four-group design (no relation) provides a means to control for this testing effect:

$$
\begin{array}{cccc}
R & O & X & O \\
R & O & & O \\
R & & X & O \\
R & & & O \\
\end{array}
$$

In this design, to determine whether differences between conditions are attributed to testing, the two groups that do not receive the pre-testing provide an opportunity to test against the other two pre-tested groups. A multifactorial analysis of the four groups, including the interaction between pre-testing and the intervention, determines the extent to which the pre-testing played a role in producing the outcome. This design is rarely used due to feasibility issues and prohibitive costs.

Instrumentation refers to differences in measurement that are not inherent in the measurement technology per se, but rather represent changes in the calibration of the measure under different circumstances and from administration to administration. An analogy is weight scales in a grocery store. Two scales may be differently calibrated. Both scales may weigh a product in kilograms, but the differences in calibration due to wear and tear over time may result in differences in the weight obtained. In social measures, the calibration is usually a human technology issue, such as research worker training, interviewing skill, data collection efficiency, and rating consistency. The variable efficacy of training service providers to interview and complete data collection forms in a reliable and valid manner may also be an issue. The confounding concern arises if these procedures differ by condition or in the interaction of condition by time in an RCT.

If the resources are available, differences in instrumentation are best controlled by proposing to hire data collectors accountable to the researcher. These data collectors collect all data for all conditions. Therefore, even if interviewing patterns change over time, particularly from practice guidelines (more efficient, greater consistency in clarifying questions, etc.), it can be assumed that the changes impact all design conditions equally. However, in many cases in which researchers are dependent on data collected by staff at the host site implementing the intervention, the human technology of data collection can be drastically different from setting to setting or from time to time, especially given the high turnover found in many service agencies. Such a situation may easily be confounded with conditions of the randomized trial through no intent of deception by the data collectors. For example, those responsible for data collection at one site may become very efficient at collecting reliable, valid data, whereas another site may change data collectors frequently or have data collectors who are unreliable or not particularly motivated to collect data, thus resulting in a large amount of missing or unreliable data. Problems of interpretation arise if these data collection confounds either suppress an effect or enhance an effect that is not present in reality. If a researcher has to use data collectors who differ by condition, extra care in data quality control procedures is likely to be considered. In addition to usual checks for completeness of data, data collectors need to be trained together to agree on ratings and data-entry decisions, and be brought together occasionally to review data quality. One reason that data collector quality may differ by site is that the sites are purposely designed to be separate by condition, in order to control for potential contamination of conditions. Thus, these considerations must be taken into account in the design of the RCT.

Controlling for Contamination of Conditions

Contamination of conditions is referred to colloquially as the *blurring of conditions, drift,* or *treatment dilution.* It is one of the most pernicious threats to the validity of a randomized trial in relatively uncontrolled field settings (Dennis, 1990). Therefore, attention to this threat deserves a great deal of attention. It should be a priority in the design process. Design decisions about the qualifications of staff to hire, geographic location for interventions, relationships among participants, and the participants pipeline all figure in examining this process. The ways in which contamination may occur are the following:

- Control condition participants gain benefit from experimental condition intervention.
- Experimental condition drifts toward control intervention (usual care).
- Changes occur in the intervention environment.

In assessing these threats, a clear conceptualization of the distinction between experimental and control provides a guide to what issues need to be addressed in designing the RCT. In the third authors study of critical time intervention (CTI) for men leaving prison, one key difference between the experimental service and the enhanced control service is that the experimental service engages the client inside prison before release and follows him into the community, whereas the control condition service works on reentry planning during the client's prison stay, but does not follow the client after release. The prison wall provides a concrete (certainly!) line for the difference between conditions.

In a study of case management for homeless individuals with mental illness leaving jail, the distinction between the ACT team experimental intervention and the individual intensive case manager intervention was more difficult to maintain. Fidelity to the ACT model requires that the team share clients as a group. Clients are not assigned to individual case managers. Our comparison to individual case managers was designed partially to test whether the team aspect had an effect along with the intensity of the ACT intervention. When in operation, the ACT team often assigned cases to individual ACT team members, because the team members believed this to be more efficient and a more effective way to serve clients who had difficulty forming relationships. Meanwhile, two of the three individual intensive case managers worked at the same agency and, by collegial agreement, often would work as a team on their combined cases (Solomon & Draine, 1995). In each case, the shift in behavior away from the intended interventions, thus blurring conditions, was driven by the professional behaviors of the individuals delivering the interventions. The case managers were acting in what they perceived to be the best interests of individual clients. Even more intensive, ongoing engagement with the providers can help build a greater appreciation for the distinctions between the intervention conditions, so that a clear intervention comparison is maintained in the RCT. Some strategies for this are reviewed in Chapter 6. The focus on maintaining the integrity of treatment conditions also generates issues relating to external generalizability, which is reviewed in Chapter 7.

Containing Contamination

Contamination refers to a situation in which individuals in the control condition, either providers or participants, may come to indirectly benefit from some social interaction with the experimental intervention. This is often a concern when the conditions of the intervention are in close proximity to one another. Examples include any intervention where both experimental and control participants are in the same setting. Consider an example in which youth in the experimental study are asked to complete homework assignments between intervention sessions, where they apply new skills with others. If the experimental and control participants are in the same service setting, the "others" could include youth in the control condition. Thus, the adherence of the youth to the experimental condition could have a potential effect of "teaching" these skills to youth in the control condition. Although the impact of the homework assignment may not be as strong an effect as participating in the full intervention, the potential effect may result in a dilution of the effect of the intervention in the final results. Generally, opportunities for information sharing by experimental and control condition participants are among the most likely to result in contamination of control conditions.

Such contamination may also take place through service providers. Health and social service professionals can learn from observing one another and adapting techniques they see in practice. If experimental condition clinicians are trained in techniques that other clinicians can observe in action or verbally communicate, a chance exists that these practices may impact the other clinicians' work, particularly when these strategies seem to produce desired outcomes. Steps to remove these threats are dependent on the resources available to the researcher. The most obvious is to make sure in the design of the RCT that interventionists and clients in the experimental condition are separated from those in the control. This may require separate physical locations for each intervention condition or different times of operation if separate locations are not feasible. However, different times of operation would likely introduce a new potential confound. Furthermore, random assignment of clients requires that each client be available for each location or time. Therefore, contamination threats may have implications for the design of an RCT and the specific randomization strategy employed.

Intervention Drift

Contamination may also be a concern among professionals who implement the service conditions. In hiring professionals to deliver services for an experimental study, both experience and an open mind toward new ways of serving clients are desirable traits. Operationally, finding both of these characteristics in the same person may be a challenge. Experienced professionals in service settings have years of experience working within complex systems. Thus, they have connections, ways of understanding rules and regulations, and accumulated practice wisdom in a professional field. In other words, what they likely know best is the treatment-as-usual (TAU) condition in the setting for the planned RCT. As described in detail in Chapter 6 on implementation, in studies of complex interventions, experienced clinicians, when facing a challenge, will fall back on this base of clinical experience time and again. The problem arises when relying on this experience may lead to drift (in which the experimental intervention moves toward looking exactly like the TAU). Chapter 6 reviews several corrections for this. In cases in which this form of contamination can be anticipated, the researcher must consider what steps will be taken to prevent contamination and plan for necessary resource allocations to assure that such preventions will be done, as this is essential to protecting the scientific validity of the RCT.

An RCT must include a protocol for assuring implementation of the experimental intervention as intended. Training and ongoing support and monitoring for the experimental intervention must be of a level of intensity that will assure that the RCT will be centrally focused on testing the intervention proposed. Regular fidelity checks are often included in the research design as part of the data collection plan to document implementation. These checks can be used as a concerted effort to correct drift from either condition. Some of this drift may be informative about the feasibility or generalizability of the intervention from one setting to another. Fidelity assessments can thus also provide in-depth contextual data on the challenges of implementing the intervention.

It is essential to consider specified procedures to minimize these threats in a research design. Conducting appropriate pilot work will provide a preliminary understanding of the intervention and the settings for the intervention, and will assist in designing controls for potential threats to internal validity within community settings. The mechanisms to address these threats must be feasible and practical, but a researcher can only do so much to keep separate groups of people who are in the same population and in physical proximity, in order to maintain their distinction. This is an especially tricky issue since these are characteristics of the very "real-world" intervention environments in which a researcher wants to demonstrate effectiveness. Thus, these threats lie at the intersection of internal and external validity. Creating a design that addresses these threats will build an understanding of the intervention in context as well as create a stronger, more defensible design.

Changes in the Intervention Environment

History is the term used to describe a threat to internal validity in which an event, such as a change in the environment (agency, community, global) may serve as an explanation for a resulting change in the outcome(s) (dependent variable) that rivals the hypothesized independent variable (Monette, Sullivan, & DeJong, 2005). Conventionally, when research methods are taught in social work programs, this concern is followed with the assertion that experimental designs offer a control for history, as both conditions are implemented simultaneously. For example, history can become a confounding factor in an RCT. As with other confounds, the complicating issue to control is not the existence of history effects per se, but rather whether the environmental change or event impacts the conditions differently.

Policy level events can be design confounds. Consider that, in many instances, randomized trials are supported with special program funding for the untested experimental intervention. The control condition of usual services may be funded through Medicaid or another billable funding source. A significant change in funding policy could impact the billable service, resulting in the control condition being either more restricted or more richly funded, thus changing the relationship to the experimental condition in one way or another. Other policy-level revisions that may differ by condition are changes in administrations that bring about changes in agency-level policies, which may support either the experimental or control condition. Given the long time period for most community-based RCTs, it can be reasonably expected that service innovations will emerge and be implemented in the host setting during the course of the study period. If this service innovation or policy change impacts both conditions equally, the researcher can be confident in the results of the RCT. Confidence in this assertion can be shaky, however, when the newly introduced service innovation interacts in some way with one condition or another to change some balance in the experimental or control services that are being compared.

Being able to change these policy-level confounds would be a rather high expectation. However, one design response to control for such confounds is to be prepared to gather data that could be used to analyze the impact of changes on the study results. Such a strategy is suggested by Dennis (1990), who has studied complex randomized community-based trials and their confounds. He suggests that a randomized trial can be thought of as nested within a quasi-experiment. The example he proposed was to nest an RCT of an innovative service enhancement within a longitudinal time series design. One would begin the time series some time before the randomized trial. His example has a six-month prospective baseline assessment phase to test the client pipeline, then a pilot period in which all participants enter into the experimental intervention, perhaps to train staff. This design approach would then provide a long baseline period to which a change in policy could be compared. Thus, longitudinal data would be available to assess the impact of the policy change during the RCT, and by incorporating this impact into analysis (Dennis, 1990).

Contamination concerns may be a particular consideration in RCTs of service system interventions, in which individuals may be assigned to an experimental intervention that is intended to have an effect on a service delivery system or on a designated population of individuals. In these cases, individuals may be the subject of the intervention, with an anticipated outcome of changed individual behavior. However, an ultimate outcome may be a change in their social environment that impacts the behavior of providers or other social actors in that environment. An example could be the use of police-based interventions for health and social concerns. In different interventions focused on police response to domestic violence and for those with mental illness, specialized police officers are trained to be available for calls that involve these concerns.

A researcher interested in these programs may want to propose an RCT of such specialized training, randomizing officers to specialized training versus a control condition with no specific training. It has been a repeated experience that once a program of specialized officers becomes known, the identification of individuals with these targeted problems (especially through police dispatchers) rises substantially (Hirschel & Buzawa, 2002; Teller, Munetz, Gil, & Ritter, 2006). This is partly due to a greater awareness and sensitivity to the issue, and partly due to the addition of a resource to help solve related problems encountered by police officers. In either case, the behavior of police personnel is changed, whether they received specialized training or not. In these cases, the contamination of conditions is likely not a technical design issue for an RCT, but a conceptual issue in understanding the interaction of the experimental intervention with how it is to be tested for effectiveness. In this case, the researcher might consider that the appropriate unit of analysis is at a level higher than the individual. Therefore, the most policy-responsive design would propose measuring the impact of the program on districts, precincts, or jurisdictions. Discussion of such higher-level randomization is not part of the plan of this text. However, the authors direct readers to work by others on these designs (Boruch et al., 2004; Boruch, 2005).

Biased Attrition

Attrition refers to the patterns of loss of research participants in follow-up waves after they are enrolled in the RCT. A researcher must be prepared to answer a number of detailed questions about the process of their RCT's implementation. How many participants are expected to be lost after baseline interviews? How many participants are likely to remain in the study providing data through all data points? The range of attrition in literature from longitudinal studies is very wide, from less than 5% to more than 50%, with attrition rates over 30% generally referred to as "high" (Ribisl et al., 1996). These rates vary greatly based on the nature of the study population, the services, and the circumstances under which individuals are recruited into the RCT. For example, the authors have consistently noted a low refusal rate for voluntary consent to research studies when consent is offered in prison or jail, usually lower than 5%, as opposed to recruitment in community settings in which the refusal rate is closer to 20%. This high agreement rate could be attributed to the overwhelming experience of boredom by most people in prison (Moser et al., 2004). For those who have studied prisoners leaving jail with follow-up studies, the first "real" refusal point is the first interview after release, at which point significant numbers engage in strategies to "not be found" or simply refuse participation. Unfortunately, at this point, this loss of participants is attrition—and not merely refusal to consent—and it may impact outcomes.

Given the longer follow-up period for study participants in community-based RCTs, a fair amount of attrition can be expected and built into the RCT design. Even if attrition does not seem a likely concern that will bias implementation, a high degree of attrition will threaten the validity at the study analysis stage. Significant attrition can introduce unmeasured heterogeneity into the experimental and/or control conditions, thus undermining the premise that the conditions are equal because of randomization. The real problem is biased attrition to one condition or another. This was a concern with the authors' RCT of individuals leaving jail who were assigned to two intensive case management conditions and the usual community services. The loss of participants at follow-up was greater for the control condition. Those who were in intensive services were easier to locate due to their involvement in such a service, but those in the control condition who were able to be found were likely to be more functionally stable. Thus, the finding of no difference among the three conditions may have been due to the type of clients who were located in the control condition (Solomon & Draine, 1995). Further, a lower overall sample size will reduce the statistical power of analysis, thus increasing type II error. In summary, a high attrition rate introduces a number of problems into understanding the results of an RCT study, and the potential for bias is only one of them.

The most basic step in controlling for attrition is to keep attrition as low as possible. A specific set of strategies that limit potential attrition needs to be considered at the design stage. Much of the guidance from the literature and from other researchers is to enact a protocol that engages individuals in the study and keeps them engaged between interviews. The locator form discussed in Chapter 6 is one means of limiting attrition. The protocol for maintaining locator information includes a plan for checking it or updating it at every opportunity. Some researchers propose and include in their budgets a paid incentive for participants to contact study staff to update locator form information.

A design strategy to reduce the impact of attrition on an RCT is to propose implementing a phase of the design in which a pre-randomization introductory phase process absorbs most of the attrition that may occur in the early months of the study (Drake, McHugo, Becker, Anthony, & Clark, 1996; Mueser et al., 2004). To some, this might be considered too much of a compromise of external validity in favor of larger effect sizes (Roberts & Pratt, 2007). More precisely, it is one of those decisions that involves a trade-off of external validity, in order to claim a bit more strength in internal validity, which is the primary focus of RCTs. The strategy is typically to engage all participants in a preparatory phase of the project before they are randomized. The preparatory phase could be a brief class in a topic related to the study, an interest meeting or two, or a wave or more of preliminary data collection. The randomization of participants into conditions is held off until after this phase is complete. Thus, those most likely to drop out of the study are given a chance to do so before their decision impacts the RCT.

In Mueser and colleagues' (2004) use of a two-session introductory research process for a randomized trial of supported employment for people with mental illness, 72% (204 out of 283) of the participants entered the randomization phase. Using this process, the researchers gained confidence that early attrition was not likely to threaten the internal validity of their study, while inserting a limitation to its overall generalizability only to those highly motivated to enter the RCT. An alternative view might be that this strategy does not undercut external validity, but rather represents the fairest comparison among the more motivated clients.

Another way to reduce attrition is through the inclusion of incentives. Given the likelihood of attrition on the first interview after release from incarceration, the CTI study pays a premium of $20 more than the base $20 for the first interview after release. Recall the aforementioned Festinger and colleague's (2005) study that examined the role of subject payments in increasing the risk of drug use among drug abuse treatment clients. The levels of incentive did not have an effect on drug use. The greater incentive payment and cash payments, as opposed to gift cards, had a positive effect on follow-up rates. The authors argue that their results support a scientific argument for larger-sum payments to subjects in order to increase the validity of study results. They also point out that more money in payments may save money in follow-up activities (Festinger et al., 2005). The amount and nature of incentive payments must be determined when designing such elements of an RCT.

As with other confounding problems, the issue with biased attrition is controlling the extent to which differences in attrition by condition may impact the results of the analysis. The first step in controlling bias is having the capacity to catch it as it emerges. An investigator can decide that field workers record all attempts at contacting participants. Next, the investigator makes a decision for close supervision of these tracking records, as these records can help in troubleshooting particular attrition problems. If data are to be regularly examined by a data safety and monitoring board or an advisory board, attrition bias can be proposed as one aspect of that board's analysis. A plan can be designed for investigators and their field coordinators to examine attrition using available study data to assure that attrition, even if evenly distributed percentage-wise among conditions, is not biased by some characteristic.

Finally, researchers can use statistical techniques that model missing data and compensate for it. Attrition by condition can be modeled at any phase of the project, and can be based on refusal rates, failure to locate rates, or combinations of these. Ribisl and colleagues (1996) warn that different techniques can generate different results. To conduct these analyses, these data must be gathered. Anticipating data collection in the design phase ensures that corrective actions can occur at implementation and that data will be available for varied analysis strategies to address these problems at the analysis phase.

Randomization Procedures

When gaining informed consent from individuals to participate in a randomized trial, researchers are often heard stating, "You will be assigned to one of the groups at random, in a way like flipping a coin." Although this is a simple way to help almost anyone understand randomization, the considerations that go into the randomization procedure amount to a bit more than merely flipping a coin. Randomization in an RCT is based on the premise that there is a planned, known chance that a person will be assigned to a particular study condition. The chance does not need to be the same for each condition. However, it must be known and be a part of the plan for allocating individuals to conditions.

Assignment to conditions is typically equal across conditions. If assignment to the condition is unequal, a design or substantive reason must exist for the difference. In some cases, the intervention may be sufficiently novel that the researchers want to have a substantial number of people in the experimental condition to power exploratory analyses of subgroups within that condition, perhaps at a ratio of 2:1. Such a decision provides statistical power for examinations by sociodemographic characteristics or the exploration of potential moderators of effectiveness. In some clinical trials, it may be that the control group receives the larger proportion of participants. Where follow-up is difficult (e.g., if control participants are less connected to the service system), control condition assignment can be made larger to assure an adequate number of individuals in the control condition at analysis, in order to account for expected attrition. Of course, in this circumstance, bias in the attrition by condition may be more of a problem than the size of the group itself at the point of analysis, as noted earlier.

In the age of computers, random number generators are readily available, although random number tables can still be found in the back of some research texts. The use of these tables and computer random number generators is preferred to physical forms of randomization, such as shuffled index cards or even the proverbial coin flipping. Some allocation methods used to assign people to condition may *seem* to be random, but are not. These include alternating assignment, taking odd and even chart numbers, dividing a group by alphabetical last name order, and the like. Although it is true that these methods introduce far less control in the allocation of individuals to services or treatment options than is usually present, these procedures are far from random. Only mathematically based procedures can truly be referred to as *random* or *randomized*, and the current availability of random number generators on the nearest computer makes this process both easy and accessible.

Even random generators cannot be considered truly random, as they are still dependent on human programming rather than some force of nature to generate their "pseudorandom" numbers. These instruments have usually been tested for lack of systematic bias in the sequencing of the numbers. These sets of standards make a difference in some areas of engineering and in statistical modeling procedures that require use of random generators. However, the scale of most community-based randomized trials is far below the level at which fine differences in the qualities of random number generators will make any substantial methodological difference. Any generator with a degree of confidence in its randomness will suffice.

Two general principles of random assignment do arise from the modeling work done on randomness and the impact on outcomes of random assignment, such as through Monte Carlo experiments. One principle is that the larger the sample size, the more confident a researcher can be that each group is generalizable to the target population. This means that larger sample sizes and larger group sizes assure greater generalizability of the samples to the populations they represent. Larger trials carry fewer concerns about using statistical means to control for potential differences among conditions. Second, given a large enough sample size, random assignment is the most reliable method for equal distribution of individual characteristics in the sample, better than the use of any intervening steps, such as stratification. If a subgroup is significantly represented in the sampling frame or recruitment pipeline (say, 20% or more in the context of a sufficiently large overall sample size), relying on randomization to allocate these individuals to conditions equally is more effective than attempting to control their distribution through stratification.

A further reason for relying exclusively on randomization at the highest level is that randomization distributes and controls for different characteristics of individuals that may impact results—both known *and* unknown. Stratification can only offer a limited control for an important variable that is known and easily measurable. Furthermore, stratifying will undercut the power of randomization in order to control for those factors that are not known or comprehended, which may potentially impact results in interaction with intervention conditions.

Stratified Randomization

Stratifying the random assignment may be useful if the overall sample size is expected to be small (100 or less), with a subpopulation of substantive interest, or when the proportion of a subpopulation of interest is extremely small (e.g., less than 20%). Stratification is utilized when random assignment may result in the allocation of participants across conditions in an imbalanced manner. If the sample size is small, randomization may not ensure equal proportions of important characteristics across conditions. If the sample size is small enough for this to be an issue, the researcher likely has a greater concern about sufficient sample size for statistical power overall.

In the second author's study of CTI for men with mental illness leaving prison, an important characteristic in the study design was whether enough individuals were being released on parole as compared to maxing-out their sentence without parole. If there were enough participants in each group, comparisons could be made on this important characteristic. Checking preliminary data, the distribution on this characteristic for prisoners with mental illness was almost exactly 50/50. Given the planned recruitment goal of 356 and the 50/50 proportion, an initial plan for stratifying random assignment by parole status was eliminated as unnecessary. However, if we were to include women in this study, there may be an argument for stratifying by gender, as women might be less than 20% of the people leaving prison.

When stratification is used, the procedure is to randomize within the stratified groups. Therefore, a randomization procedure must be generated, such as including lists of random numbers for each subgroup. This level of greater complexity also presents more opportunities for randomization to be compromised. Further, technically, the generalizability is within each stratum of random assignment, not across the whole sample as representative of the population.

Cluster Randomization

In some cases, randomization occurs at the group or cluster level, in which intact groups are randomized with all eligible and consenting individuals within a particular group entering the assigned condition. Hence, this approach is referred to as a *cluster-randomized trial*. This randomization strategy can be a specific response to concerns about contamination of interventions, as individuals randomized to different conditions may not be in the same setting. One can randomize practices, health plans, or geographical areas to name a few (Donner & Klur, 2004; Mazor, Sabin, Boudreau, Goodman, et al., 2007). In the human immunodeficiency virus (HIV) prevention intervention in which the first author is involved, case managers were randomized. This procedure was employed to reduce the possibility of contamination by the case manager serving clients from both conditions. This approach is also used for greater efficiency by serving everyone in a given service intervention in one location. In other instances, if much of the data are routinely collected, it is not feasible to gain consent from each individual, and the intervention is a change in policy or guideline, then cluster-randomized design is cost- and time-efficient (Mazor, et al, 2007). However, these designs require larger sample sizes to compensate for the limited degrees of freedom and variance inflation imposed by clustering.

Blocked Randomization

At times, particularly in community-based trials in which teams of intervention providers are prepared to provide service, a pressing need arises to ensure an adequate number of individuals are assigned to each condition at any given time. Of course, if left to random chance, it is possible that the first 20 cases of recruited participants would be assigned to the control condition. This situation can be particularly problematic for interventions that are based on group processes, as those delivering the intervention typically need to wait for sufficient numbers of group members to run the intervention. Blocked randomization can be proposed as a strategy to assure an even distribution of new clients to all conditions as enrollment is occurring, while preserving the predicted likelihood of being assigned to one condition or another (Cavanaugh, 2007). In blocked randomization, assignment allocation sheets are made up for smaller units, perhaps 10 at a time. Where assignment is 50/50, providers in an experimental condition can reliably expect that, given this procedure, of each 10 new participants, 5 will be their clients. Therefore, following-up on the group intervention example, group leaders can reasonably plan for when groups will be operational during the course of the RCT.

Blinding

In most biomedical fields that utilize RCTs, participants and treatment providers as well as investigators are *blinded* to the assignment of the participant to the study condition (i.e., providers, participants, nor investigators know whether clients are in the experimental or control condition). This blinding procedure is employed to ensure that as little bias as possible enters through social interactions that may impact the results of the trial. The goal here is to limit/control bias should individuals providing services to the participants know the assigned treatment condition, and similarly, to protect participants from influencing outcomes due to their knowing the condition to which they have been assigned. To ensure the blinding, steps can be taken to remove providers and research workers from the allocation of participants to conditions. For example, in most drug trials, the clinician working on the trial orders a drug from a specialized research pharmacy, and the drug for that individual arrives at the clinic without an indication of whether it is the active experimental drug or a placebo. All treatment is provided to the participant in the clinic as if the drug they are receiving is active, with precautions against potential side effects and psychosocial supports provided to all participants.

However, in community-based RCTs of complex psychosocial interventions, it is obvious how the interventions are delivered. Service providers cannot deliver different educational group strategies while "blinded." Rarely can participants be blinded, given that the consent describes the different service interventions under study, and the participant can accurately surmise from his own experience to which condition he has been assigned. Similarly, the researcher is well aware of the assignment. This is particularly true of random assignment to structural social service options. Therefore, random assignment procedures in most community-based psychosocial RCTs are generally observable to all, except at recruitment, when assignment to condition is generally not known to anyone until after baseline interviews and assessments are complete and random assignment takes place.

However, Gellis and his colleagues (2007) were able to blind interviewers in his pilot study of Brief Problem-Solving Therapy in Home Care targeted at older adults with severe depressive symptoms in acute home care setting delivered by clinical social workers. Interviewers were blinded to treatment assignment in order reduce bias on outcomes. This type of blinding may be possible, contingent on the nature of the questions asked. When conducting a fidelity assessment, the blinding may be violated by the participants' responses.

Randomization in Practice

In most community-based psychosocial RCTs, random assignment is not conducted until baseline interviews and assessment are completed. The initial assessments are completed with no prior knowledge of the condition to which the participant will be assigned. Typically, the potential participant is presented with a consent form and is engaged in a consent process. In the consent process, the potential participant is told what the conditions in the study are, that assignment is random, what the odds are of being assigned to each condition, and what will happen in each condition. Baseline interviews are conducted and, once completed, a researcher may call a coordinating office or consult a laptop computer program to find out the condition to which the individual is assigned.

Random assignment is usually designed to be centrally controlled in large trials. It is likely based on sequential assignment of participants as they are enrolled in the RCT. Multiple workers may be doing baselines at the same time in different locations with different participants, and the order in which they call a coordinator is linked to which condition the study participant will be assigned. The coordinator is typically working from a computerized random number–generated list of assignments to condition, and he will simply enter the individual's identification number into a database for the next open slot, which results in assignment to the specific condition. This separation of interface from participants and the random assignment mechanism is a protection against the random assignment process being subverted, as when a risk exists of field workers and providers manipulating random assignment for a "needy" client to suit the preferences of providers, participants, and even research workers. This is well-documented in all types of RCT research, notably in randomized studies of arrest for domestic violence, in which police officers were able to subvert random assignment because the process was transparent to them, and they had the ability to manipulate assignment to the condition that they believed was in the best interest of the participant (Sherman & Berk, 1984).

Even in circumstances in which remote connection to a coordinator is not feasible, centralized control of random assignment can still be maintained. In studies of services to people leaving prison or jail, recruitment, enrollment, and baseline interviewing typically takes place inside the prison or jail before release. In this case, an envelope procedure, much like those used with index cards in previous generations of randomized trials, is useful, as computers are not allowed to be brought into these facilities. The coordinator of the randomization process generates the order of assignment, and then places the assignments in envelopes that are numbered in order. Once a baseline interview is complete, the next sequential envelope is opened and the participant is informed of his assignment. However, this process is not perfect, as it needs to accommodate the possibility of more than one field worker enrolling participants in multiple facilities concurrently. In these instances, the research workers have different envelopes. If they are opened out of order, the reasons are recorded and the sequence continues with that constraint.

In summary, the random assignment process must be carefully designed and implemented in order to ensure true randomness in procedures. To the extent possible, the simplest random assignment strategy should drive the process. Given the importance of random assignment for RCT validity, any intervening steps to randomization, such as stratification or block assignment, have to be considered and clearly justified. Procedures for random assignment must be centrally controlled and be designed to protect against subversions by providers, participants, or research field workers.

Sampling

RCT methods are focused on internal validity. Most introductory research texts describe how internal and external validity exist in tension, and detail steps to be taken to ensure that internal validity is not undercut by external validity, and vice versa. RCT methods are generally considered the "gold standard" of empirical support for internal validity (i.e., the effectiveness of interventions and cause-and-effect arguments). The gold standard for external validity, by comparison, is the population-based random sample. Like the RCT, this method relies on randomness as the basis for the strength of its external validity. It is very rare, however, for a study to have both a randomly selected population-based sample and random assignment. One could think of scenarios in which this is possible, but in most community-based settings, such a strategy would be untenable.

Because the nature of social services is so context dependent, the strongest of EBPs are reliant on the resources and peculiarities of a service setting for implementation. Moreover, each RCT implementation is shaped by these changing circumstances. One of the context-driven aspects of a service setting is its pipeline of clients. From where do clients come, and how are they engaged? This is often a defining characteristic of an intervention. One could create a scenario in which multiple sites might recruit from a sampling frame of clients who are then randomly referred to different service options. The process itself would be so different from most naturalistic processes of service delivery that it is likely that the sampling procedure would shape the nature of the service and engagement process, such that the study results would only be generalizable to that specific process. Furthermore, a good deal of the U.S. federal research funding streams have been depleted over the past 20 years for multi-site service trials, many of which faltered on their inability to control the heterogeneity of service contexts around and within the interventions (Cocozza et al., 2000; Lattimore, Broner, Sherman, Frisman, & Shafer, 2003; Obert et al., 2005). Such efforts were driven largely by policy makers who were anxious about the lack of data on service-level interventions and were looking for a strategy to increase their available evidence base quickly. However, the nature of such an evidence base is iterative. The RCT evidence base for community-based psychosocial intervention models needs to prioritize internal validity in the design process. This necessitates planning for a depth of information on the context of a study that allows others to understand its limitations and arguments for external validity. These procedures will be discussed in the following chapter.

Capacity for a Fully Powered Randomized Controlled Trial

Community-based psychosocial RCTs of health and social services are reliant on naturalistic sampling opportunities for implementation. One of the key elements of preliminary work for an RCT is to understand the pipeline of clients through a system. Pipeline studies were described in some detail in Chapter 3, on planning. The design issue is this: At what point of the pipeline is it both feasible and conceptually important to recruit participants into the randomized trial? Specifying and operationalizing the point at which participants will be recruited into the RCT carries significance for the intervention pipeline—and thus the population to which results will be generalized. Therefore, part of design includes specifying the point of referral and its significance for the intervention, as well as the feasibility of garnering an adequate sample from that point for the RCT.

The astute researcher will generally anticipate problems in recruitment and will want to have empirical support for the capacity of a research setting to provide the necessary number of participants for the RCT. Slow and cumbersome recruitment is often reported in RCT studies (Boruch, Rindskopf, Anderson, Amidjaya, & Jansson, 1979; Dennis, 1990). Rigorous research designs anticipate questions about recruitment problems, especially in complex systems. Data from a pilot study of recruitment or a pipeline study that show the availability of the required number of individuals who meet study criteria (taking into account expected numbers of those refusing to participate and those lost through attrition) will provide direction for designing feasible recruitment and retention strategies to achieve the required participants for an RCT. These data will then be used to support a recruitment strategy based on these referral patterns.

Inclusion and Exclusion Criteria

In developing an RCT, the conscientious social work researcher has used the literature as a guide, conceptualized an intervention model in a particular setting, and has explored the setting for how the intervention may best fit. The researcher has used this information to guide a preliminary study of pipeline (i.e., client availability) in the specific setting, particularly through the proposed recruitment point of the service system, in order to know the flow of clients. The next step is to use all this information to support the establishment of sampling criteria for the proposed RCT. If all the information is used well, the sampling criteria will be driven by the interaction of these data and the conceptualization of the intervention.

Defining these criteria is important for the RCT, as they often set the limitations to the external validity of the study results. Short of being able to take a random population sample, these criteria define the population to which study results can be generalized. Criteria for inclusion in a sample conventionally are defined in terms of both inclusion criteria and exclusion criteria, and each criterion needs to be operationally defined, just as is done with every variable in the RCT. For example, diagnostic criteria need to be operationalized as to whether chart diagnosis, self-report, or a diagnostic screening instrument will be used. These criteria generally will be specific to the intervention model to be tested. However, some broad categories of consideration apply to most studies. For inclusion criteria, consider:

- **Age.** Chronologic age is a factor in a number of interventions, particularly those that are specific to youth or older people. Age may have implications in terms of legal policies, ethical guidelines for research, and benefits policies that impact the service setting environment.
- **Diagnoses.** Specificity of diagnoses is usually more specific in controlled clinical studies than in community-based psychosocial RCTs. The typically broader criteria in community-based studies reinforce a degree of external validity, as service systems rarely use diagnostic criteria as tightly as those for clinical efficacy trials. In generating criteria for inclusion, be certain the criteria are grounded in the previous evidence base for the intervention. Also, consider how the diagnostic criteria may interact with the operation of the proposed service context for the RCT. One serious consideration will be to understand that seemingly similar diagnostic criteria established by one service system may not correspond with the understanding of diagnosis in another system. This situation is seen in the intersection of the justice and behavioral health systems, where different organizational cultures use diagnosis and treatment for different purposes. A misunderstanding of these interactions may result in serious underestimates of available study participants (Blank, 2006). In jails, for instance, the context creates different needs for diagnoses than for services outside the jail. There is less need to tease apart the cocaine or opiate addiction from mental illness, for example, so the path of least resistance is to label someone an addict and not wait for detox to sort it out from serious mental illness. Such a procedure would create a systematic bias against finding individuals with mental illness who also have problems in addiction.

- **Language considerations.** Given the great diversity of U.S. culture in both urban and rural settings, use of language other than English in health and social services is commonplace. In many circumstances, the reliance on the researcher being proficient only in English is insufficient justification for an English-only inclusion criterion. Such a decision needs to be grounded in data on the population itself to justify its appropriateness.
- **Geographic considerations.** Many interventions are geographically specific, and criteria should include geographic considerations if they are important.

It is less common to have exclusion criteria in effectiveness RCTs than in efficacy trials, as RCTs are not as limiting as efficacy studies; for example, ruling out all comorbidities is not usually necessary.

For exclusion criteria, consider:

- **Vulnerable populations.** Prisoners, youth, and pregnant women carry additional regulatory and ethical expectations when they are included in research. Researchers should decide whether excluding them will conceptually impact the validity of an RCT. Major considerations are whether the intervention will incorporate activities with the client in jail or prison, whether youth may be emancipated or able to make their own decisions about research and/or treatment (a state-by-state legal question in the U.S.), and the extent to which pregnancy may be a consideration in the intervention.
- **Individuals with disorders or comorbid conditions that will likely not benefit from the service model.** In many behavioral health studies, organic brain injury–based disorders are excluded because of differences in etiology and treatment.
- **Differing system status levels may be an important exclusion criterion.** For example, in the authors probation and parole study (not an RCT, but an example of this phenomenon), some probationers were not required to personally report to a probation office. Because interpersonal interaction was important for this study, nonreporting probation was an exclusionary criterion.

Inclusion Criteria for CTI Study (no exclusion criteria)

1. Male age 18 and older
2. Leaving a NJDOC prison with a release date within two to three months
3. Relocating to Camden County
4. Actively classified as a special-needs prisoner
5. Diagnosis (determined by interviewer screening with the MINI) of schizophrenia spectrum disorder, bipolar disorder, major mood disorder or depression (including dysthymia), anxiety disorder, or PTSD
6. Voluntary informed consent

Sampling Method and Recruitment Procedures

As indicated previously, nonprobability sampling methods are the dominant form of sampling in RCTs, including community-based psychosocial RCTs. Often a purposive sample of individuals in a particular circumstance—in jail, in foster care, or those individuals desiring help with employment—is used. Researchers find these individuals by going to the places where they congregate. Essentially, these are samples of convenience or availability samples with specific criteria. Often, these samples are a specific type of sample referred to as *consecutive sampling*, whereby all individuals who meet study criteria are recruited as they enter the service setting recruitment point. Given that sampling for community-based psychosocial RCTs often occurs as individuals enter a specific point in the service, it is common to have consecutive-type samples.

To facilitate referrals into the RCT, the researcher should have research staff on site at the referral setting, often in constant communication with the agency staff who are making referrals. This level of research staff availability will ensure that questions about whether or not to refer an individual will be answered, which may facilitate more referrals to the RCT. A specific referral process needs to be designed clearly. Such a process may include a form to complete, or may use a contact person at an agency as a central point of referral for screening. This alludes to a previous discussion in Chapter 3, about negotiating a setting. Samples for RCTs may also be recruited from the general population. Some interventions are not dependent on formal service systems as a context, and thus a purposive sampling strategy will differ, with planned advertising or recruitment targeted to attract eligible individuals. Quotas may also be used for randomized trials. *Quota sampling* may be related to stratified randomization. A total sample proposed for a stratified randomization will likely include a pre-set number of slots for each level of stratification. In sampling, these slots amount to quotas. As with the stratified random sampling discussion, the use of quotas should be clearly justified.

In most circumstances, a researcher's sampling methods often result in a combination of purposive, quota, and even *snowball sampling*, in which individuals often refer friends, who can then be assessed in terms of meeting criteria. Given these patterns, the specification of the referral patterns and recruitment strategies is important to allow documentation of the full sampling frame that is represented and to argue for the generalizability of the sample and hence the results of the RCT.

Sample Size and Power

Statistical power with regard to RCTs is the capacity of a research design to detect a difference in outcomes between the experimental condition and the control condition, assuming a difference exists. The primary component of power over which a researcher has direct control is sample size (N): the more N; the more power. Other design factors are key determinants of power. These determinants begin with conceptualization. Will the intervention model have the potency and capacity to make the change that is hypothesized? This argument is grounded in previous research related to the intervention, as well as in the anticipated implementation of the intervention itself and its comparison condition. This potency of difference between conditions is grounded in the significance of your RCT. Designing aspects that will likely ensure faithful implementation of the intervention is also related to greater power, provided the hypothesized effect is true. If the interventions for the conditions are faithfully implemented, the difference between them is more likely to be detected.

Other factors in statistical power include the quality of measures to be used and the stringency of statistical tests proposed for analysis. More reliable measures increase statistical power (which will be discussed further under measurement). Power is also enhanced by a number of researcher design decisions and researcher commitments to a strongly implemented RCT. These statistical considerations cannot make up for an intervention that is conceptually flawed, or that is simply not going to engender empirical support no matter how high in quality other aspects of the study may be.

Operationalization of Experimental and Control Interventions

The independent variable in an RCT is whether a participant was assigned to the experimental or control condition. In this variable, a simple indicator variable, 1 or 0, is employed to indicate whether or not an individual was assigned to the experimental treatment (1) or control (0). To fully operationalize the independent variable, the researcher characterizes the intervention thoroughly and makes clear distinctions between the experimental intervention and its control condition.

In an RCT, the best-case scenario is to have an experimental intervention condition developed to the point at which it becomes manualized. Whereas the 1 or 0 dummy variable is the operationalization of the experimental intervention for statistical analysis purposes, the manual is the operationalization of the experimental intervention in practice. Like operationalizing other concepts in the study, the manual is a step-by-step process that indicates how one will proceed in implementing the intervention (see Chapter 3 regarding the elements of a treatment manual). The RCT design should have a clear role for the manual in operationalizing the intervention and for fidelity assessment, to assure that the primary independent variable (i.e., the "1" in the "1, 0" experimental-control condition variable) is reliably proposed.

A rigorous research design also carefully addresses the operationalization of the "0" in the "1, 0" variable—that is, the control condition. This side of the "1, 0" variable generally represents the usual care/treatment

(TAU). In these situations, the investigator is still responsible for opera-tionalizing what the "0" means, even if the investigator is not responsible for the implementation of the control condition intervention itself. The point is to fully operationalize the "1, 0" variable, so that what is being tested by the primary independent variable is thoroughly understood. A TAU condition will typically not be manualized. However, the investiga-tor is responsible for having sufficient information about the TAU so as to be able to comprehend the comparability of the interventions, as well as the essential differences that are hypothesized. Consequently, practice guidelines or a less structured manual will be helpful when it comes to implementation of the control condition of the RCT.

If the investigator is providing a benign intervention, a manual may be developed as a way of ensuring that the benign control intervention will be fully implemented while staying within the bounds of its concep-tualization. Having such a manual as a reference guide may be a check against intervention drift, previously mentioned as a possible confound. Recall that intervention drift involves the gradual change in intervention conditions to a point at which the two conditions are more alike than desired, thus undercutting the difference in the experimental interven-tion to be tested by the RCT. For the control condition, the undesired drift may result from incorporating aspects of the experimental condition.

Outcome Measures and Data Points

Early in this chapter, the design of an RCT was referred to as the opera-tionalization of the intervention's effectiveness. Looking at Figure 4.2, one sees that operationalizing effectiveness includes outcome measures. When conceptualizing any sort of model, a reasonable expectation is that the model is fully realized in operation. Indeed, every item in the right box is measured as an outcome in the CTI study. The mediator is measured, and CTI is operationalized with fidelity measures, a manual, and an enhanced usual-services control condition that is limited in its potential impact on outcomes, as the usual service does not provide planning or support services after release from prison. The outcome measures were selected based on several areas of focus that were considered important:

- Mental health outcomes that were empirically justified in the literature on case management, community integration, and recovery
- Criminal justice outcomes from this domain of literature
- Specific outcomes identified in the prior literature on CTI
- Measures that capture the change mechanism that may explain the outcome attributed to CTI

Conceptualizing these areas of measurement captures the multiple aspects of CTI for prisoners that are of interest to policy makers, practitioners, and researchers in social work, criminal justice, and mental health. The crucial feature of measurement selection is to demonstrate that the conceptual model is represented by the measurement protocol, and that the measurement plan and data collection provide for adequate data to test hypotheses derived from the conceptual model.

The failure to have a well-conceptualized intervention model that is tested by the research design is one of the *main* downfalls encountered in the literature on community-based psychosocial intervention research. There should be virtually no mysteries in a well-designed study. Every concept must be in the conceptual model and included in the hypotheses. Every study concept needs to be operationalized in the measurement section. Relationships implied by the conceptual model and the study hypotheses, including mediators and moderators, must be measured and then tested in the analysis. There is no room for surprise concepts, those that suddenly pop up in the measurement section.

In selecting measures, technical considerations concern the qualities of those measures. Researchers must select measures that meet standards for reliability and validity in the population under study. Although validity is essential, reliability is of a specific importance to assure the statistical power of the analysis. Unreliable measures can introduce error and reduce the capacity of an outcome model to detect differences. The investigator has to choose measures that have a demonstrated capacity to show change over time, and within the time period in which change will be measured. In the CTI study, for example, the previous work on CTI showed effects in nine months and at 18 months (nine months after close of intervention) (Susser et al., 1997). For this reason, many of the same measures as in previous studies of CTI are incorporated into this study with a different population, given their relevance to the population. The capacity of a measure to capture change is both technical and theoretical. Measuring concepts, in which great change is unlikely to happen quickly, may result in disappointing outcomes, as change may occur slowly. An example of this can occur with the concept of quality of life (QOL). Some QOL measures can detect change in a relatively short period of time, such as greater satisfaction with a new housing situation; however, overall positive outcomes of life satisfaction may be more difficult to detect within a limited time frame. Given that social workers are ultimately interested in such broader outcomes, these measures are still worth considering for data collection.

Sometimes, a researcher may decide on more frequent data points, closer together, to allow for the assessment of intervention process and outcomes in a different way than more global measures at more distance points in time. Such assessments may be important for interventions in which behavioral changes are expected to occur more quickly, and the process of change and movement toward ultimate outcomes of improved symptoms and functioning can be captured with more frequent data points. Of course, this results in greater data collection costs, if collected by primary data collectors. More frequent data points can generate a finer-grained association between intervention activities and distal outcomes.

Given the relationship between measurement and conceptualization, strategies for determining study data points are driven by different ways of thinking about the intervention, process, and outcome. For example, in the coping literature, responses to measurement items about coping over time are different from responses to items asking about coping behaviors in discrete time periods, such as every day or weekly (Folkman & Moskowitz, 2004). Each of these operationalizations will result in a different idea about coping, and knowing these implications and how they interact with the specified data points will be important in understanding what the researcher will learn from an RCT.

The selection of measures must be sensitive to validity as well. This includes consideration of the measure being valid for the population to be served, for the level of change expected within the time frame, and for cultural appropriateness. Remember, when testing the hypotheses, it is not the concepts themselves that are tested, but the variables derived from measures. Consequently, the congruence must be very high between the measures that are selected for a study and the concepts used to conceptualize the study. Otherwise the hypotheses will not be rigorously tested.

Data Analysis

Testing of hypotheses is the final step in operationalizing the RCT. Moving beyond ANOVA (analysis of variance), the classic model for testing the effectiveness of an intervention is a *regression model*, with control variables that are likely to impact outcomes, using each outcome measure in turn regressed on a dummy variable for experimental versus control condition. This approach has the interpretive advantage of expressing the impact of the intervention in terms of units of outcome. One critical caveat is the current expectation that analyses be conducted on an intent-to-treat basis. *Intent-to-treat* refers to grouping participants for purposes of analysis based on their original assignment to the treatment or control group. The alternative to this approach is removing those participants who were considered noncompliant, incomplete in the receipt of the intervention, or somehow out-of-line with ideal expectations of random assignment. The temptation to take the latter approach is understandable. One can hear an experimental intervention social worker saying, "But they didn't even come and give it a chance!" or "They only came once!" The ideal, however, does not represent the actual delivery of services, where whole segments of a population may only partially participate or perhaps participate not at all in services that are thought to be beneficial. Thus, the intent-to-treat approach is considered a more rigorous test that yields a more conservative estimate of the effect, and one that is more conceptually valid in modeling how service interventions tend to operate in the real world.

Within an intent-to-treat framework, other variables can be used to assess or control for the extent to which participants engage in RCT service interventions. Fidelity measures may provide some assessment of the extent to which an intervention was delivered as planned, given variables available from a fidelity measure at an individual and/or time varying level. Also, compliance, adherence, or engagement measures can be used to assess the extent to which showing up more than once even matters in the final analysis. These "dosage effects" must be conceptualized carefully so as not to be regarded as substituting for the main test of the independent variable in the RCT, the central point of the intent-to-treat analysis.

Analytic strategies have advanced substantially to include multilevel modeling and generalized estimating equations (GEE) models that can more readily capture change over time, given enough data points, which may be another reason to collect more data points. In addition to these models, advances in the estimation of missing data allow for the inclusion of cases that may have otherwise been excluded in the past.

In all of these analytic decisions, one of the most useful tools is a capable and sensible statistical consultant. The researcher cannot be expected to have all the required expertise, especially in applying statistical knowledge to real-world effectiveness trials. The role of the statistical consultant cannot be relegated to helping to design the analysis and then waiting to turn on the computer for the analysis once data are collected. A good statistical consultant is an expert research methodologist who understands the tools of statistics in the context of research design. Therefore, a statistical consultant needs to be present in the first meetings of the research team, and must be included in every step of the planning, design, and implementation of the study. Day-to-day decisions about data collection can have analytic implications known to an experienced statistical consultant. Therefore, the consultant can discuss alternatives, from high-tech (e.g., missing data modeling as a fallback to not having all the questions answered in a survey) to low-tech strategies (whether to increase subject payments to decrease attrition). Once the statistical consultant has been involved in all phases of the study, she not only sees data, but also understands whence these data came.

Alternatives to Conventional Randomized Controlled Trial Design

There are limits to the RCT design. It may be surprising to some, more obvious to others, but we must admit it is true. The strongest arguments against RCTs have to do with the reactivity of the participants toward the randomized trial itself. In other words, some aspects of the results may be attributable to the fact that they are obtained from a randomized trial. While randomized trials are often regarded as the gold standard of internal validity, a variety of factors are seen as threatening that fortress of internal validity (Corrigan & Salzer, 2003). Examples include:

- Highly selective samples attributed to restrictive entry criteria, such as a requirement that individuals be in their first episode of a problem (diagnosis, arrest, etc). This may interact with the service conditions. For example, first-time recipients of criminal justice rehabilitation programs are more likely to have more faith in their effectiveness than those who have already been in criminal justice rehabilitation programs (Marlowe, 2006). Therefore, if the sample is limited to first-time offenders, there may be a greater incentive to stay in an RCT if assigned to the experimental rather than the control condition, which may bias results.
- Highly selective samples based on the fact that some individuals are more likely to have access to an RCT recruitment effort, a result of such factors as proximity to a research center that might be biased toward urban settings or the tendency to volunteer.
- Preferences interacting with actual services delivered. Individuals with a preference for one or more study condition may be more likely to drop out of an RCT if they do not obtain their preference, therefore biasing the comparison as randomized.
- Randomized trials of complex interventions do not account for the accumulative qualities of intervention service elements or phases of the experimental intervention.

A number of alternative randomized trial designs have been proposed that address these challenges as well as others (TenHave, Coyne,

Salzer, & Katz, 2003). Some of these alternatives incorporate participant preferences into the randomization process. Others address sequences of treatment options, and may introduce preferences as well. Examples include the following strategies:

- **Fixed adaptive designs**, in which individuals are assigned to conditions, but their progress through the interventions is driven by the need for more or less intensive treatment over time.
- **Randomized adaptive designs**, in which shifts or changes in service condition are driven by randomizations to choices that are shaped by participant outcome, participant preference, or provider preference.
- **Encouragement or randomized-consent trials**, in which individuals are encouraged to participate in one service option or the other, but are not constricted to their selected option.
- **Randomized preferences**, in which participants decide whether they will allow themselves to be randomized, or simply choose their service option (TenHave, Coyne, Salzer, & Katz, 2003).

As in the conventional RCT, each of these options has a number of iterations and possible design twists. For example, the degree of certainty of preference may figure into whether someone is randomized at all, or whether to measure the concept (participants' preference) and use this preference variable as a factor in analysis. Anyone with basic statistical sensibilities will intuitively see that these alternative models likely involve a more sophisticated set of statistical skills than may be available to the typical intervention researcher, so specialized consultation is definitely in order.

It is important to note that these alternative models have been challenging to the conventional research design expectations at federal funding agencies. Although funding sources value innovation, they are also inherently conservative in terms of methodological innovation.

Conclusion

Nils Bohr, the noted 20th-century physicist, once defined an expert as someone who had made all the mistakes there are to make in a narrowly defined field. Most of what one can learn regarding how to design an RCT comes from lessons gained from experience. We have covered in this chapter a combination of the conventional wisdom from the long-accepted design traditions of randomized trials and the lessons we have garnered from our experiences and those of colleagues in the unique application of RCTs to community-based psychosocial interventions. Although each of the issues we discussed can be covered in a book-length treatment of greater depth, this chapter hopefully presents how the basic issues of design, feasibility, measurement, sampling, and analysis intersect to create a whole design to answer a policy and/or practice questions for psychosocial treatments.

What remains, to follow from the Bohr quote, is to make more mistakes. This requires more people to be engaged in the challenges of research design in complex settings, which are far less controlled than the clinical settings in which most RCT methods were developed. Hopefully, this creates more expertise and an ever-growing community of scholars who contribute to the research literature, in both methods and in terms of innovative interventions. The ultimate gain will be the clients of community agencies, who benefit from more effective community-based psychosocial interventions.

For Further Reading

Dattalo, P. (2008). *Determining sample size.* New York: Oxford University Press.

Fowler, F. (1995). *Improving survey questions: Design and evaluation.* Thousand Oaks, CA: Sage Publications.

Evans, C., Ilstad, S. (eds.). (2002). *Small clinical trials: Issues and challenges.* Washington, D.C.: Institute of Medicine, National Academy Press.

Kazdin, A. (2003). *Research design in clinical psychology.* Boston: Allyn and Bacon.

Nezu, A. & Nezu, C. (eds.). (2008). *Evidence-based outcome research: A practical guide to conducting randomized controlled trials for psychosocial interventions.* New York: Oxford University Press.

Schwarz, N. & Sudman, S. (eds.). (1996). *Answering questions.* San Francisco: Jossey-Bass Publishers.

Shadish, W., Cook, T., & Campbell, D. (2002). *Experimental and quasi-experimental designs.* Boston: Houghton Mifflin Company.

6

Implementing the Randomized Controlled Trial

It is important that implementation issues are considered in advance. The evaluation research literature demonstrates that the treatment of social programs as "black boxes" is inappropriate. Dobson and Cook (1980) noted that "if treatments are not clearly specified and if the services implied by those treatments are not delivered in a way that is consistent with program objectives, it is likely that evaluation results will be less than useful, or meaningless" (p. 270). They indicate that many investigators worry about type I and type II error, but that type III error, which is measuring something that does not exist or a service program that is inadequately implemented, is not considered. The lack of attention to what is in the "black box" has been corrected in community-based psychosocial RCT interventions through the borrowing of fidelity assessment from psychotherapy research. However, the implementation of these assessments is vital in avoiding type III errors.

Implementing randomized controlled trials (RCTs) is concerned with ensuring both the integrity of the research design as well as the intervention itself. Implementation of the research protocol means recruiting and retaining the number of required eligible subjects, randomly assigning without bias, and collecting data reliably at the conceptually appropriate time points. Implementation of the intervention concerns adherence to the intervention with regard to both delivery of the intervention by providers and participation of the recipients enrolled (Fraser, 2004). Managing these two aspects of the RCT requires a delicate balance. Modification may need to be made as the study is conducted (McAulilffe & Ashery, 1993). The researcher cannot be so rigid to the science that this rigidity affects the ability to maintain the integrity of the intervention by either the providers or the recipients. Flexibility is required along with thoughtful decision-making while considering the requirements of the ensuing science as well as the practicalities of the real-world community-based setting and the clinical needs of clients. As a community-based psychosocial RCT researcher, one must be cognizant of reasonable research demands, such that they do not compromise the psychosocial intervention itself (Gueron, 2000).

This chapter examines the importance of the interplay of the environmental setting and the community-based psychosocial intervention. Considerations as to how to manage a shift in the intervention and policies as well as staffing changes during the conduct of the RCT are discussed. Furthermore, training and supervision of staff for implementing the intervention are essential to ensuring the integrity of each of these aspects of the RCT. Issues of implementing fidelity assessments and the means to assess and ensure the protection of the control condition from contamination of the experimental intervention are implementation priorities. The utility of qualitative methods in assessing the implementation, in addition to the environmental contextual factors that may impact the implementation of the intervention and the outcomes, is also examined.

Preparing the Setting for Implementing the Randomized Controlled Trial

As we discussed in Chapter 3, the development of the intervention must be conducted in partnership with the setting, rather than imposing a top-down approach. However, the reality is that not everyone who will ultimately be involved in the RCT's implementation will have actually participated in the development of the intervention. Furthermore, given the high turnover rate in agency personnel, those who may have been involved in the design of the intervention may no longer be at the agency at the point of the RCT execution.

Before embarking on the actual implementation of the RCT, the investigator needs to prepare the setting for this undertaking. The nature of preparation will vary contingent on the type of setting and the actual design of the protocol. For example, many community-based psychosocial interventions are conducted in agencies where existing staff are to incorporate the intervention into their ongoing agency responsibilities. In this type of situation, a good deal of preparation for these settings may be required of the researcher, more than when the researcher hires staff to conduct the experimental intervention. However, even if staff is being hired from funds specifically designated for purposes of the RCT, the agency staff needs to understand the RCT's rationale and operation. Also, it is likely that staff other than those directly involved in the conduct of the study will be impacted by demands of the RCT. The researcher must be cognizant that preparation of the control condition is essential. Even if providers are to continue performing their jobs as they currently do, the RCT may still require supplementary paperwork and/or additional tasks, such as recruiting participants and obtaining consents or signed release-of-information forms. Even if the intervention is to be conducted in locations where the staff is accustomed to conducting RCTs, preparation of the setting is still necessary, particularly since there may be concerns about conflict of interests regarding other RCTs perhaps competing for the same participants.

When presenting the RCT to agency personnel, it may prove helpful to consider the following:

1. **Inform the setting with sufficient lead time for preparation, but not so far in advance that details/plans will be forgotten.** Not everyone who will be affected by the RCT was likely involved in its planning. Consideration must be given as to the optimal time to inform providers and administrators about the RCT. You do not want to make formal presentations to the individuals responsible for conducting key tasks for the RCT so far in

advance of actually implementing the study that they will forget or think that the RCT will not actually happen. At the same time, you do not want to inform setting staff the day before the RCT is to begin. When considering timing, it is important to realize that implementation also includes training the staff. Generally, it may not be wise to have setting administrators present the information about the RCT to setting staff without you present. The researcher should attend the staff meeting when the RCT will be presented, ensuring that enough time is available to respond to questions. An investigator needs to be confident of the accuracy of study information that is communicated to the setting staff.

2. **Informing agency personnel**. Should the researcher inform everyone at a staff meeting or at individual group meetings (e.g., supervisors, experimental intervention providers, and control condition providers)? It is best to jointly decide with agency administrators on the most effective means of informing setting staff. In the current atmosphere of limited resources, agency administrators are quite concerned about loss of billing time. Presently, a number of agencies, at least in the mental health arena, employ a sizeable number of contract workers and, consequently, it may not be feasible to inform these providers at a meeting, for it is likely to be quite costly to the agency to do so. The researcher must consider carefully what information is required and when and how to inform all involved in a cost-efficient manner.

3. **Jointly present the RCT with key administrators and staff**. A unified front needs to be communicated to staff that not only the researchers but also the administration of the setting considers this RCT to be important and beneficial to the agency. The more the administrators can explain the study the better, as this will indicate that they understand the study and believe in its importance. However, they may not be able to explain the many intricacies of the RCT. Have administrators present as much information about the study as they feel comfortable with, but work cooperatively with them, so that they do not feel that they are placed in an uncomfortable position.

4. **Remember, the investigator has to "sell" the RCT in terms of the benefits to the setting, the providers, and the clients—not solely in terms of gaining new knowledge.** Providers will be concerned as to what the RCT, specifically the intervention, means to them and their clients. In some instances, it may be a more intensive and individualized service for clients or one that targets a need that would otherwise not have been addressed.

5. **Don't oversell what can realistically be delivered.** You do not want to mislead setting administrators and staff regarding what the RCT can actually deliver (Gueron, 2000). As was evident in Chapter 3, the investigator must understand the community service setting and what can realistically be accomplished.

6. **Be sure that you understand the providers' perspective.** As much as you possibly can, try to think from the providers' perspective, so that you can understand their concerns (Gueron, 2000). Addressing their concerns in your presentation will be helpful in their believing that you understand their position, needs, and other issues, and that you are knowledgeable about their setting and their clients.

7. **Be sensitive regarding the language and the examples that you employ.** Use familiar terminology to explain research terms such as "random assignment" and "control group." If you do use these terms, be sure to define them clearly. Provide examples that are relevant to the agency setting.

8. **Turn any lack of clarity into an advantage.** When questions are raised about some aspect of the study that you had not considered or about which you may be uncertain, indicate that the issue is important and of concern and that setting administrators and staff can help in the process of figuring out how the issue can be addressed (Gueron, 2000). However, remember, do not make promises that you cannot follow through on, because that may undermine your credibility.

9. **Try to anticipate questions and issues that are likely to arise and raise them yourself.** This communicates to your audience that you understand the implications of these issues for their setting

and that you are confident of being able to address them (Gueron, 2000).

10. **Be prepared to address the issue of random assignment in a straightforward manner.** Someone is likely to raise the issue of denying the experimental service to those in the control group. Explain the reason for this design requirement and address what is likely to be the concerns underlying the questions being raised (Gueron, 2000).

11. **Try to counter any negative momentum.** If there seems to be any negative concerns, it is best to try to stop this by indicating that the issue will be taken under advisement with administrators and with input from providers.

12. **A positive frame of mind is critical: Remember—you need them more than they need you.** Approach comments and concerns in a positive and friendly manner, rather than being defensive. You need administrators and providers to carry out your RCT, whether it is to help with recruitment, provide data, or to conduct the intervention. Try not to say "no" to their suggestions, unless it deals with a central element of the protocol, such as random assignment (Gueron, 2000). Remember, regardless of how little work you think the RCT may be to setting personnel, it still requires more than they are currently doing, and most often an RCT is more involved than either they or you may realize.

The usefulness of these considerations will vary, contingent on a variety of factors. For example, in one randomized design in which two of the authors were involved, the grant and the local governmental-match paid for both the control and experimental condition, although the two teams of providers were located in separate agencies. Explaining the research and intervention was conducted as part of the training for the case managers in both intervention conditions. The administrators in both agencies had been involved in the development and writing of the grant application, and the providers were specifically hired for the RCT. Implementing the RCT was the job description under which they were hired.

In another example, the providers and administrators of the two experimental interventions, family consultation and group family education workshop for families of individuals with severe mental illness, developed two specific intervention conditions for the RCT and had sought out the first author to evaluate these interventions. Initially, setting administrators were opposed to using a randomized design, but after the first author attempted without success to craft a nonrandomized design that was scientifically strong, they came to trust the researcher enough to be convinced of the need for the RCT. Working closely together in the process, setting personnel came to understand the RCT intimately and to appreciate its strengths for meeting their objectives, for they had input into all decisions regarding design (random assignment), measurement, and interventions. Consequently, they were quite capable of explaining the protocol to the other providers. For the purposes of good science, one modification was required to this RCT: facilitators of the group workshop were requested not to provide any informal consultation to attendees at the end of the workshop. These interactional processes with attendees were uncovered during the monitoring of the fidelity of the intervention, and it was believed that this type of intervention with family members would result in less of a distinction between the two intervention conditions. Workshop facilitators were resistant to complying with this request, as they believed that these informal discussions with attendees, which often included advising them on their personal issues, were extremely important. However, the administrators who were also providers were able to convince the facilitators of the need for this modification.

In another RCT in which the first author is involved, agency staff was incorporating the experimental intervention into their work and others were not. Those who were not delivering the intervention were still providing process data to ensure no spillover effect. In this situation, researchers met initially with the administrators and supervisors of the providers and then met individually with the two teams, one doing the experimental intervention and one not.

In preparing for the implementation of the randomized trial of Critical Time Intervention (CTI) for men with mental illness leaving prison, the third author needed to negotiate with multiple settings and layers of authority in a diversity of systems. Although the administration of the prison system and the top leadership of mental health services were convinced of the importance of the intervention, researchers were left with the task of selling the program to the administrators of each prison and each prison mental health service. Even with the endorsement of the prison system headquarters, the superintendent of a prison could respond with, "yes, I saw that memo but tell me what that means to me—how it will help me run my jail." Thankfully, experience has taught us to expect this pragmatic approach in systems, and we were prepared with answers. Even in the mental health service units inside individual prisons, our main source of referral are the front-line mental health workers. After nearly a year in the field, we are still not completely sure the word has reached this level of these organizations. Repeated reminders to administrators are important in getting the word out. However, our most effective strategy is "strike when the iron is hot." Getting a phone call from a front-line worker at a prison whom we had not yet heard from gives us a chance to make a pitch directly to him and to encourage him to tell his colleagues about the resource offered by the CTI trial. It is important to point out that, in an environment in which a resource like CTI is valued, the randomized trial aspect may not be a drawback. Our response is to remind staff that, although the chances are 50/50 that their client will get the less intensive service, every client will get something more than what they are currently receiving.

These examples demonstrate that preparing the settings for the RCT implementation vary greatly, contingent on the involvement of the staff in the design of the RCT, the nature of the setting, and what is being asked of staff in a given situation. RCTs that are more complex, in terms of involving a number of sites, such as the CTI example, certainly complicate the preparation process.

Ongoing Cooperation of Researchers and Intervention Settings

After preparing the setting for implementation of the RCT, the collaborative relationship between the providers, administrators, and researchers must be on-going to ensure continued cooperation. Good communication and the active involvement of the providers in implementing the RCT is crucial (Asscher, Dekovic, van der Lann, et al., 2007). This process will take a good deal of time on the part of both researchers and site personnel. It is best to schedule bi-weekly or at least monthly meetings with key administrators and/or providers and the researchers. In the beginning, these meetings should occur more frequently, as a variety of issues will arise as implementation proceeds that will not have been anticipated. It is most efficient, if possible, to include key agency personnel who are in the position to make decisions without having to check with higher-level administrators. This checking process can delay the implementation of changes that may need to occur immediately. Furthermore, if the person has to seek approval from higher-level administrators, this situation will put him in a position of having to convince another administrator of the need for the change. The person may not feel equipped to make the necessary arguments to convince his superior.

Arranging these kinds of meetings will be difficult when numerous sites are involved. The first author was able to conduct monthly meetings with two RCTs with which she was involved, as there was only one agency involved in each of the RCTs. The key researchers (e.g., the research coordinator) met with the Director of Outpatient Programs and the supervisors of the agency interventionists and control providers on a monthly basis. Solutions to emerging problems were solved jointly or at least attempted to be worked out at these meetings. In one of these RCTs, the first author eventually had to terminate the RCT at the site, as the agency was too chaotic and consequently, unable to implement agreed-upon changes. (The lack of intervention implementation became apparent when doing the first follow-up interview with participants and assessing recipients' perception of the intervention.) Major issues that were discussed at these meetings were recruitment of participants, intervention implementation (or more likely the lack of implementation of the experimental intervention), and staff turnover. For example, one issue addressed was that, when staff left agency employment, procedures had to be put in place to ensure that those assigned to the experimental intervention (in this RCT, case managers were randomly assigned to deliver the experimental intervention or not) were reassigned to an experimental case manager.

This assignment procedure was a concern because a lag often occurred between employee termination and hiring of new staff and then subsequently training the new hire in the experimental intervention. Thus, when the caseloads of the terminated case manager were distributed, a concerted effort on the part of the agency had to be made to ensure that the integrity of the RCT was maintained. Updates of RCT progress were given at each meeting, along with specific intervention activities delivered by each case manager. Case managers discussed implementation problems, and strategies for taking corrective actions were worked out jointly.

In some RCTs, it may be necessary to hold meetings separately with each site, as it may be difficult to coordinate the timing of meetings convenient to all sites. In addition, traveling to a meeting can be costly in terms of staff time. Furthermore, implementation issues may vary by sites and, even if similar problems occur, often solutions to these problems may well differ by agency or even by sites of the same agency.

Specific efforts are essential to maintain the cooperation of the providers. In the human immunodeficiency virus (HIV) prevention intervention, every effort was made to be responsive to concerns raised by experimental providers in terms of trying to meet their practical needs in implementing the intervention. For example, since the intervention was often delivered in the community and required a good deal of equipment, case managers were given wheeled briefcases to make it easy for them to transport the materials. Eventually, we gave the workers a $3 incentive for every hour of the intervention they delivered. This incentive was deemed necessary, as many of the experimental providers were delivering only a limited amount of the intervention.

Use of Computer Technology for Recruitment and Tracking

Recruitment

Computers and electronic communication provide new opportunities for recruitment into studies and tools for tracking and retaining participants. Depending on the nature of the RCT and the population from which an investigator is recruiting, the Internet can reach a wide range of participants. As with any application, the technology is not the gadget (computer) alone, but rather the gadget interacting with the social environment. In using computers for recruitment, one needs to consider the intersection of the recruitment methodology with the experimental and control conditions as delivered, as well as with the RCT protocol. The advantage of many Internet-based recruitment strategies is that the "flyer" can be much more carefully targeted to an audience of individuals who would be interested in the RCT. For example, with interventions that are focused on general support for individuals with a particular concern—who are thought to have reliable access to computer technology and the Internet—the use of listservs or support websites can make sense in targeting the population of interest. However, if entry criteria are very particular, such strategies may overload the investigator with referrals that do not meet criteria.

Consider the low-tech use of flyers on the bulletin board of an agency, the advertisement on the public transit bus, or public service announcements on radio or TV. A primary benefit of this strategy is that it provides a voluntary means for potential participants to initiate contact with the researcher. Such an approach addresses some concerns that are raised in ethical reviews about how participants are approached. Just as with flyers or ads, recruitment materials delivered over the Internet should not over-promise results from the intervention or the RCT, thus maintaining the stance of equipoise about the results. These materials should not overplay the role of financial incentive—although a mention of the incentive is likely important.

Tracking Participants

Attention to the retention and tracking of research participants can meet with good success. To achieve success requires developing a specific procedure for tracking participants, along with a tracking form that is to be completed for each participant upon enrollment in the RCT. Ribisl and colleagues (1996) developed a comprehensive list of retention and tracking techniques for longitudinal research studies that are relevant for the data collection portion of RCTs. This list is an excellent starting place, but not every item is relevant for all RCT studies. Upon developing an initial protocol and a tracking form, it is wise to have the procedures reviewed by others who have conducted research on similar populations, providers working with the population, and members of the population. Having a protocol set up in advance will enable the researcher to obtain the necessary release-of-information forms signed in advance of needing them, as some of these sources will not provide information without a signed release form. Also, by virtue of having a well-delineated plan, the job of locating and continuing to engage participants becomes a less daunting task, as the necessary resources are more likely to be available when needed (Sullivan, Rumptz, Campbell, Eby, & Davidson 1996). Table 6.1 provides a list of data elements that could be collected at baseline and subsequent interview points to help with tracking and locating participants for follow-up visits. The suggested data collected and strategies for maintaining follow-up information build on those in the table found in the paper by Ribisl and colleagues (1996), with information used by the authors and seen in other studies.

Index cards were once used to track participants, and the third author still has the tin box of index cards he used to track the subjects from the first study he worked on with the first author on a randomized trial of services to homeless people with serious mental illness leaving jail. The cards were used to sort participants by condition, referral source, or referral date. The cards could be pulled for interviews due in the coming week or month, and replaced once interviews were complete. The cards contain the names, aliases, prison system ID numbers, contact information, release dates from jail, and if needed, jail incarceration dates. (Don't fret about confidentiality—they are in a locked drawer.) In a simple study of 100 or 200 participants, this may still be a manageable way to track clients.

However, with any greater degree of complexity, computer technology presents distinct advantages. The complexity of a project will likely determine the extent to which a computer application for tracking and following up with participants needs expert programming assistance. In many cases, working knowledge of a program like Microsoft Access can

Table 6.1. Comprehensive Listing of Retention and Tracking Information and Techniques

Data Collected

Demographic and identifying Information:
- All names (first, last, middle, married, etc.), aliases, nicknames
- Name change plans, past name changes
- ID numbers, Social Security, Medicaid/Medicare, Drivers License
- Date and location of birth
- Home addresses, mailing addresses, phone numbers (i.e., cell phones and e-mails)
- All names and relationships of people who live at the same location
- Work: Employers, occupations (present and past)
- Veterans status and benefits, dates and locations of services
- Education: Schools, current student status, all levels of school
- Plans to move or change any status in near or distant future

Relatives, information from multiple people at different locations:
- Full names, addresses, phone numbers
- Dates of birth
- Similar information on significant others of relatives and friends
- Information on representative payee, pastors or other clergy
- Landlord contact information
- Names of people who take messages, or who can relay messages
- Places to stay other than home during the day or at night

Professional contacts for contact information:
- Case managers for all service systems (education, health, mental health, social services, child welfare, employment, etc.)
- Probation and parole officers, noting probation times and incarceration dates
- Treatment programs, day programs, drop-in centers, missions frequented; names of contacts at these locations

Incidental contacts (all information, locations, specific people for contact):
- First stop after release from jail or hospitalization
- Where to go when out of money
- Where to eat meals when hungry
- Where to sleep when homeless

(continued)

Table 6.1. (*continued*)

Techniques to Enhance Locator Information

- Specific information used to make each follow-up, recorded to have written documentation of most useful locator information
- Validity of information checked whenever possible with collateral contacts such as relatives, case managers, etc.
- Participants asked to update contact information with every research contact
- Offer incentive payments for contacting study to update current contact information

provide the tools one needs. Such databases can be used to manage all the data collection sources of the study, such as primary interviews, chart reviews, collateral interviews, and administrative data. The database can also include information from a *locator form*—a working document of all possible contact information that can help the research team find a participant when needed. This database will be linked to retention strategies reviewed in the next section.

A computer application to support tracking needs to be easy to maintain by novice computer users. These tracking systems must produce up-to-date reports of data to be collected, follow-up visits to make, and work reports by interviewer, if project size is sufficient to have multiple field workers. In cases in which the RCT may be done entirely over the Internet, protocols may be developed for electronic reminders of when participants are required to complete online assessments. Prompts may also be issued to remind an investigator to use another device to follow up on a participant who seems lost to follow-up: the telephone.

Monitoring Recruitment

Using the tracking system, the researcher needs to monitor recruitment to ensure that sample accrual is meeting its timely projections (Del Boca & Darkes, 2007). Researchers must be aware, as soon as possible, if the recruitment is not on schedule; otherwise, it may be too late to take effective corrective action (Ashery & McAuliffe, 1992). If recruitment is slower than projected, it may mean that the RCT will not meet the required sample size. Also, if a big push is done late in the study, it may well result in some participants not completing the intervention or the inability to obtain the proposed outcome data for some participants. Both will affect the power of the study analyses and, consequently, affect the construct validity of the study findings.

It is best to maintain as much control of the recruitment as is ethically and feasibly possible. The most effective RCT recruitment with which two of the authors (Solomon and Draine) were involved was a family education RCT. A half-time recruiter went to agencies and met with family members. The recruiter was well-known to family members in the area, as her daughter had committed a highly publicized, violent crime, and the recruiter was also active in local family organizations. When she conducted recruitment, she explained that, if she had had such an intervention as this family education when she was dealing with this incident, it would have helped her greatly. This statement encouraged many family members to participate, particularly since it was coming from someone who had experience with problems similar to their own. Members of the target population can be quite effective recruiters. This study was ahead of scheduled recruitment and enrolled 25 more participants than planned. As in this RCT, whenever a study depends on volunteers or a referring network, the researchers having direct contact with potential participants are the most effective means of recruiting participants. Over-enrollment is a rather unusual situation, as many RCTs have problems recruiting participants. In some cases, additional sites or other programs in a given site' need to be added to meet the required sample size.

Relying on referrals from providers can be a very slow process and may not occur at all. Providers do not make referrals for a variety of reasons, including seeing the RCT program as competition, wariness of research generally, resistance to random assignment, lack of understanding of the nature of the intervention, having a higher priority to serve their clients than to spend time on the research, or just forgetting to do the recruiting (Ashery & McAuliffe, 1993; Del Boca & Darkes, 2007). Frequently, agencies need to maintain some control over recruitment, given issues of confidentiality and access to potential participants. In-service training and ongoing collaboration may help to engender trust and overcome some of these resistances. However, there may be creative ways for researchers to control and perform more of the recruitment.

Providers often do not want to perform recruitment tasks, thus providing incentive for agencies to give more control of recruitment to the researchers. Recruitment is just one more responsibility that providers have to perform without reducing any of their many existing responsibilities. Recruitment takes time and costs the agency money. Therefore, creative suggestions, within ethical bounds, that researchers take over this task may be welcomed when timed right and approached sensitively.

Monitoring Retention

Even if providers must engage in the referral process, they should not be conducting eligibility determinations for the study, as the researcher needs to know the characteristics of the entire client pool (Petersilia, 1989). In some cases, providers will refer ineligible clients, whereas in other cases, a provider may want to remove a difficult client from his caseload or may believe the client will benefit from the experimental intervention. If providers have to implement study recruitment, they need to obtain a signed release-of-information, so that the researchers can be given the necessary information to be able to contact potential clients, determine eligibility, explain the RCT, and gain informed consents. Generally, providers should not obtain the consents. They are often not invested in explaining the study and are not always knowledgeable about the study and/or comfortable enough to answer questions about the protocol.

When community-based recruitment strategies rely on agency and service system staff to identify and refer clients who may be eligible to the researcher, the researcher should define preliminary screening criteria for referral, so that the staff members understand whom to refer to the researcher. These criteria should be easily observable or obtainable and cast a wide net. Making the screening criteria wide is beneficial on a couple of levels. It lessens the burden on service collaborators, who may not be able or willing to make fine distinctions. Second, if the criteria are easily observable in day-to-day operation, they are more likely to be implemented. If at all possible, use the system's usual categorization. Once referred to the research team, the burden is on the researcher to confirm a narrower diagnostic category.

Every effort must be made to obtain outcome data from all participants, even if they have dropped out of the experimental or control interventions, as these data are required for outcome analyses. Ensuring retention of participants in the research portion of the RCT requires thoughtful consideration of research staffing for both recruitment and retention. The following should be considered: Will the same data collectors be used for both conditions? Will the same collectors do all assessment points with the same participant (this helps in maintaining rapport with participants; some even request the same interviewer)? What qualifications and experience do these collectors need to have, and how will they be supervised and monitored? Desmond and his colleagues (1995) identified ten effective follow-up procedures (enhanced from our own experience):

1. **Collect complete locator information at study entrance**. The relevant data for the particular RCT must be completed during enrollment or at the baseline interview. You may have a separate form for locator data, or the questions may be incorporated into your interview or data collection form and then transferred to a tracking database.

2. **Inform participants that they will be followed and at what time intervals**. Informing participants that they will be followed should be incorporated into the consent procedures. Also, explaining what efforts will be conducted to contact them is important information for participants to be aware of at entrance into the RCT.

3. **Review locator information at subsequent data collection points**. Participants in community-based psychosocial RCTs tend to be highly mobile, and their lives tend to be chaotic. Noting if any of the locator information has changed at each data collection point is important to maintain contact with participants.

4. **Offer adequate incentives**. The researcher needs to work out with providers in some instances to determine what constitutes

an acceptable incentive. However, the researcher must be able to provide some type of real incentive to enhance follow-up. A bonus for completing all data collection points can be offered.

5. **Employ effective research data collectors.** The personal characteristics of those tracking and collecting follow-up data are key to the successful retention of participants: "Traits such as assertiveness, tactfulness, tenacity, competitiveness, and ingenuity can determine to a great extent the effectiveness of follow-up" (Desmond, et al., 1995, p. 97). Consideration may also be given to matching collector–participant on demographic characteristics.

6. **Document all follow-up activities in detail.** Data collectors need to record in the tracking system all efforts made and strategies used to contact the participant.

7. **Exploit the contact information obtained.** When the researcher is unable to directly contact the participant, use both the formal and informal contact sources provided by the participant at study entrance and update locator form at each data collection contact. The researcher needs a well-defined procedure for contacting participants. This means specifying what kinds of contact methods will be used initially, and then proceeding through various options. Decisions regarding when contacts have been exhausted need to be clearly defined. Also, even if a participant could not be contacted at previous data points, this does not mean that attempts to contact that participant should not be made at subsequent data points.

8. **Conduct follow-up data collection to reasonably accommodate the participant as much as possible.** Meet the participant in the community at a mutually agreed-upon location, rather than depending on the participant to come to the research office for the interview. However, the location needs to be one in which the interviewer feels safe and the participant is comfortable and likely to appear for the interview. If necessary and feasible, more than one interviewer can go together to conduct the interview. Arrangements can also be made with agencies to provide private space on an as-needed basis to conduct interviews. Often,

conducting interviews at the service site is a good idea, as the participant is familiar with the setting and accustomed to going there.

9. **Allocate enough resources for travel.** These resources include both time and funds for traveling a geographical distance in situations in which participants have moved or are relocated to an institutional setting within a reasonable distance. Researchers need to define the time period before and after the due date within which it is acceptable to conduct the interview.

10. **Allow ample time for tracking down participants.** Patience and persistence are key attributes here; doubling the size of the follow-up staff will not necessarily cut the time required in half (Desmond, et al., 1995, p. 97).

The discussion thus far has included procedures to ensure that participants remain in the research portion of the RCT, but one cannot forget that continuing in the intervention is an important aspect of the RCT. In the recruitment process, emphasizing and ensuring that participants understand the significance and relevance of the study is vitally important (Davis, Broome, & Cox, 2002). Outlining the benefits and expectations of participation in the RCT may enhance retention (Davis et al., 2002). Making minor modifications, such as cutting the amount of service required, may increase the attractiveness of both the experimental and control condition, if the researcher finds that too many study participants are dropping out of the RCT's interventions. Training providers in both conditions includes teaching about issues of engagement, retention, and relationship building, which are important factors in retaining individuals in the intervention (Cotter, Burke, Loeber, & Navratil, 2002; Davis, et al., 2002; Sullivan, et al., 1996). Demonstrating trust includes reminding participants about protections in place to ensure that data are kept confidential.

Building in outreach efforts to those not showing for services can be an effective strategy for reconnecting participants to the service intervention. RCT interventions that target high-risk groups often require novel thinking about many aspects of an RCT. For example, researchers should consider giving up their usual professional office environment in favor of one that is welcoming to individuals who are likely to be participants in their RCTs. In several studies known to the authors in which the target populations are engaged in drug use or prostitution, the waiting room and intervention space is more accessible to these clients, and may even be places for clients to occasionally hang out and meet acquaintances. Although this does not exactly approach the level of being an extension of street life, the purpose of this kind of arrangement is to increase the likelihood that a person might come to the office for service as well as for occasional visits. Thus, contact is maintained, hopefully engagement in service is also maintained, and perhaps the locator form gets updated just in time for a follow-up interview.

Training and Supervising Experimental Intervention Staff

Hiring the most qualified providers is imperative to effective implementation of the experimental intervention. Remember, the concern in implementing the intervention is not just about adherence, but also about competence. Highly qualified providers should be a criterion for the control condition as well. However, in a number of community-based psychosocial RCTs, staff is not specifically hired for the RCT. But should the researcher have such control, every effort should be made to select the most qualified of existing staff for both conditions, so that the providers' characteristics are controlled for as much as possible. Otherwise, these varying qualifications by condition can be design confounds.

Training of experimental intervention staff must include human subject protections, an overview of the purpose and conceptual basis of the study, the basic design of the RCT, and the operationalization of the experimental intervention. Should the staff be involved in recruitment, eligibility determination, or data collection, they will need to be trained in these areas as well. An attitudinal change may also be required for interventions that have higher expectations for client functioning than providers may believe the clients are capable. Modifying attitudes is far more difficult than teaching new skills. The training in terms of the experimental intervention involves didactic instruction concerning the intervention, program philosophy, and program goals and principles, as well as practice experience in delivering the intervention, preferably with target population clients; at the least, role-played practice should occur (Del Boca & Darkes, 2007). Training should include concrete examples along with referring to the material (Witte & Wilber, 1997). Should manualized training protocols be available, such material will save much time and effort. If the experimental intervention is a relatively well-regarded one (although not manualized), there may exist training materials that can be employed or adapted. Use as much as these materials as is feasible, but make sure that the existing training materials are consistent with the intervention manual. Although the training materials may be titled the same as the RCT intervention model, they may not meet the standards delineated in the intervention manual without modification.

One essential research issue that must be addressed during training is random assignment, as many practitioners frequently resist random assignment, given that they believe that they know, both intuitively and from clinical experience, what is the most beneficial treatment for their clients. They are often opposed to denying an available treatment to their clients and find denial ethically irresponsible. If providers are unconvinced of the need for random assignment, they may find a means to undermine the random assignment procedure. They can be extremely creative in manipulating the experiment to place their clients in what they believe will be the most beneficial treatment for that individual (Petersilia, 1989). A compelling argument for random assignment is to appeal to providers' self-interest, particularly for difficult clients with whom they may have had little success in discovering what works for these clients (Petersilia, 1989).

The intervention manual needs to be reviewed as part of the training. Homework assignments may also be given if the training covers more than one day. It requires a good deal of motivation for providers to spend their own time learning an intervention that they may be resistant to implementing in the first place. The use of audio or videotapes for providers to practice and/or learn the intervention is not likely to happen, unless time and resources are allocated specifically for this purpose by the agency.

Hiring an expert trainer is sometimes a possibility for well-regarded or manualized interventions, but the researcher still needs to consider how to provide ongoing support to providers as they implement the intervention. In some instances, the expert trainer may provide this type of service, including periodic booster trainings and possibly on-site or telephone support.

Virtually no research has been done to determine the most effective means for training providers to deliver a new intervention. However, with the recent emphasis on implementing evidence-based practice (EBP), there is a burgeoning new area of research on the implementation of EBPs. From this literature, it is quite apparent that training is not a one-time occurrence of a few hours or a few days. Training is an ongoing process. How long and how frequent the training is dependent upon the complexity of the intervention. Training includes engaging the support of service providers for the likely usefulness of the intervention for their clients, teaching them how to do the intervention, and finally supporting them in performing the new practice, which includes keeping them motivated to do so (Torrey, Lynde, & Gorman, 2005). Over time, providers come to appreciate the availability of ongoing consultants who monitor and advise them in the implementation. Eventually, these consultants come to be viewed as "coaches, resources, and aids," whereas initially they are often viewed as intruders (Aarons & Palinkas, 2007). The amount of ongoing technical support will also vary by the nature of the intervention. Recognizing a provider's successes in implementing the intervention is important.

Clinical supervision of providers during the RCT is critical to maintaining the fidelity of the intervention. Such supervision can include regularly scheduled meetings during which performance and individual cases are reviewed (Del Boca & Darkes, 2007). These meetings also serve to build support among the service providers, as well as with the researchers, in the implementation of the intervention.

Furthermore, the researcher needs to make provisions for training new staff, as staff turnover is inevitable, whether the providers are agency employees or hired by the researcher to implement the RCT. A "train the trainers" approach (i.e., designating specific providers to train new staff) may be a consideration, depending on the nature of the intervention. Booster sessions are also likely to be essential to ensuring the ongoing integrity of the intervention.

Experimental intervention providers usually need to be trained on the use of fidelity forms. Researchers need to monitor these forms to ensure that the intervention is being delivered as intended. These forms should be collected frequently, such as weekly or bi-weekly, so that the researcher can take corrective action quickly. These forms may offer direction in terms of additional training needs. Also, close supervision of providers is necessary to ensure that no slippage occurs in established ways of functioning. Unless providers are closely monitored, "they may unconsciously undermine a clinical trial by introducing elements of an approach they feel is effective, even if it is inconsistent with the protocol" (McAuliffe & Ashery, 1993, p. 46). Establishing consistent clinical practice and policies may help to keep providers on track with the experimental intervention, because many providers are attached to a particular approach, and are accustomed to making their own decisions and responding to the immediacy of client needs (McAuliffe & Ashery, 1993). In the current environment of high caseloads, providers are oriented to responding to crises, as opposed to being proactive. Therefore, depending on the nature of the intervention, providers may never get around to implementing the intervention if it appears to have a low priority in what they see as their job responsibilities.

In ongoing supervision, the supervisor must provide examples and refer to the manual, curriculum, or workbook in offering feedback. Witt and Wilber (1997) noted that four problems are common to adherence of manual-guided interventions: (1) strict conformance to the manual, (2) failure to adapt the intervention to a given client, (3) looseness in conforming to the manual, and (4) contamination or drift of the intervention. Strict conformance to the manual tends to be overcome as the providers become more experienced with the intervention. An important role of the supervisor is to offer suggested alternatives that are appropriate for given clients and are consistent with the experimental intervention. The job of the supervisor is to help the provider see that the manual is not merely a collection of activities and techniques, but also of concepts and principles that are flexible to meet the needs of clients. It is best that supervision for the experimental intervention is provided by those invested in the experimental intervention, which may be RCT research staff or trained agency personnel. However, if trained agency staff, these staff should also have experience in delivering the intervention and an investment in maintaining the integrity of the intervention.

Training and Monitoring Control Condition Staff

Training of control-condition staff is usually less involved, as these providers frequently continue to do what they are already doing. If the control is an inert intervention, such as a healthy lifestyle, the intervention will likely still involve some training. The primary training that the control condition needs is in eligibility determination and recruitment and in the completion of data collection forms. Usually, providers will be required to complete some forms to assess the extent that this condition differs from the experimental intervention, and that no spillover occurs from the experimental intervention to the control condition. As easy as the completion of forms may seem, such as being merely a checklist, they still require training and monitoring to ensure that they are completed correctly. All forms must be reviewed carefully in the beginning to be confident of the validity of the responses. If they are not completed accurately, the researcher needs to ask questions of the providers and offer corrective feedback. These fidelity or *leakage forms* may need to be collected with the same frequency as those from the experimental providers. Since interaction between control and experimental providers often occurs, the researcher must monitor the forms to determine what corrective actions may be required should the control providers be utilizing some of the strategies of the experimental intervention.

Hiring, Training, and Supervising Research Staff

Hiring the research coordinator first is preferable, with this person then assisting in hiring and training the research assistants, recruiters, and/ or data collectors. The research coordinator should have some research experience, understand research methods, and should have some practice experience. Master-level social workers with practice experience are usually the best qualified for research coordinator positions, as they have service experience and are also trained in research methods. It is preferable that the research staff have some experience with the study target population.

Training for the research staff usually includes the rationale for the RCT, overview of the study, human subject protections, recruitment, tracking and randomization procedures, and review of all data collection materials. In reviewing data collection forms, whether interviews, questionnaires, or record extraction forms, be sure that the intent of the questions or items, procedures for recording, and review of all forms are clearly understood by the research staff. Some measures employed in RCTs may have packaged training sessions available that research assistants can attend, such as training in the use of diagnostic assessment instruments for eligibility screening. Therefore, research personnel may be sent elsewhere for training on specific aspects of the study methods.

A research assistant cannot collect data until she has completed required Institutional Review Board (IRB) training. Dependent on the study population, research personnel may have to be taught how to conduct a risk assessment for suicide or harming someone else, and then how to access crisis services and/or psychiatric hospitalization. In addition, research personnel may have to be trained in how to handle issues of child abuse, because social workers as well as many other professional providers are mandated reporters.

Frequently, the research staff are involved in the fidelity assessment and monitoring of the intervention. They may be involved in providing ongoing support and technical assistance for the experimental and control providers in the completion of fidelity forms and the implementation of the interventions. The research staff will then need to be trained in these study requirements. With more clinically complex interventions, the researcher needs to assess what qualifications are needed for research staff to be able to provide support to those implementing the experimental intervention, or whether specific intervention support people should be hired. These technical supporters must be individuals who have worked with the target population and have used the intervention or at least engaged in a similar type of intervention.

Efforts to Ensure Integrity of Randomized Controlled Trial

In Chapter 3, we discussed the development of fidelity assessments. Here, we address issues that concern the implementation of those fidelity assessments. Initially, one needs to decide at what points the assessments will be conducted. Given that RCT experimental interventions frequently are initiated for the purpose of research, it takes time for the program or service to be fully operational. One factor that affects the operationalization of the intervention is the pace at which participants are recruited. The rate of recruitment determines when the program has a complete complement of clients being served. In addition, it takes time for the providers to be fully comfortable and able to perform the service or program intervention. Mature programs are likely to be very different from developing programs with regard to fidelity. The time points for assessing fidelity should be determined with consideration of these factors, as measurement of the developing as well as the mature program is important for statistical analyses. It does become questionable as to whether the researcher is truly assessing the intervention when the intervention is designed to serve ten clients per team member, but is only serving two (Solomon, 1997).

In addition, both the time points and the frequency of assessments need to be determined from different perspectives—from both those delivering the intervention and from the recipients—as the integrity of the intervention concerns both the delivery and the receipt of the intervention. Researchers must recognize and try to account for the fact that implementation and fidelity are developmental processes. Without conceptualizing and measuring these changes, they remain a source of error (McGrew, Bond, Dietzen, & Salyers, 1994).

Fidelity assessments of community-based psychosocial interventions have focused on "program characteristics and essential components, such as organizational structure, staffing patterns, and service delivery characteristics" (Paulson, Post, Herinckx, & Risser, 2002, p. 121). In other words, program-level performance indicators, such assessments, may include obtaining data on the clients being served at a given point in time. For example, if the program is serving more clients than specified by the program model, this could affect the integrity of the intervention (Solomon, 1997). The assessment of the intervention's implementation includes not only the degree to which program service elements are delivered, but also the amount of these elements that a given participant received. In some cases, administrative reporting or billing information systems may provide some of the essential data for making an assessment of implementation. In other cases, treatment logs, which categorize service activities that specifically match the critical aspects of the particular intervention, have been employed (Orwin, 2000). If the researcher can use data that are already required, it will increase the likelihood of obtaining that data.

In many community-based psychosocial interventions, no particular number of sessions is specified, but rather the amount and nature of the service is defined by the needs of the given client. Thus, these programs are "needs-based" treatment, whereby the type and degree of services provided is contingent on the clinical assessment of the client's needs (Dobson & Cook, 1980). Consequently, the nature and amount of client contact with providers may be essential to assess the degree to which a given client received the intervention. In some situations, the number of referrals or appointments kept may be important to assessing fidelity. In the first and third authors' RCT on family education, attendance records were kept for all participants of each educational session. However, as Orwin and colleagues (1998) noted, collecting individual client-level data can be "expensive, intrusive, or otherwise impractical to obtain. Cruder data, for example, presence versus absence of a given service, are often more feasible to collect, as well as more likely to be available archivally" (p. 246). These types of data can be used to assess spillover effects as well. Although these crude data may not be ideal, they may be better than obtaining no data at all.

It is also important to obtain an assessment of the study participants' perspective in terms of what they believed they received. In the social participation RCT, a parallel checklist was used for clients. However, this was not completed for each contact, but as part of the follow-up interview for collecting outcome data. The questions asked assessed what program service activities the client engaged in with the case manager in the past six months, given that follow-up interviews were collected at six and 12 months.

In some instances, site visits by researchers are made to assess program implementation. Many of these process assessments entail the use of qualitative methods. These procedures may include observations of the program and in-depth interviews with staff and clients by a team of researchers. In addition, data collection may include reviewing records, fiscal information, and other relevant materials. The team members each complete a fidelity form that is comprised of a series of items that conform to program service components or elements. Subsequently, interrater reliability is determined (Blakely, Mayer, Gottschalk, Schmitt, et al., 1987). These procedures are similar to what Mowbray and her colleagues did to develop the Consumer Drop-In Centers (CDI) fidelity measure (as discussed in Chapter 3).

Ethnographic methods have been employed to shadow service providers, as a means of directly observing the delivery of the intervention. Paulson and colleagues (1999) conducted an RCT of consumer and nonconsumer delivered Assertive Community Treatment (ACT) that employed participant observation, in which case managers were accompanied on visits to clients to assess the differences in practice patterns. This *shadowing* procedure was combined with quantitative methods, specifically activity logs (Paulson, Herinckx, Demmler, et al., 1999). Focus groups are also another qualitative method used to assess the fidelity of the intervention, as well as to determine spillover effects (Solomon, 1997). The use of participant diaries is yet another method that has been employed with RCTs, as an approach to gaining insight into aspects of the interventions that are not open to observation. The format can vary from highly structured to more open approach (Sharkey, Maciver, Cameron, et al., 2005). Qualitative process assessment of the implementation of the program over time can serve as a quality control mechanism and provide data to take corrective actions when the program is drifting away from the proposed intervention. Combining process data with quantitative fidelity scales strengthens the ability to assess the degree of implementation of an intervention (Strange, Allen, Oakley, et al., 2006). These process methods indicate the need for a qualitative researcher to be a member of the RCT research team.

In Chapter 3, methods were discussed for delineating the service elements and activities necessary to develop a manual. These methods, such as focus groups, Delphi method, and concept mapping can be used to assess what was actually implemented. Some of these approaches are a combination of qualitative and quantitative approaches. Concept mapping, for example, has been used to assess the fidelity of a psychiatric rehabilitation for homeless persons with severe mental illness. This study also determined in what ways the intervention was adapted to the local environment (Shern, Trochim, & LaComb, 1995).

Assessing Environmental Context

Glisson and colleagues have conducted extensive research in the child welfare area on organizational culture and climate and its impact on interventions (Glisson, Dukes, & Green, 2006; Hemmelgarn, Glisson, & James, 2006). They note that "the social context of an organization helps to determine what types of interventions will be chosen, how these interventions will be implemented, the way decisions will be made, and how problems will be solved. Furthermore, the influence of an organization's social context on the choice, approach, and everyday implementation of an intervention may maximize or minimize the effectiveness" (Hemmelgarn, et al., 2006, p. 75). The way that providers function and relate to their clients is greatly influenced by the organization's contextual characteristics. These researchers offer a number of strategies for taking into account these organizational variables, such as using randomized blocked designs when a number of organizations are involved in the study or measuring these constructs and then statistically controlling for their potential effects.

Recent research has found that organizational culture and climate are key factors in the effective implementation of service interventions (Hemmelgarn et al., 2006). The support of the organization or agency to the implementation of the RCT is paramount to its success. This support cannot be just in the presence of the researchers, but also in the daily operation of the organization—a factor that, unfortunately, researchers have little, if any, control over. Supervisors of the service providers should be trained in the intervention. Mistakenly, in the HIV prevention intervention in which the first author was involved, it was believed that the supervisors' time should be spared by not having them participate in the training of the experimental intervention. This lack of training resulted in their being unable to supervise staff appropriately.

Community-based psychosocial RCTs do not function in isolation, but are imbedded within a larger social context. These social contexts play a major role in the effectiveness of the experimental intervention (Orwin, 2000). This is best illustrated with service interventions that have case management components, which are dependent on referring participants to other service resources in the environment. Consequently, the effectiveness of such interventions may have far more to do with the service environment than with the experimental intervention. Availability of services in the environment may not just affect provider behavior but also client participants' behavior. For example, in substance abuse treatment interventions, it is important to assess the use of self-help groups by participants, because the degree of attendance in these programs may affect participants' outcomes. In the previously mentioned family educational intervention, attendance at other informational programs, including National Alliance for Mental Illness (NAMI) meetings, was collected during the follow-up interviews with participants. Participation in family support and advocacy groups did affect outcomes of the intervention (Solomon, Draine, Mannion, & Meisel, 1996).

Similarly, systematically keeping track of those changes within the organization and the organizational environment that may affect the outcomes of study participants is necessary. Organizational policy changes, such as eligibility requirements for service or performance standards, may influence the way the service is delivered and consequently, influence client outcomes. Assessing environmental context becomes even more complicated when the RCT is implemented in more than one site. This information should be systematically recorded by date. Knowing these dates may help with the interpretation of data when outcomes seem to change over time. Some studies have found site effects on outcomes (Del Boca & Darkes, 2007). Therefore, site-specific characteristics need to be measured and certainly at least systematically recorded by date, so that they are not forgotten at the time of outcome analysis.

Since, in many psychosocial RCTs, the researchers have no control over the selection of providers, it is imperative to obtain data on provider characteristics. These data may include experience with the target population and with the type of intervention, as well education and years of practice experience. In the psychotherapy field, researchers are concerned with the "nonspecific factors" that may affect outcomes. Nonspecific factors are those other than the "active ingredients" of the experimental interventions—factors such as empathy, warmth, genuineness, and alliance, as well as provider characteristics and their competency in delivering the intervention. Scales exist for measuring many of these factors, although most were originally developed for psychotherapy research. Some have been adapted for service interventions, such as the Working Alliance Inventory for use by case managers, rather than therapists (Solomon, Draine, & Delaney, 1995).

A mixture of quantitative and qualitative methods can be utilized. In the HIV prevention intervention of the first author, interest was focused on what, if anything, was being done by the agency in terms of educating clients about HIV prevention before implementation of the RCT, so a *rapid assessment* was conducted. The rapid assessment included in-depth interviews with and focus groups for providers and clients, and agency observations to determine the availability of information booklets on HIV prevention (Solomon, Tennille, Lipsett, Plumb, & Blank, 2007). The same procedure was conducted at the end of the RCT to determine if the intervention had an effect on the organization in terms of its educating clients about HIV prevention. From the focus groups, it was determined that some spillover effect had occurred on control case managers' behavior in terms of providing some information about HIV prevention.

Conclusion

Implementation of an RCT requires close attention to not only the research activities of recruitment, retention, and data collection but also to the intervention itself. The realities of service environments are that the front-line staff who will be executing the intervention may not have even been employees of the setting/agency at the planning stage of the RCT. Researchers must work collaboratively with setting personnel on procedures for implementing the intervention to ensure that they as researchers understand and respect the environmental context and that the providers appreciate the requirements and restrictions of research. The success of the RCT is dependent not only on a well-designed study, but also on a sound translation of this vision into the real world of practice. This translation will draw on one's social work skills in negotiation and advocacy.

Decisions regarding hiring, selecting, training, and supervising of research personnel, as well as intervention personnel, must be thoughtfully considered within the given parameters of the setting, as each contributes to the success of implementing the intended RCT. The researcher needs to be vigilant about monitoring and assessing the recruitment and retention of participants, intervention fidelity, and the service context, in order to efficiently implement corrective actions. A variety of strategies in each of these domains were discussed, including tracking procedures, ongoing training, and continual monitoring of both the experimental and control condition from the vantage point of the provider and the recipient. Qualitative inquiry has a key role in RCTs.

For Further Reading

Morgan, D. (1996). *Focus groups as qualitative research.* Thousand Oaks, CA: Sage Publications, Inc.

Thyer, B. (ed.). (2001). *The handbook of social work research methods.* Thousand Oaks, CA: Sage Publications, Inc.

7

Generalizing Randomized Controlled Trial Outcomes to Community Practice Settings

Thus far, much of the text has focused on the internal validity of randomized controlled trial (RCT) design. This seems reasonable, as the primary reason why RCTs are considered the "gold standard" of efficacy and effectiveness research is because they provide the strongest case for drawing causal inferences. However, by maximizing internal validity through detailing inclusion and exclusion criteria, monitoring an intervention with a structured protocol, selecting and training the most qualified providers, employing a relatively short follow-up period, and using proximal rather than more distal outcomes, the RCT sacrifices external validity for increased confidence in the outcome effect being produced by the experimental intervention.

External validity, the generalizability or the applicability of the results produced by the RCT to the everyday practice world, includes how closely the study sample, practice setting, study providers, role of the provider in decision-making, and role of client preferences within the study resemble those of actual practice (Persaud & Mamdani, 2006). This comparability with routine practice determines the generalizability of the RCT's findings to other clients, providers, settings, and times than those in which the community-based psychosocial RCT was conducted (McHugo, Drake, Brunette, et al., 2006).

In the domain of medical RCTs, much has been written about the gap between research and its application to practice. The number of evidence-based practices (EBPs) that have been translated into daily agency protocols and practices is discouragingly limited (Glasgow, Green, Klesges, et al., 2006). Although there are a variety of reasons for this situation, including system and organizational factors, as well as provider characteristics, the primary reason—one that is important in the current context—is the lack of relevance of RCT findings to the practice arena. Granted, community-based psychosocial effectiveness RCTs are somewhat closer to the realities of practice, with its less rigid inclusion criteria and settings more comparable to usual care environments, than are efficacy studies. Still, community-based psychosocial RCTs are conducted under the most ideal circumstances possible, rather than dealing with the messy vagaries of the practice environment.

This chapter demonstrates the relevance of RCTs to building a sound, scientific basis for social work services and programs, so that social work practitioners can select the most effective interventions for their clients. Methods for establishing the external validity of RCTs are discussed, along with the responsibilities of social work researchers in reporting the results of RCTs to increase their usefulness to practice application. Furthermore, the use of systematic reviews in creating generalizable knowledge for practitioner decision making is presented, and the contributions of RCTs to the development of EBPs is reviewed.

Defining External Validity and Related Forms of Validity

In the context of an RCT, external validity is generally defined as the extent to which the experimental intervention can be applied to other clients, settings, and times, and can be expected to have similar outcomes when delivered by other investigators at another time and in other settings. Therefore, external validity is concerned with whether the intervention itself can be replicated with a high degree of confidence and whether the intervention is likely to result in similar outcomes in different environments or with different clients (Brass, Nunez-Neto, & Williams, 2006). Frequently, the terms *generalizability*, *replicability*, and *repeatability* are used interchangeably with external validity.

Two related forms of validity of relevance to RCT external validity are ecological validity and construct validity. *Ecological validity* is related to the degree to which the methods, intervention, and setting of an experiment approximate the real-life practice circumstances being studied (McHugo, et al., 2006). The greater the extent to which the RCT estimates the situations to which one wants to generalize, the greater the extent that the RCT has ecological validity. Thus, ecological validity is not the same as external validity (although these two are frequently confused), but it certainly contributes to external validity. Because community-based psychosocial RCTs frequently have relatively high ecological validity due to the type of practice settings in which they are conducted and the heterogeneity of the samples, they are likely to have a high degree of external validity. However, the RCT experimental intervention may be based on using a highly structured manual. If this manual does not reflect the procedures employed in the practice setting, the study is somewhat limited in ecological validity. Consequently, the study results are less applicable to the practice arena.

Construct validity is concerned with the interpretation of the study findings. This type of validity has to do with the relationship of the particular measures, operations of the intervention, and setting in which data were collected to the higher-order theoretical concepts that these data represent. For example, a client educational intervention measures an outcome regarding attitudes toward adhering to prescribed medication, but does not measure actual behavioral adherence to prescribed medications. A positive change in attitudes is found for those in the experimental educational intervention with regard to medication compliance. However, to interpret this result as the intervention leading to improvement in medication adherence, which is ultimately the target construct of interest, may be of questionable construct validity. There is likely a correlation between attitudes and behaviors regarding adherence to medication, but these two constructs are not the same concept.

Procedures for Achieving External Validity in Randomized Controlled Trials

Unfortunately, it is difficult to achieve external validity within an RCT, given the trade-offs that are made in ensuring internal validity. In many regards, a single-site RCT is essentially a case study. Although these RCTs employ quantitative methods, they are still based on one site, with all its idiosyncrasies. Consequently, the application of the results of RCTs to other situations and environments is somewhat limited, but can contribute to the iterative process of theory building.

One approach to external validity is to capitalize on methods that are intended to be used for single sites. The case study method, for example, takes as its unit of analysis a single case in a particular setting (Yin, 2003). Utilizing this design, a researcher collects all of the information that can be used to understand a specific case and its setting. These sources may include observations and interviews, quantitative data, documents, policies, and procedures. All these sources of data together provide insight into what may be unique about the setting. The multiple sources of information also provide a researcher with data to compare and contrast this setting with other potential settings. Therefore, the informed reader, with enough information and analysis by the researcher, can make his own assessment of generalizability to another setting.

Likewise, an RCT researcher may pursue the same strategy as in a case study. The "case," however, is the intervention or program. The setting is the organizational, system, community, and policy context. The research begins with the data collected from clients on background characteristics, service use, and outcome. In addition, fidelity assessment provides an opportunity to address the implementation of an intervention, but could also provide more contextual detail on the challenges of a particular replication of an intervention model for a new setting. Researchers can spend time observing the intervention and interviewing some clients and service providers (both experimental and control) in-depth. Contextual information can be collected about those specific policies in the service setting that enhance resources available or create barriers for clients and service providers. Finally, these multiple sources of data can be used to describe how a setting is similar to other settings, and how it is different. The researcher can use these data to provide their own analysis of the extent of external validity, and the reader is provided with sufficient information to judge that assessment.

For the reason of greater generalizability, as well as greater statistical power, increasing emphasis has been placed on multi-site RCTs, particularly for effectiveness studies in mental health services (Kraemer, 2000). A multi-site RCT requires more than two sites, with separate staff all implementing the same treatment and protocol procedures. One designated organization is charged with the tasks and responsibilities of accruing, processing, and analyzing data from participating sites (Kraemer, 2000). The advantages of multi-site RCTs are enhanced external validity; greater statistical power, particularly, when studying rare events in outcomes (such as mortality or arrests); greater variance in the outcome measure; and an increased rate of recruitment with more timely results (Weinberger, Oddone, Henderson, et al., 2001). There are, of course, numerous pitfalls and challenges to conducting multi-site RCTs that are both operational and scientific. Multi-site studies have a principal investigator at each site, which requires agreement from all involved parties on the standardization of procedures, so that all sites are comparable regarding eligibility criteria, intervention, usual care, and data collection (Kraemer, 2000; Weinberger, et al., 2001). These studies can be costly, and caution must be exercised before undertaking such a large-scale effort. Kraemer (2000) notes that, at times, multi-site RCTs are proposed before the necessary single-study RCTs are conducted. She notes, "[T]o propose a multi-site RCT before the research question and the approaches to take are clear from an accumulation of single-site RCTs may result in a poorly designed and inadequately [designed] multi-site RCT that not only would waste a great deal of time, effort, and funding that could have been better invested elsewhere but also might mislead the entire field for some time" (Kraemer, 2000, p. 535).

Thus, multi-site RCTs are not a quick fix to increasing external validity, but for interventions that have the appropriate preliminary work, they may prove useful. However, these investigations cannot be implemented feasibly by the lone researcher. Generally, these studies occur through a funding source, such as a federal agency, issuing a specific announcement to which individual investigators respond with a written proposal. These funding mechanisms are generally cooperative agreements in which the staff of the federal agency maintains primary control over the entire study, as opposed to a grant arrangement in which the principal investigator has more freedom in decision making regarding design and implementation. Once the sites are selected, based on scientific merit of the applications, a coordinating center is also selected (similarly based on competitive review of proposals), and the principal investigators from all participating sites meet to make decisions on the standardized protocol. Much time and effort goes into the final protocol, as well as many compromises. Procedures are also put in place to ensure that the established protocol is implemented as agreed upon by all parties.

The more feasible means for an individual investigator to achieve increased external validity is to replicate an already completed RCT. The new RCT may be conducted with a slightly different target population and will likely be conducted in a different setting from the original RCT. Given the case study nature of RCTs, the repeatability of the experimental intervention under diverse circumstances will enhance the external validity of the findings should the outcomes be equally positive. The repeatability of similar RCTs is essential to the conduct of meta-analyses and in building an evidence base, as discussed later. Justification for study replication is that the initial research shows promise, assuming a positive response, and therefore requires more accumulated evidence, under different circumstances, with different participants, or another target population. If the initial study results are not positive, there may be a need for a well-designed test, improvements in implementation, or conceptual modifications.

An RCT can fail for five primary reasons that may require corrective action in future studies: theory failure, implementation failure, measurement failure, design failure, and a lack of statistical power. If an argument can be made for any of these reasons in analyzing failed RCTs, then compensating for these deficiencies is a justification for another modified RCT to correct for the failure(s). Using these five potential problems as a guide is a good approach to critically assess failed RCTs.

In addition, if existing RCTs were exclusively conducted by the intervention developers, there is a need for studies conducted by an independent investigator, in order to control for possible allegiance bias (Littell, 2005). Independent replications of the initial RCT's positive findings increase confidence in their validity.

Neglect of External Validity in Randomized Controlled Trials

A variety of ranking systems have been developed to assess the level of evidence in order to assist clinical decision-makers. For example, Chapter 1 discussed the hierarchy of evidence for establishing EBPs. For the most part, these ranking systems have focused primarily on evaluating internal validity, leaving external validity to be determined by the practitioner in the process of application (Persaud & Mamdani, 2006). The most frequent criticism leveled at RCTs by practitioners is the lack of external validity. This is often the primary reason given for the limited use of practice guidelines and EBP (Rothwell, 2005, 2006). Determining the external validity of an RCT requires clinical expertise rather than simply methodological knowledge (Rothwell, 2006). It is unrealistic to expect that the results of an RCT will apply to all clients in every situation. At the same time, RCTs need to be designed and reported in a manner that permits practitioners to evaluate to which clients and situations the results can be applied reasonably (Rothwell, 2005). Without the ability to assess RCTs regarding their application, there is little purpose in conducting them. The inherent reason for conducting RCTs is to increase practice knowledge and ultimately enhance the quality of services, so as to improve client outcomes. Consequently, transparency of reporting the study protocol with all of its intricacies is essential to achieve effective practice application and study replication.

Factors Affecting External Validity

A variety of factors affect the external validity of studies. These factors have been categorized as follows: setting (e.g., type of service program, service delivery setting, or country; Rothwell, 2005), reach (e.g., participation rate and representativeness), program or policy implementation (e.g., levels of interventionist expertise and training, consistency of delivery, degree of adaptation to local circumstances), outcomes (e.g., impact on costs, quality of life, and adverse consequences), and maintenance and sustainability (e.g., which components are institutionalized or modified over time; Glasgow, et al., 2006, p. 106).

The RCT setting often causes concern, given that it is conducted in a specific environment that is likely not representative of most routine practice settings by virtue of the fact that the RCT is being conducted within it. Furthermore, differences in service delivery systems can affect external validity. For instance, the available service options may affect the nature of who is served in a given program. The national and local policies related to service eligibility and program funding criteria can affect the nature of services provided and clients served. Also, available services can affect who is willing to participate in an RCT. For example, in an RCT of families of adults with severe mental illnesses, Dixon (personal communication, May 15, 2008) has found biased recruitment in her RCT. Only those willing to forgo the experimental intervention for a period of time are enrolling in the study, as the experimental intervention, Family-to-Family, sponsored by the National Alliance for Mental Illness, is widely offered in the study community. Thus, there is no incentive for potential participants to take part in the study.

Generally, many RCTs employ samples of convenience, as opposed to using random sampling from a specific target population. In addition, RCTs have specific inclusion and exclusion criteria that limit the findings to only a portion of those individuals served in routine practice settings. However, before study eligibility criteria are applied in a given setting, prior stages of selection occur that further constrain the sample representativeness. The study setting determines the extent to which individuals who meet the study criteria are served in that setting. For example, if you are studying psychiatric clients and you are utilizing an inpatient setting for recruitment, only a portion of psychiatric clients receives services in hospitals today. Also, the availability of service options and alternatives in a given environment affects who receives services in a specific service site.

Furthermore, the use of run-in periods and enrichment strategies (i.e., actively recruiting those most likely to respond well to the intervention) further confine sample representativeness (Rothwell, 2005).

Critiques of the applicability of RCTs to the practice environment focus on those who deliver the interventions being perhaps more experienced and educated than the staff of many social work agencies. The clinical relevance of the outcomes is also frequently questioned. For example, what does scoring two points higher on a self-efficacy, self-esteem, or quality-of-life measure for experimental participants compared to controls mean clinically? Often, outcome measures of RCTs are presented as scales that do not translate well into the practice environment (Kazdin, 2006). For this reason, careful thought has to be given to RCT outcome measures in relation to external validity of findings, in order for these results to be useful to relevant practice settings. Concerns are also raised about the feasibility of the intervention to other settings and to routine clinical practice. RCT experimental interventions may require a high degree of expertise to implement, a good deal of funds, and changes in the organizational structure and policies. For these reasons, it may not be feasible to easily implement RCT interventions without an infusion of funds and major organizational policy and program modifications. The sustainability of the experimental intervention, even in the host setting, is frequently at issue. If an experimental psychosocial intervention that is determined to be effective is unable to be continued upon conclusion of the RCT in the host environment, it is questionable whether other environmental settings are in a position to institute such a program or intervention.

Reporting Criteria for Internal and External Validity

With the recent emphasis on the use of empirically supported interventions in clinical practice, the focus for most ranking systems of evidence has been on internal validity. The need for researchers and practitioners to be able to evaluate the RCT has resulted in established standards for the reporting of RCTs in medical and health care journals. Moher and colleagues (2001) noted that "a report of a randomized controlled trial should convey to the reader, in a transparent manner, why the study was undertaken, and how it was conducted, and analyzed" (p. 1191). In the mid-1990s, an international independent initiative to improve reporting requirements of RCTs was undertaken. This effort resulted in the Consolidated Standards of Reporting Trials (CONSORT). The CONSORT statement consists of a checklist and a flow diagram for reporting an RCT. This statement is continually monitored by biomedical publications and has been periodically revised when weaknesses in reporting become apparent. The 22-item checklist includes requirements under each of the major sections of a journal article: Title and Abstract, Introduction, Methods, Results, and Discussion. We include this checklist, as it gives a clear indication of what needs to be reported when presenting an RCT, and these criteria are also relevant to reporting the community-based psychosocial RCT (Figure 7.1). The flow chart of participants throughout the RCT is helpful in clarifying what the sample sizes are at the various points in the study (Figure 7.2). This information is important to communicate to others because, inevitably, in any RCT, the analyses of outcomes are on a very different sample size than the numbers who were randomly allocated to conditions. Consequently, the RCT's results may not be relevant even to those originally eligible for the study, as was the situation with two of the authors' forensic assertive community treatment (ACT) RCT (Figure 7.3). Moher and colleagues (2001) reported that "preliminary data indicate that the use of CONSORT does indeed help to improve the quality of reports of RCTs" (p. 1191).

The high degree of internal validity of RCTs resulted in the acceptance of the above criteria. However, a consequence of the widespread adoption of these standards has provoked the question of developing such standards for external validity. Such similar requirements might not only improve the quality but also the relevance of the evidence base (Glasgow, et al., 2006). Information related to contextual factors that are consistent with the categories of information just discussed that affect external validity (e.g., the setting, sample representativeness, implementation issues, and outcomes of relevance to practitioners and other decision-makers) has been suggested as reporting criteria requirements for evaluating the external validity of RCTs.

Paper Section and Topic	Item	Descriptor
Title and Abstract	1	How participants were allocated to interventions (e.g., "random allocation," "randomized," or "randomly assigned").
Introduction Background	2	Scientific background and explanation of rationale.
Methods Participants	3	Eligibility criteria for participants and the settings and locations where the data were collected.
Interventions	4	Precise details of the interventions intended for each group and how and when they were actually administered.
Objectives	5	Specific objectives and hypotheses.
Outcomes	6	Clearly defined primary and secondary outcome measures and, when applicable, any methods used to enhance the quality of measurements (e.g., multiple observations, training of assessors).
Sample Size	7	How sample size was determined and, when applicable, explanation of any interim analyses and stopping rules.
Randomization – Sequence Generation	8	Method used to generate the random allocation sequence, including details of any restrictions (e.g., blocking, stratification).
Randomization – Allocation Concealment	9	Method used to implement the random allocation sequence (e.g., numbered containers or central telephone), clarifying whether the sequence was concealed until interventions were assigned.
Randomization – Implementation	10	Who generated the allocation sequence, who enrolled participants, and who assigned participants to their groups.
Blinding (masking)	11	Whether or not participants, those administering the interventions, and those assessing the outcomes were blinded to group assignment. If done, how the success of blinding was evaluated.
Statistical Methods	12	Statistical methods used to compare groups for primary outcome(s); Methods for additional analyses, such as subgroup analyses and adjusted analyses.
Results Participant Flow	13	Flow of participants through each stage (a diagram is strongly recommended). Specifically, for each group report the numbers of participants randomly assigned, receiving intended treatment, completing the study protocol, and analyzed for the primary outcome. Describe protocol deviations from study as planned, together with reasons.
Recruitment	14	Dates defining the periods of recruitment and follow-up.
Baseline Data	15	Baseline demographic and clinical characteristics of each group.
Numbers Analyzed	16	Number of participants (denominator) in each group included in each analysis and whether the analysis was by "intention-to-treat". State the results in absolute numbers when feasible (e.g., 10/20, not 50%).
Outcomes and Estimation	17	For each primary and secondary outcome, a summary of results for each group, and the estimated effect size and its precision (e.g., 95% confidence interval).
Ancillary Analyses	18	Address multiplicity by reporting any other analyses performed, including subgroup analyses and adjusted analyses, indicating those pre-specified and those exploratory.
Adverse Events	19	All important adverse events or side effects in each intervention group.
Discussion Interpretation	20	Interpretation of the results, taking into account study hypotheses, sources of potential bias or imprecision and the dangers associated with multiplicity of analyses and outcomes.
Generalizability	21	Generalizability (external validity) of the trial findings.
Overall Evidence	22	General interpretation of the results in the context of current evidence.

Figure 7.1. CONSORT Checklist (http://www.consort-statement.org/)

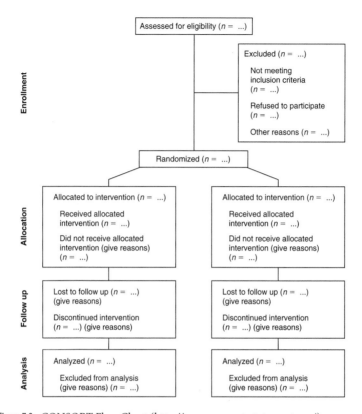

Figure 7.2. CONSORT Flow Chart (http://www.consort-statement.org/)

Importance and Relevance of Randomized Controlled Trials to Systematic Reviews

A primary means of increasing the applicability of RCTs is to combine the results of multiple RCT studies through the conduct of systematic reviews. By combining RCTs, the variance of settings, study designs, and implementation enhances the external validity of the pooled findings. Systematic reviews help practitioners to make sense of a variety of RCT studies with varying outcomes and, at times, divergent findings on the same topic. These reviews summarize a large body of research evidence and help to explain differing findings among studies on the same or similar interventions. The defining characteristics of systematic reviews are

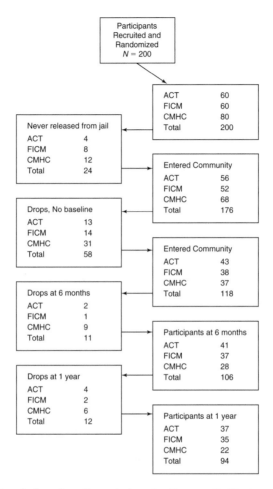

Figure 7.3. Sample flow chart: Forensic Assertive Community Treatment (ACT) randomized controlled trial

that they are explicit and rigorous regarding the procedures used to identify and combine independent studies. When the studies are summarized, but not statistically combined, the reviews are called *narrative summaries* or *qualitative syntheses*. Some do not see these as systematic, but more haphazard (Littell, Corcoran, & Pillai, 2008). The conclusions of qualitative reviews are considered to be open to more bias from the reviewer than are quantitative ones, and to be affected by large-scale studies.

Quantitative syntheses employ statistical procedures to aggregate the results of two or more studies addressing a given intervention. *Quantitative reviews* are generally referred to as *meta-analyses*. Meta-analytic reviews usually use the effect sizes of individual study results. Because the review process may be subject to bias, as with any research "systematic reviews use transparent procedures to identify, assess, and synthesize results of research on a particular topic. These procedures are defined in advance and are documented so that others can critically appraise and/ or replicate the review" (Littell, 2005, p. 449). As with the CONSORT, the Quality of Reporting of Meta-Analyses (QUOROM) addresses the standard for improving the quality of reporting for RCT meta-analyses. The QUOROM includes a checklist and a flow diagram. The checklist describes how to present the abstract, introduction, methods, results, and discussion sections of a meta-analysis report. The flow diagram provides information about the numbers of RCTs identified, included, and excluded, and the reasons for the exclusion of trials (Moher, Cook, Eastwood, et al., 1999).

Littell (2005) recently reported on the lessons she learned from conducting a meta-analysis that focused on multisystemic therapy (MST) RCTs. MST is a short-term, intensive, family- and community-based treatment program designed to produce positive changes in youth who have severe psychosocial and behavioral problems and are at risk for out-of-home placement. She noted that most prior reviews have concluded that MST is an effective intervention program. Based on these reviews, MST is considered an EBP and has been promoted by numerous federal agencies, such as the Substance Abuse and Mental Health Services Administration (SAMHSA) and the National Institute of Mental Health (NIMH), as well as foundations such as the Annie E. Casey Foundation. Contrary to prior reviews, Littell and her colleagues' preliminary results found "few if any significant effects on measured outcomes, compared with usual services or alternative treatments" (Littell, 2005, p. 457). Her preliminary conclusions have caused some controversy, resulting in a rebuttal by the developer and promoter of MST to her article (Henggeler, Schoenwald, Swenson, & Borduin, 2006) and a subsequent response by Littell (2006) in *Children and Youth Services Review*, the journal that published her meta-analysis. Some of the issues under contention stem from the lack of clarity of RCT reporting; for example, inconsistent reporting on the number of cases that were randomly assigned; lack of clarity of randomization procedures; implementation issues, such as unstandardized observation periods in the RCTs; and loss of participants at follow-up.

The Contribution of Randomized Controlled Trials to Evidence-Based Practice

One RCT does not create an evidence base for a given intervention. It is only when enough RCTs are available to be able to conduct systematic reviews that include meta-analytic reviews of a specific intervention can conclusions of the effectiveness of the interventions be made. Thus, there is a need for a relatively sizeable number of RCTs in a given intervention area in order to establish an evidence base of specific interventions. Unfortunately, limited RCTs have been conducted on social work interventions. Social workers have conducted RCTs, but often these interventions are not social work interventions per se, although they may be closely aligned with social work, such as the previously mentioned RCTs on family education and ACT. Cavanaugh's (2007) RCT that examines the effectiveness of dialectical behavior educational workshop for males at risk of intimate partner violence combines social work, psychology, and public health frameworks. MST was developed by a psychologist, but is consistent with a social work approach and philosophy.

Hopefully, texts such as this book will encourage social workers to conduct RCTs on social work interventions, so that the profession can begin to build its own evidence base.

Cost Effectiveness in Randomized Controlled Trials

One of the issues related to wider dissemination of effective interventions is whether they are cost effective. Given the limited resources of social and behavioral health services, the interest in further application of a successful intervention is its cost effectiveness. In cost-effectiveness analysis, the monetary costs of the interventions are assessed, but the monetary benefits of the interventions are not. Cost-effectiveness analysis examines intervention costs per unit of a specific outcome (Rubin & Babbie, 2008). For example, Rothbard and colleagues (2008) conducted a cost-effectiveness analysis of cognitive therapy (CT) versus treatment as usual (TAU) in the community for the prevention of repeat suicide attempts. The number of suicide attempts for CT was 28 out of 60 participants and 57 out of 60 for TAU. The direct and indirect costs for CT were $8,781 and for TAU $7,752, while annual cost to avert a suicide attempt was $2,129.

To conduct a cost-effectiveness analysis, planning is required from the beginning of the study, as it requires an extensive collection of data, including all treatment costs both from the program and other services, depending on the nature of the service and the population. Having a member of the research team with expertise in designing and conducting the cost analysis is essential.

Cost–benefit analysis makes an effort "to monetize the program's outcome in addition to its costs" (Rubin & Babbie, 2008 p. 316). However, a cost–benefit analysis is complicated, because it is often quite difficult to allocate dollar amounts to some outcome benefits, such as the burden in terms of emotional strain placed on family members of persons with a psychiatric disability (Weisbrod, Test, & Stein, 1980). The problem regarding cost allocation is due to value issues. Consequently, it is more common to conduct cost-effectiveness assessments than cost–benefit analyses, as they are more feasible and less controversial (Rubin & Babbie, 2008).

Conclusion

Given the essential case study approach of an RCT, the researcher has control only over a limited number of factors. However, reporting the study must be made as transparent as possible, so that others employing the study findings are clearly aware of the intricacies of the design and implementation of the RCT. With increased clarity of reporting, there will likely be increased consistency in the conclusions of systematic reviews, thus avoiding problems that Littell (2005) encountered in her review of MST. Furthermore, practitioners will have a better understanding to whom and under what conditions the outcomes of the RCTs apply.

We hope that, in the future, when planning, designing, and implementing an RCT that you heed our message: Do not make community-based psychosocial RCTs so complex and expensive that they cannot later be used to inform practice because community service agencies are unable to match the funding or feasibly implement the intervention. The ultimate purpose of community-based psychosocial RCTs is to provide more effective services for vulnerable populations. Therefore, to have applicability beyond your RCT, an intervention must be practical within the nature of the current service arenas. Designing such studies draws on many social work research and practice skills, and the nature of these research skills go well beyond quantitative research methods. RCTs are best conducted by a team of individuals with diverse expertise, including such realms as qualitative methods, statistics, and cost-effectiveness analysis. It is important to note that well-planned, designed, and implemented RCTs have implications for both social work practice and social policy. RCTs offer direction for whom, what, and how we deliver services, as well as where we should allocate our limited resources.

For Further Reading

Littell, J., Corcoran, J., Pillai, V. (2008). *Systematic reviews and meta-analysis*. New York: Oxford University Press.

Lipsey, M., & Wilson, D. (2001). *Practical meta-analysis*. Thousand Oaks, CA: Sage Publications.

Glossary

Adverse Event: An untoward or undesirable event experienced by a research participant.

Allegiance Bias: Loyalty of the developer of an intervention that may result in demonstrating the effectiveness of the intervention.

Assent Form: A simple and brief consent form that a child can understand and sign prior to entrance into a research study. Content needs to parallel a consent form.

Attrition: Departure of an enrolled participant from a research study before it is completed, which may result in a threat to the internal validity of the RCT.

Beneficence: Ethical principle of research that requires the researcher to maximize possible benefits to participants while minimizing any potential risks or harm.

Blinding: A procedure where investigators, providers and/or participants are naïve to the condition to which the participants are assigned. Blinding may include "double blind," in which neither participant nor the provider is aware of assignment. "Single blind" occurs when only the investigator is aware of which intervention the participant is receiving, but the participant is unaware of assignment. Blinding is utilized to control for potential bias from knowledge of assignment that may affect responses of participant or provider, or assessment of the outcome(s).

Blocked Randomization: A procedure that balances the assignment of participants to the intervention conditions of the RCT at the end of each block.

Certificates of Confidentiality: A certificate issued by the National Institute of Health to protect identifiable research data from forced release to other parties. These certificates allow researchers to refuse releasing information about the identification of the participants, even under court subpoena, in any federal, state, or local, civil, criminal, administrative, legislative, or other proceedings, with a few exceptions.

Cluster Randomization: When the unit of randomization occurs at the group or cluster level in which intact groups are randomized with all individuals within a particular group entering the assigned condition. One can randomize practices, health plans, or providers to control for potential contamination between study conditions.

Concept Mapping: Employs a group process to brainstorming about a topic, procedures for sorting and rating the emerged items, and multivariate techniques to develop clusters regarding the items, with the final output being a concept map (that is, a visual display of the categories in relation to each other) that the group then interprets.

Confidentiality: An agreement by the researcher to protect a study participant's personal information by ensuring under what, if any, specific circumstances this information will be disclosed.

Confound: An alternative possible variable or extraneous variable that may affect the RCT outcome variable.

Consecutive Sampling: A form of convenience sampling in which all available and eligible subjects are recruited as they enter the service setting.

Consent Form: A form that a research participant signs prior to entrance into an RCT that provides information about the research study that is necessary in order to make an informed decision as to whether to participate or not. It includes the purpose, duration of participation, nature of procedures, risks, benefits, and available alternative treatments or therapies. For RCTs, the form needs to specify that assignment to treatment or intervention or control condition will be done randomly.

Construct Validity: In the context of RCTs, this refers to the interpretation of the effect that was demonstrated (that is, whether the interpretation of the findings is consistent with operationalization of the constructs).

Contamination, Diffusion, or Imitation of Treatment: In RCTs, when providers inadvertently deliver aspects of the experimental intervention to controls or recipients of the control condition receive some of elements of the intervention intended for the experimental participants, thus reducing the planned differences between conditions.

Control Condition or Group: A group of participants who do not receive the intervention that is being tested and are similar in all other characteristics to the experimental group.

Convenience or Availability Sampling: A method of selecting sample elements based on their ready access. This sampling procedure is frequently used in RCTs.

Data Safety and Monitoring Board: A committee comprised of members with expertise necessary to protect the safety of participants in an RCT and to ensure the validity and integrity of data, independent of the researchers conducting the trial. This committee provides oversight and monitoring during the conduct of the trial.

Delphi Method: A structured procedure for generating ideas from a group of individuals and, through rounds of controlled feedback, to come to a consensus on the topic.

Dosage: The amount of the experimental intervention participants receive in terms of quantity of services or service elements.

Dummy, Inert, or Bogus Intervention: The control condition in an RCT, which is expected to provide no benefit, but employed for scientific reason of controlling for the internal validity threat of attention.

Ecological Validity: Relates to the degree to which the methods, interventions, and setting of an experiment approximate the real-life practice circumstances being studied.

Effectiveness Studies: RCTs conducted under "real-world" conditions. The criteria of efficacy studies are relaxed to achieve greater sample representativeness to treatment populations and application of results to community-based service settings.

Efficacy Studies: RCTs conducted under "ideal conditions," highly controlled research environments, with rigid inclusion criteria, manualized intervention, and blinding to control for reactivity effects of providers and participants.

Equipoise: An ethical requirement of RCTs that there is a substantial degree of uncertainty as to which treatment or intervention will benefit the study participant more.

Ethnographic Methods: In the context of an RCT, a qualitative approach in which one provides a detailed in-depth description of the intervention operations and practices, as well as the social environment by the researcher spending extensive time in the setting.

Evidence-Based Practice or Empirically Supported Intervention: A practice or intervention consistently demonstrates improved client outcomes based on scientific evidence (i.e., a number of RCTs conducted by independent teams of researchers).

Exclusion Criteria: Characteristics of the population that determine that the potential participant is ineligible to enter the RCT.

Experimental Condition or Group: A group of participants who receive the intervention that is being evaluated and should characteristically be similar to the control group in all other aspects.

Experimental Design: A research method that employs random assignment or randomization of units to experimental and control conditions following a pretest of the outcome, introducing the experimental intervention to the experimental condition, withholding this intervention from the control condition, and comparing the outcome or post-test between the experimental and control condition.

External Validity: The extent to which the findings of an RCT can be generalized to other settings and populations beyond those from which the study was conducted.

Fidelity Assessment: Determining whether the intervention was conducted as planned and is consistent with service or program elements delineated in the manual, including structures and goals.

Fidelity Measure: A scale or tool that assesses the adequacy of implementation of a service or program or a means to quantify the degree to which the service elements in a program or service are implemented.

Focus Group: A qualitative research approach in which a small group (commonly 6–12 individuals) of selected individuals are brought together to have a guided discussion on a specific topic.

History: A threat to internal validity where an event and/or a change in the environment (agency, community, global) may also provide an explanation for resulting change in the outcome rather than merely the experimental intervention.

Hypothesis: Empirically testable statement of a relationship of the intervention to specific theorized outcomes.

Inclusion Criteria: Characteristics of the target population that determine whether the potential participant is eligible to be entered into the RCT.

In-depth Interviews: An extensive interview on a one-to-one basis in which a particular topic is explored closely.

Instrumentation: A threat to internal validity that results from differences in measurement that are not inherent in the measurement technology per se, but rather changes in the calibration of the measure under different circumstances and/or changes in procedures from administration to administration. Thus, the outcome of the RCT may be due to these changes rather than the experimental intervention.

Intent-to-Treat Analysis: Grouping participants for purposes of analysis based on their original assignment to the experimental intervention or the control group, regardless of whether the participant received the intervention or not. This procedure is done to preserve the original randomization and avoid potential selection bias from loss of participants. This approach is favored in effectiveness RCTs as it mirrors the adherence in practice.

Internal Validity: The extent to which the results or outcomes of an RCT were the result of the experimental intervention rather than other extraneous factors.

Intervention Drift or Spill-over Effect: A situation in which, over the course of the RCT, the experimental intervention moves toward looking exactly like the treatment as usual, in other words the control condition.

Intervention Manual or Treatment Manual: Details specifically the experimental intervention and provides careful guidelines for intervention implementation. In addition the manuals specifies the standards for evaluating adherence to the intervention, offers guidelines for training, provides quality assurance and monitoring standards, facilitates replication, and stimulates dissemination and transfer of an effective intervention.

Justice: Ethical principle of research that requires research participants undertaking the burden of risk to be representative of the group who will receive the benefits derived from the research being conducted.

Leakage Scale or Form: A measure that captures the degree to which participants in the control condition receive services planned only for the experimental intervention.

Locator Form: A working document of all possible contact information that can help the research team find a participant when he is needed.

Mediator: Variable that is hypothesized to help make change happen; a conceptual link in the middle of a cause and effect argument, which is some times referred to as an intervening or process variable.

Meta-analyses: Statistical procedures for analyzing and synthesizing the outcomes of multiple studies, or multiple RCTs, on a particular topic.

Moderator: A variable that interacts with the intervention in such a way that the interaction of the moderator variable with the intervention has different effects (or strengths of effect) on the outcome.

Multi-factorial Designs: Group designs in which two or more interventions with two or more levels for each intervention are examined (e.g., 2 × 2 designs, with four groups). These designs encompass the combination of the interventions, so that the main effects of each intervention, as well as the interaction of the different interventions can be evaluated.

Multisite RCT: More than two sites conduct the same RCT with same intervention and protocol procedures.

Nonspecific Factors: Other factors than the 'active' ingredients of the experimental interventions, such as empathy, warmth, genuineness, and alliance, as well as provider competency in providing the intervention.

Nominal Group Process: Controlled means of generating creative ideas, in which group members write down their ideas, which are subsequently discussed and prioritized one at a time by the group.

Participant Observation: A qualitative method in which the researcher is both a part of and participant in the situations, groups, and individual's lives that are being studied.

Placebo: An inactive intervention given to a control condition for purposes of comparison to experimental intervention to determine the effectiveness of the experimental intervention.

Placebo Effect: A measurable or observed positive effect of attention to or treating the participant on the participant's outcome.

Pilot Study: Preliminary testing of the procedures of a research study prior to conducting the full-scale study. Usually done on a small scale to see if recruitment and methods work and are practical and feasible, including whether the intervention seems to produce the intended effect.

Pipeline: "Directs attention to how, why, and when individuals may be included in the experiment or excluded, and to the number of individuals who enter or exit the study at any given point" (Boruch, 1997, p. 88).

Population: All possible cases that the research is focused on studying.

Practice Guidelines: "A set of systematically complied and organized statements of empirically tested knowledge and procedures to help practitioners select and implement interventions that are most effective and appropriate for attaining the desired outcomes" (Rosen & Proctor, 2003, p. 1).

Pre-experimental Design: A one-group design that does not control for factors other than the intervention that may have an impact on the outcome(s).

Program Evaluation: A systematic approach to assess goals, processes, and outcomes of programs, interventions, and policies that may employ experimental designs in assessing outcomes.

Program Manual: Delineates the core elements and structures of the program, as well as the various roles of the different providers. Program manuals are similar to treatment manuals, see *Treatment Manual.*

Purposive Sampling: A type of convenience sampling in which participants are selected based on the judgment of the investigator and prior knowledge as most appropriate for the purposes of testing the intervention.

Quasi-experimental Design: A research method that employs comparison conditions that are not randomly assigned. Lack of random assignment is the major distinction from an experimental design.

Qualitative Research Methods: Focus on in-depth understanding and deeper meanings of human experience and the social environment and processes of implementation. Common methods include focus groups, participant observation, and ethnographic methods.

Quota Sampling: A type of nonprobability sampling technique used to include a pre-set number of participants for each level or category of stratification. See *Stratified Randomization.*

Random Assignment or Randomization: Chance allocation of units to conditions in an RCT. Units may be at the micro, mezzo, or macro level (i.e., individuals, organizations, or counties).

Randomized Controlled Trial (RCT): A true experiment whereby study participants are assigned by chance, following a pretest, to at least two conditions: An experimental treatment or intervention, and a control intervention used for purposes of comparison on study outcomes.

Release of Information Form: A form signed by a service client who agrees that the service agency can release information from the clinical and/or service record to a third party, in this case a researcher.

Reliability: The consistency with which a measure yields the same results each time it is used under the same circumstances.

Respect: An ethical principle of research that refers to the right of autonomous individuals to make their own decisions regarding their treatment and participation in research, and to the obligation of clinicians and researchers to protect individuals with diminished autonomy.

Statistical Power: Ability to detect a difference between outcomes of conditions in an RCT when there is a difference. In RCTs, power is a measure of the degree of certainty in avoiding a false-negative conclusion that an experimental intervention is ineffective when it is effective.

Stratified Randomization: Participants are grouped into strata of a given characteristic and then randomly assigned by strata to the RCT conditions. This procedure is employed to ensure that equal numbers of participants with a given characteristic that may affect the outcome are distributed across all conditions of the RCT.

Systematic Review: Explicit and rigorous procedures, a specific plan or protocol, for identifying and combining a number of independent studies (e.g., RCTs) on the same or similar topic.

Testing [AQ1]: A threat to internal validity that results from taking the same test repeated times during the study. The outcome of the RCT may occur due to repeated exposure to the test rather than from the experimental intervention.

Train-the-Trainers: An approach to training providers that designates specific providers to train new staff.

Treatment Differentiation: Ensuring that the intervention differs from other similar treatments or services.

Treatment Manual: Specifies the intervention, provides standards for evaluating adherence to the intervention, offers guidance for training, provides quality assurance standards, facilitates replication, and stimulates dissemination and transfer of effective interventions. These manuals often include a brief literature review, general guidelines for establishing a therapeutic relationship, descriptions of specific techniques and content, suggestions for structurally sequencing activities, and strategies for dealing with special problems, implementation issues, and termination.

Treatment-as-Usual (TAU): Conventionally offered treatment or service interventions of accepted standards of care. Commonly used as a control condition in an RCT rather than no service.

Type III Error: Measuring an intervention that does not exist or a service program that is inadequately implemented.

Validity: The extent to which a measure reflects the theoretical meaning of the concept of interest.

Waiting List Control: Participants assigned to this control design complete their research purpose before receiving the experimental treatment. This condition is used in lieu of no treatment or intervention control.

References

Aarons, G., Palinkas, L. (2007). Implementation of evidence-based practice in child welfare: Service provider perspective. *Administration Policy in Mental Health & Mental Health Services Research, 34,* 411–419.

Ajzen, I., & Fishbein, M. (1980). Understanding attitudes and predicting social behavior. *Journal of Health Services, 27*(1), 177–199.

Armitage, C. J., & Conner, M. (2001). Efficacy of the theory of planned behaviour: A meta-analytic review. *British Journal of Social Psychology,* 40, 471–499.

Ashery, R., & McAuliffe, W. (1992). Implementation issues and techniques in randomized trials of outpatient psychosocial treatments for drug abusers: Recruitment of subjects. *American Journal of Drug and Alcohol Abuse, 18,* 305–329.

Asscher, J., Dekovic, M., van der Lann, P., Prins, P., & van Arum, S. (2007). Implementing randomized experiments in criminal justice settings: An evaluation of multi-systemic therapy in the Netherlands. *Journal of Experimental Criminology, 3,* 113–129.

Babcock, J. C., Green, C. E., & Robie, C. (2004). Does batterers' treatment work? A meta-analytic review of domestic violence treatment. *Clinical Psychology Review, 23*(8), 1023–1053.

Baron, R. M., & Kenny, D. A. (1986). The moderator-mediator variable distinction in social psychological research: Conceptual, strategic, and statistical considerations. *Journal of Personality & Social Psychology, 51*(6), 1173–1182.

Bellg, A., Borrelli, B., Resnick, B., Hecht, J., Minicucci, D., Ory, M., Ogedegbe, G., Orwig, D., Ernst, D., Czajkowski, S. (2004). Enhancing treatment fidelity in health behavior change studies: Best practices and recommendations from the NIH Behavior Change Consortium. *Health Psychology, 23,* 443–451.

Bilson, A. (2004). *Evidence-based practice and social work practice: International research and policy perspectives.* London: Whiting & Birch.

Blagys, M. D., & Hilsenroth, M. J. (2002). Distinctive activities of cognitive-behavioral therapy. A review of the comparative psychotherapy process literature. *Clinical Psychology Review, 22*(5), 671–706.

Blakely, C., Mayer, J., Gottschalk, R., Schmitt, N., Davidson, W., Roitman, D., & Emshoff, J. (1987). The fidelity-adaptation debate: Implications for the implementation of public sector social programs. *American Journal of Community Psychology, 13,* 253–268.

Blank, A. E. (2006). Access for some, justice for any? The allocation of mental health services to people with mental illness leaving jail. Ph.D. Dissertation, University of Pennsylvania, United States—Pennsylvania. Dissertations & Theses @ University of Pennsylvania database. (Publication No. AAT 3246142).

Bond, G., Evans, L., Salyers, M., Williams, J., Kim, H-W. (2000). Measurement of fidelity in psychiatric rehabilitation. *Mental Health Services Research, 2,* 75–87.

Bond, G., Williams, J., Evans, L., Salyers, M., Kim, H-W, Sharpe, H., Leff, S. (Nov. 2000). *Psychiatric Rehabilitation Fidelity Toolkit,* Cambridge, MA, Human Services Research Institute.

Boruch, R. (1997). *Randomized experiments for planning and evaluation: A practical guide.* Thousand Oaks: Sage Publications.

Boruch, R. F. (2005). Better Evaluation for Evidence-based policy: Place randomized trials in education, criminology, welfare, and health. *Annals of the American Academy of Political and Social Science, 599,* 6–18.

Boruch, R. F., Rindskopf, D., Anderson, P. S., Amidjaya, I. R., & Jansson, D. M. (1979). Randomized experiments for evaluating and planning local programs: A summary on appropriateness and feasibility. *Public Administration Review, 39,* 36–40.

Boruch, R., May, H., Turner, H., Lavenberg, J., Petrosino, A., deMoya, D., et al. (2004). Estimating the effects of interventions that are deployed in many places: Place-randomized trials. *American Behavioral Scientist, 47,* 608–633.

Bourdieu, P. (1986). Forms of capital (R. Nice, Trans.). In J. E. Richardson (Ed.), *Handbook of theory of research for the sociology of education.* Westport Connecticut: Greenwood Press.

Brass, C., Nunez-Neto, B, & Williams, E. (March 7, 2006). *Congress and Program Evaluation: An Overview of Randomized Controlled Trials (RCTs) and Related Issues.* Congressional Research Services. The Library of Congress.

Briggs, H., & Rzipnicki, T. (2004). *Using evidence in social work practice: Behavioral perspectives.* Chicago: Lyceum Books.

Bruns, E., Burchard, J., Suter, J., Leverentz-Brady, K., Force, M. (2004). Assessing fidelity to a community-based treatment for youth: The Wraparound Fidelity Index. *Journal of Emotional and Behavioral Disorders*, 12, 79–89.

Bull, S., Lloyd, L, Rietmeijer, C., & McFarlane, M. (2004). Recruitment and retention of an online sample for an HIV prevention intervention targeting men who have sex with men: The Smart Sex Quest Project. *AIDS CARE*, 16, 931–943.

Burns, T., Firn, M. (2003). *Assertive outreach in mental health: A manual for practitioners*. New York: Oxford University Press.

Carroll, K., Nuro, K. (2002). One size cannot fit all: A stage model for psychotherapy manual development. *Clinical Psychology: Science and Practice*, 9, 396–406.

Carroll, K., Nuro, K. (1997). The use and development of treatment manuals. In K. Carroll, (Ed.). *Improving compliance with alcoholism treatment*. Bethesda, MD: National Institute of Alcohol Abuse and Alcoholism, pp. 53–72.

Carroll, K., Rounsaville, B. (2008). Efficacy and effectiveness in developing treatment manuals. In A. Nezu, & C. Nezu. (Eds.), *Evidence-based outcome research*. New York: Oxford University Press.

Cavanaugh, M. M. (2007). An exploration of the feasibility and utility of the Dialectical Psychoeducational Workshop (DPEW) as a preventative intervention for males at potential risk of intimate partner violence. Ph.D. dissertation, University of Pennsylvania. ProQuest Digital Dissertations database. (Publication No. AAT 3260886).

Chambless, D., & Ollendick, T. (2001). Empirically supported psychological interventions: Controversies and evidence. *Annual Review of Psychology* 52, 685–716.

Clarke, G. N., Herinckx, H. A., Kinney, R. F., Paulson, R. I., Cutler, D. L., Lewis, K., et al. (2000). Psychiatric hospitalizations, arrests, emergency room visits, and homelessness of clients with serious and persistent mental illness: Findings from a randomized trial of two ACT programs vs. usual care. *Mental Health Services Research, 2*(3), 155–164.

Cocozza, J. J., Steadman, H. J., Dennis, D. L., Blasinsky, M., Randolph, F. L., Johnsen, M., et al. (2000). Successful systems integration strategies: The access program for persons who are homeless and mentally ill. *Administration and Policy in Mental Health, 27*(6), 395–407.

Cohen, S., Gottlieb, B. H., & Underwood, L. G. (2000). Social relationships and health. In S. Cohen, L. G. Underwood & B. H. Gottlieb (Eds.), *Social support measurement and intervention: A guide for health and social scientists.* (pp. 3–25). New York: Oxford University Press.

Coleman, J. S. (1988). Social capital in the creation of human capital. *American Journal of Sociology, 94*(Supplement), S95–S120.

Corrigan, P. W., & Salzer, M. S. (2003). The conflict between random assignment and treatment preference: Implications for internal validity. *Evaluation and Program Planning, 26,* 109–121.

Cosden, M., Ellens, J. K., Schnell, J. L., Yamini-Diouf, Y., & Wolfe, M. M. (2003). Evaluation of a mental health treatment court with assertive community treatment. *Behavioral Sciences and the Law, 2,* 415–427.

Cosden, M., Ellens, J., Schnell, J., & Yamini-Diouf, Y. (2005). Efficacy of a mental health treatment court with assertive community treatment. *Behavioral Sciences and the Law, 23,* 199–214.

Cotter, R., Burke, J., Loeber, R., & Navratil, J. (2002). Innovative retention methods in longitudinal research: A case study of the Developmental Trends Study. *Journal of Child and Family Studies,* 11, 485–498.

Crepaz, N., Lyles, C. M., Wolitski, R. J., Passin, W. F., Rama, S. M., Herbst, J. H., et al. (2006). Do prevention interventions reduce HIV risk behaviours among people living with HIV? A meta-analytic review of controlled trials. *Aids, 20*(2), 143–157.

Davis, L, Broome, M., & Cox, R. (2002). Maximizing retention in community-based clinical trials. *Journal of Nursing Scholarship, 34,* 47–53.

Del Boca, F., Darkes, F. (2007). Enhancing the validity and utility of randomized clinical trials in addictions treatment research: II. participant samples and assessment. *Addiction, 102,* 1194–1203.

Dennis, M. L. (1990). Assessing the validity of randomized field experiments: An example from drug abuse treatment research. *Evaluation Review, 14,* 347–373.

Desmond, D., Maddux, J., Johnson, T., & Confer, B. (1995). Obtaining follow-up interviews for treatment evaluation. *Journal of substance Abuse Treatment, 12,* 95–102.

DeVillis, B. M., & DeVellis, R. F. (2000). Self efficacy and health. In A. Baum, T. A. Revenson & J. E. Singer (Eds.), *Handbook of Health Psychology* (pp. 235–247). Mahwah, NJ: Erlbaum.

DiClemente, C. C., & Hughes, S. O. (1990). Stages of change profiles in outpatient alcoholism treatment. *Journal of Substance Abuse, 2*(2), 217–235.

Dobson, D., Cook, T. (1980). Avoiding Type III error in program evaluation: Results from a field experiment. *Evaluation and Program Planning,* 3, 269–276.

Donner, A., & Klur, N. (2004). Pitfalls of and controversies in cluster randomization trials. *American Journal of Public Health,* 94, 416–422.

Draine, J., & Herman, D. (2007). Critical time intervention for reentry from prison. *Psychiatric Services,* 58, 1577–1581.

Drake, R. E., McHugo, G. J., Becker, D. R., Anthony, W. A., & Clark, R. E. (1996). The New Hampshire study of supported employment for people with severe mental illness. *Journal of Consulting & Clinical Psychology, 64*(2), 391–399.

Drake, R., McHugo, G., Bebout, R., Becker, D., Harris, M., Bond, G., et al. (1999). A randomized clinical trial of supported employment for inner-city patients with severe mental illness. *Archives of General Psychiatry*, 56, 627–633.

Drake, R., McHugo, G., Becker, D, Anthony, W., & Clark, R. (1996). The New Hampshire Study of Supported Employment for people with severe mental illness: Vocational outcomes. *Journal of Consulting and Clinical Psychology*, 64, 391–399.

Festinger, D., Marlow, D., Croft, J., Dugosh, K., Mastro, N., Lee, P., DeMatteo, D., & Patapsi, N. (2005). Do research payments precipitate drug use or coerce participation? *Drug and Alcohol Dependence*, 78, 275–281.

Fishbein, M., & Ajzen, I. (1975). *Belief, attitude, intention and behavior.* Reading, MA: Addison-Wesley.

Flander, M., Burns, T. (2000). A Delphi approach to describing service models of community mental health practice. *Psychiatric Services*, 51, 656–658.

Folkman, S., & Moskowitz, J. T. (2004). Coping: Pitfalls and promise. *Annual Review of Psychology, 55*, 745–774.

Fox, M., Martin, P., & Green, G. (2007). *Doing practitioner research.* London: Sage Publications.

Fraser, M. (2003). Intervention research in social work: A basis for evidence-based practice and practice guidelines. In A. Rosen, & E. Proctor. (Eds.), *Developing practice guidelines for Social Work intervention.* New York: Columbia University Press.

Fraser, M. (2004). Intervention research in social work: Recent advances and continuing challenges. *Research in Social Work Practice, 14*, 210–222.

Gellis, Z., McGinty, J., Horowitz, A., Bruce, M., Misener, E. (2007). Problem-solving therapy for late-life depression in home care: A randomized field trial. *American Journal of Geriatric Psychiatry, 15*, 968–978.

Gibbs, L. (1991). *Scientific reasoning for social workers.* New York: Macmillan.

Glasgow, R., Green, L., Klesges, L., Abrams, D., Fisher, E., Goldstein, M., Hayman, L., Ockene, J., & Orleans, C. (2006). External validity: We need to do more. *Annals of Behavioral Medicine*, 31, 105–108.

Glisson, C., Dukes, D., Green, P. (2006). The effects of the ARC organizational intervention on caseworker turnover, climate, and culture in children's service systems. *Child Abuse & Neglect, 30*, 855–880.

Godin, G., & Kok, G. (1996). The theory of planned behavior: A review of its applications to health-related behaviors. *American Journal of Health Promotion*, 11, 87–98.

Goldfinger, S., Schutt, R., Tolomicenko. G., Seidman, L., Penk, W., Turner, W., et al., (1999). Housing placement and subsequent days homeless among formerly homeless adults with mental illness. *Psychiatric Services*, 50, 674–679.

Good, M., Schuler, L. (1997). Subject retention in a controlled clinical trial. *Journal of Advanced Nursing, 26,* 351–355.

Groopman, J. (2007). *How doctors think.* New York: Houghton-Mifflin.

Gueron, J. (January 2000). The politics of random assignment: Implementing studies and impacting policy. *Working Paper.* New York: Manpower Demonstration Research Corporation.

Havik, O., & VandenBos, G. (1996). Limitations of manualized psychotherapy for everyday clinical practice. *Clinical Psychology: Science and Practice, 3,* 264–267.

Hemmelgarn, A., Glisson, C., & James, L. (2006). Organizational culture and climate: Implications for services and interventions research. *Clinical Psychology: Science and Practice, 13,* 73–89.

Henggeler, S., Schoenwald, S., Swenson, C., & Borduin, C. (2006). Methodological critique and meta-analysis as Trojan Horse, *Children and Youth Services Review, 28,* 447–457.

Herbst, J. H., Beeker, C., Mathew, A., McNally, T., Passin, W. F., Kay, L. S., et al. (2007). The effectiveness of individual-, group-, and community-level HIV behavioral risk-reduction interventions for adult men who have sex with men: A systematic review. *American Journal of Preventative Medicine, 32*(4 Suppl), S38–67.

Herbst, J. H., Kay, L. S., Passin, W. F., Lyles, C. M., Crepaz, N., & Marin, B. V. (2007). A systematic review and meta-analysis of behavioral interventions to reduce HIV risk behaviors of Hispanics in the United States and Puerto Rico. *AIDS Behavior, 11,* 25–47.

Herinckx, H. A., Kinney, R. F., Clarke, G. N., & Paulson, R. I. (1997). Assertive community treatment versus usual care in engaging and retaining clients with severe mental illness. *Psychiatric Services, 48*(10), 1297–1306.

Hirschel, D., & Buzawa, E. (2002). Understanding the context of dual arrest with directions for future research. *Violence Against Women, 8,* 1449–1473.

Hoffrage, U., Linsey, S., Herwig, R., Gigerenzer, G. (2000). Communicating statistical information. *Science, 290,* 2261–2262.

Hohmann, A. (1999). A contextual model for clinical mental health effectiveness research. *Mental Health Services Research 1,* 83–91.

Holter, M., Mowbray, C., Bellamy, C., MacFarlane, P., Dukarshi, J. (2004). Critical ingredients of consumer-run services: Results of a national survey. *Community Mental Health Journal, 40,* 47–63.

Howard, M., Jenson, J. (2003). Clinical guidelines and evidence-based practice in medicine, psychology, and allied professions. In A. Rosen, & E. Proctor. (Eds.), *Developing practice guidelines for Social Work intervention.* New York: Columbia University Press.

Howard, M., McMillen, C., & Pollio, D. (2003). Teaching evidence-based practice: Toward a new paradigm for social work education. *Research on Social Work Practice*, 13, 234–259.

Kanter, J. (1996). Engaging significant others: The Tom Sawyer approach to case management. *Psychiatric Services*, 47(8), 799–801.

Kaufman, C., Schulberg, H., & Schooler, N. (1994). Self-help group participation among people with severe mental illness. *Prevention in Human Services*, 11, 315–331.

Kazdin, A. (2003). *Research design in clinical psychology.* Boston: Allyn and Bacon.

Kazdin, A. (2006). Arbitrary metrics. *American Psychologist*, 61, 42–49.

Kraemer, H. (2000). Pitfalls of multisite randomized clinical trials of efficacy and effectiveness. *Schizophrenia Bulletin*, 26, 533–541.

Kraemer, H., Mintz, J., Noda, A, Tinklenberg, J., Yesavage, J. (2006). Caution regarding the use of pilot studies to guide power calculations for study proposals, *Archive of General Psychiatry*, 63, 484–489.

Lancaster, G., Dodd, S., Williamson, P. (2004). Design and analysis of pilot studies: Recommendations for good practice. *Journal of Evaluation in Clinical Practice*, 10, 307–312.

Lattimore, P. K., Broner, N., Sherman, R., Frisman, L., & Shafer, M. S. (2003). A comparison of prebooking and postbooking diversion programs for mentally ill substance using individuals with justice involvement. *Journal of Contemporary Criminal Justice*, 19, 30–64.

Lazarus, R. S., DeLongis, A., Folkman, S., & Gruen, R. (1985). Stress and adaptational outcomes. The problem of confounded measures. *American Psychologist*, 40(7), 770–785.

Linehan, M. M. (1993). *Skills training manual for treating borderline disorder.* New York: Guilford Press.

Littell, J. (2005). Lessons from a systematic review of effects of multisystemic therapy. *Children and Youth Services Review*, 27, 445–463.

Littell, J. (2006). The case for multisystemic therapy: Evidence or orthodoxy? *Children and Youth Services Review*, 28, 458–472.

Littell, J., Corcoran, J., & Pillai, V. (2008). *Systematic review and meta-analysis.* New York: Oxford University Press.

Marlowe, D. B. (2006). When "what works" never did: Dodging the "Scarlet M" in correctional rehabilitation. *Criminology and Public Policy*, 5(2), 339–346.

Marshall, T., & Solomon, P. (2004). Confidentiality intervention: Effects on provider-consumer-family collaboration. *Research on Social Work Practice*, 14, 3–13.

Mazor, K., Sabin, J., Boudreau, D., Goodman, M., Gurwitz, J., Herrinton, L., Raebel, M., et al. (2007). Cluster randomized trials opportunities and barriers identified by leaders of eight health plans. *Medical Care*, 45, Suppl 2, S29–S37.

McAuliffe, W, & Ashery, R. (1993). Implementation issues and techniques in randomized trials of outpatient psychosocial treatments for drug abusers, II. clinical and Administrative Issues. *American Journal of Drug and Alcohol Abuse, 19*, 35–50.

McDonald, A., Knight, R., Campbell, M., Entwistle, V., Grant, A., Cook, J., Elbourne, D., Francis, D., Garcia, J, Roberts, I., Snowdon, C. (2006). What influences recruitment to randomized controlled trials? A review of trials funded by two UK funding agencies. *Trials, 7*:9 doi:10.1186/1745–6215–7–9.

McFarlane, W. R., Dixon, L., Lukens, E., & Lucksted, A. (2003). Family psychoeducation and schizophrenia: A review of the literature. *Journal of Marital and Family Therapy, 29*(2), 223–245.

McGrew, J., & Bond, G. (1995). Critical ingredients of Assertive Community Treatment: Judgments of the experts. *Journal of Mental Health Administration, 22*, 113–125.

McGrew, J., Bond, G., Dietzen, L, & Salyers, M. (1994). Measuring the fidelity of implementation of a mental health program model. *Journal of Consulting and Clinical Psychology, 62*, 670–678.

McHugo, G., Drake, R., Brunette, M., Xie, H., Essock, S., & Green, A. (2006). Enhancing validity in Co-occurring Disorders Treatment Research. *Schizophrenia Bulletin, 32*, 655–665.

McKay, M. (2006). Commentary on increasing access to child mental health services for urban children and their caregivers. In L. Alexander, & P. Solomon, (Eds.), *The research process in the human services*. Belmont, CA: Thomson Brooks/Cole.

McKay, M., Stoewe, J., McCadam, K., & Gonzales, J. (1998). Increasing access to child mental health services for urban children and their caregivers, *Health and Social Work, 23*, 9–15.

McNeece, C., & Thyer, B. (2004). Evidence-based practice and social work. *Journal of Evidence-Based Social Work, 1*, 7–25.

Miklowitz, D., & Hooley, J. (1998). Developing family psychoeducational treatments for patients with bipolar and other severe psychiatric disorders: A pathway from basic research to clinical trials. *Journal of Marital and Family Therapy, 24*, 419–435.

Moher, D., Cook, D., Eastwood, S., Okin, I., Rennie, & D., Stroup, D. (1999). Improving the quality of reports of meta-analyses of randomized controlled trials: The QUORUM statement. *The Lancet, 354*, 1896–1900.

Moher, D., Schulz, K., & Altman, D. (2001). The CONSORT statement: Revised recommendations for improving the quality of reports of parallel-group randomized trials. *The Lancet, 357*, 1191–1194.

Moncher, F., & Prinz, R. (1991). Treatment fidelity in outcome studies. *Clinical Psychology Review, 11*, 247–266.

Monette, D. R., Sullivan, T. J., & DeJong, C. R. (2005). *Applied social research: A tool for the human services* (6th ed.). Belmont, CA: Wadsworth/Thompson.

Moser, D. J., Arndt, S., Kanz, J. E., Benjamin, M. L., Bayless, J. D., Reese, R. L., et al. (2004). Coercion and informed consent in research involving prisoners. *Comprehensive Psychiatry, 45,* 1–9.

Mowbray, C., Bybee, D., Holter, M., Lewandowski, L. (2006). Validation of a fidelity rating instrument for consumer-operated services. *American Journal of Evaluation,* 24, 315–340.

Mowbray, C., Holter, M., Mowbray, O, & Bybee, D. (2005b). Consumer-run drop-in centers and Clubhouses: Comparison of services and resources in a statewide sample. *Psychological Services,* 2, 54–64.

Mowbray, C., Holter, M., Stark, L., Pfeffer, C., & Bybee, D. (2005a). A fidelity rating instrument for consumer-run drop-in centers (FRI-CRDI). *Research on Social Work Practice,*15, 278–290.

Mowbray, C., Holter, M., Teague, G., & Bybee, D. (2003). Fidelity criteria: Development, measurement, and validation. *American Journal of Evaluation,* 24, 315–340.

Mueser, K. T., Clark, R. E., Haines, M., Drake, R. E., McHugo, G. J., Bond, G. R., et al. (2004). The Hartford study of supported employment for persons with severe mental illness. *Journal of Consulting & Clinical Psychology, 72*(3), 479–490.

National Institutes of Health. NIH Policy for Data and Safety Monitoring. Release date June 10, 1998.

Nezu, A., & Nezu, C. (2008). *Evidence-based outcome research.* New York: Oxford University Press.

Oakley, A., Wiggins, M., Turner, H., Rajan, L., & Barker, M. (2003). Including culturally diverse in health research: A case study of an urban trial of social support. *Ethnicity & Health,* 8, 29–39.

Obert, J. L., Brown, A. H., Zweben, J., Christian, D., Delmhorst, J., Minsky, S., et al. (2005). When treatment meets research: Clinical perspectives from the CSAT Methamphetamine Treatment Project. *Journal of Substance Abuse Treatment, 28,* 231–237.

Orwin, R. (2000). Methodological challenges in study design and implementation: Assessing program fidelity in substance abuse health services research. *Addiction,* 95 (S3), S309–S327.

Orwin, R., Sonnefeld, L., Cordray, D., Pion, G., & Perl, H. (1998). Constructing: Quantitative Implementation scales from categorical service data. *Evaluation Review,* 22, 245–288.

Paulson, R., Herinckx, H., Demmler, J., Clarke, G., Cutler, D., & Birecree, E. (1999). Comparing practice patterns of consumer and non-consumer mental health service providers. *Community Mental Health Journal, 35*(3), 251–269.

Paulson, R., Post, R., Herinckx, H., & Risser, P. (2002). Beyond components: Using fidelity scales to measure and assure choice in program implementation and quality assurance. *Community Mental Health Journal, 38,* 119–128.

Pearlin, L. I., & Schooler, C. (1978). The structure of coping. *Journal of Health and Social Behavior, 19*(1), 2–21.

Persaud, N., & Mamdani, M. (2006). External validity: The neglected dimension in evidence ranking. *Journal of Evaluation in Clinical Practice,* 12, 450–453.

Petersilia, J. (1989). Implementing randomized experiments: Lessons from BJA's intensive supervision project. *Evaluation Review, 13,* 435–458.

Piantadosi, S. (1997). *Clinical trials: Methodological perspective.* New York: John Wiley & Sons, Inc.

Pollio, D. E., Spitznagel, E. L., North, C. S., Thompson, S., & Foster, D. A. (2000). Service use over time and achievement of stable housing in a mentally ill homeless population. *Psychiatric Services, 51*(12), 1536–1543.

Portes, A. (1998). Social Capital: Its origins and applications in modern sociology. *Annual Review of Sociology, 24,* 1–24.

Proctor, E., Rosen, A. (2003). The structure and function of social work practice guidelines. In A. Rosen, & E. Proctor, (Eds.), *Developing practice guidelines for Social work intervention.* New York: Columbia University Press.

Putnam, R. D. (2000). *Bowling alone.* New York: Simon and Shuster.

Regehr, C., Stern, S., & Shlonsky, A. (2007). Operationalizing evidence-based practice: The development of an Institute for Evidenced-Based Social Work Practice. *Research in Social Work Practice,* 17, 408–416.

Rendell, J., Licht, R. (2007). Under recruitment of patients for clinical trials: An illustrative example of a failed study. *Acta Pscychiatrica Scandinavica,* 115, 337–339.

Ribisl, K. M., Walton, M. A., Mowbray, C. T., Luke, D. A., Davidson, W. S., & Bootsmiller, B. J. (1996). Minimizing participant attrition in panel studies through the use of effective retention and tracking strategies: Review and recommendations. *Evaluation and Program Planning, 19,* 1–25.

Roberts, A., & Yeager, K. (Eds.) (2006). *Foundations of evidence-based social work practice.* New York: Oxford University Press.

Roberts, M. M., & Pratt, C. W. (2007). Putative evidence of employment readiness. *Psychiatric Rehabilitation Journal, 30,* 175–181.

Rosen, A. Proctor, E. (2003). Practice guidelines and the challenge of effective practice. In A. Rosen, & E. Proctor, (Eds.), *Developing practice guidelines for Social Work intervention.* New York: Columbia University Press.

Rosenstock, I. M., Strecher, V. J., & Becker, M. H. (1988). Social learning theory and the Health Belief Model. *Health Education Quarterly, 15*(2), 175–183.

Rothbard, A., Koisumi, N., Brown, G., Sosjan, D., & Beck, A. (2008). *Cost effectiveness of cognitive therapy intervention for the prevention of repeat suicide attempts.* Lecture notes, University of Pennsylvania, Philadelphia.

Rothwell, P. (2005). External validity of randomized controlled trials: "To whom do the results of this trial apply?" *The Lancet*, 365, 82–93.

Rothwell, P. (2006). Factors that can affect the external validity of randomized controlled trial. *PLoS Clinical Trials*, 1(1): e9. DOI: 10.1371/journal.pctr. 0010009.

Rubin, A., & Babbie, E. (2007). *Essential research methods for social work*. Belmont, CA: Wadsworth/Thompson.

Rubin, A., Babbie, E. (2008). *Research methods for social work*. Belmont, CA, Thomson: Brooks/Cole.

Sackett, D., Richardson, W., Rosenberg, W., & Haynes, R. (1997). *Evidence-based medicine: How to practice and teach EBM*. New York: Churchill Livingstone.

Sarason, B. R., Sarason, I. G., & Gurung, R. A. R. (2001). Close personal relationships and health outcomes: A key to the role of social support. In B. R. Sarason & S. W. Duck (Eds.), *Personal relationships: Implications for clinical and community psychology*. Canada: Wiley.

Schmidt, L., Gill, K., Solomon, P., Pratt, C. (2008). Comparison of service outcomes of case management teams with and without a consumer provider. *American Journal of Rehabilitation Skills, 11*.

Sharkey, S., Maciver, S., Cameron, D., Reynolds, W., Lauder, W., & Veitch, T. (2005). An exploration of factors affecting the implementation of a randomized controlled trial of a transitional discharge model for people with a serious mental illness. *Journal of Psychiatric and Mental Health Nursing, 12*, 51–56.

Sherman, L. W., & Berk, R. A. (1984). The specific deterrent effects of arrest for domestic assault. *American Sociology Review, 49*, 261–272.

Shern, D., Trochim, W., & LaComb, C. (1995). The use of concept mapping for assessing fidelity of model transfer: An example from psychiatric rehabilitation. *Evaluation and Program Planning, 18*, 143–153.

Shlonsky, A., & Gibbs, L (2006). Will the real evidence-based practice please stand up? In A. Roberts, & K. Yeager, (Eds.), *Foundations of evidence-based social work practice*. New York: Oxford University Press.

Solomon, P. (1997). Issues in designing and conducting randomized human service trials: Lessons from the field. *Journal of Social Service Research, 22*, 57–71.

Solomon, P. (2004). Peer support/peer provided services underlying processes, benefits, and critical ingredients. *Psychiatric Rehabilitation Journal, 27*(4), 392–401.

Solomon, P., & Draine, J. (1995). One-year outcomes of a randomized trial of case management with seriously mentally ill clients leaving jail. *Evaluation Review*, 19, 256–273.

Solomon, P., & Draine, J. (1995). The efficacy of a consumer case management team: 2–year outcomes of a randomized trial. *Journal of Mental Health Administration, 22*(2), 135–146.

Solomon, P., & Draine, J. (2006). Commentary on "Predicting incarceration of psychiatric probation and parole" in Alexander, L., Solomon, P. (eds.) *The research process in the human services: Behind the scenes.* Belmont, CA: Wadsworth/Thomson Learning.

Solomon, P., Draine, J., & Delaney, M. (1995). The working alliance and consumer case management. *The Journal of Mental Health Administration, 22,* 126–134.

Solomon, P., Draine, J., Mannion, E., & Meisel, M. (1996). Impact of brief family psychoeducation on self-efficacy. *Schizophrenia Bulletin,* 22, 41–50.

Solomon, P., Draine, J., Mannion, E., & Meisel, M. (1997). Effectiveness of two models of brief family education: Retaining gains of family members of adults with serious mental illness. *American Journal of Orthopsychiatry,* 67, 177–186.

Solomon, P., Tennille, J., Lipsett, D., Plumb, E., & Blank, M. (2007). Rapid Assessment of HIV prevention programming in a community mental health center. *Journal of Prevention and Intervention in the Community, 33,* 137–151.

Sormanti, M., Pereira, L., El-Bassel, N., Witte, S., & Gilbert, L. (2001). The role of community consultants in designing an HIV prevention intervention. *AIDS Education and Prevention,* 13, 311–328.

Startup, M., Jackson, M. C., & Startup, S. (2006). Insight and recovery from acute psychotic episodes: The effects of cognitive behavior therapy and premature termination of treatment. *Journal of Nervous and Mental Disease, 194*(10), 740–745.

Strange, V., Allen, E., Oakley, A., Bonell, C., Johnson, A, Stephenson, J. (2006). Integrating process with outcome data in a randomized controlled trial of sex education. *Evaluation, 12,* 330–352.

Strauss, J. S., & Carpenter, W. T., Jr. (1972). The prediction of outcome in schizophrenia. I. Characteristics of outcome. *Archives of General Psychiatry, 27*(6), 739–746.

Strauss, J. S., & Carpenter, W. T., Jr. (1977). Prediction of outcome in schizophrenia. III. Five-year outcome and its predictors. *Archives of General Psychiatry, 34*(2), 159–163.

Sullivan, C., Rumptz, M., Campbell, R., Eby, K., Davidson II, W. (1996). Retaining participants in longitudinal community research: A comprehensive protocol. *Journal of Applied Behavioral Science,* 32, 262–276.

Susser, E., Valencia, E., Conover, S., Felix, A., Tsai, W. Y., & Wyatt, R. J. (1997). Preventing recurrent homelessness among mentally ill men: A "critical time" intervention after discharge from a shelter. *American Journal of Public Health,* 87, 256–262.

Sutton, S. (2001). Back to the drawing board? A review of applications of the transtheoretical model to substance use. *Addiction, 96*(1), 175–186.

Teller, J. L., Munetz, M. R., Gil, K. M., & Ritter, C. (2006). Crisis Intervention Team training for police officers responding to mental disturbance calls. *Psychiatric Services, 57,* 232–237.

TenHave, T. R., Coyne, J., Salzer, M., & Katz, I. (2003). Research to improve the quality of care for depression: Alternatives to the simple randomized clinical trial. *General Hospital Psychiatry, 25,* 115–123.

The National Commission for the Protection of Human Subjects of Biomedical and Behavioral Research (April 18, 1979). The Belmont Report.

Torrey, W., Lynde, D., & Gorman, P. (2005). Promoting the implementation of practices that are supported by research: The National Implementing Evidence-Based Practice Project. *Child and Adolescent Psychiatric Clinics of North America, 14,* 297–306.

Trochim, W., Cook, J., & Setze, P. (1994). Using concept mapping to develop a conceptual framework of staff's views of a supported employment program for individuals with severe mental illness. *Journal of Consulting and Clinical Psychology, 62,* 766–775.

Tsemberis, S., Gulcur, I., & Nakae, M. (2004). Housing First, consumer choice, and harm reduction for homeless individuals with psychiatric disabilities. *American Journal of Public Health, 94,* 651–656.

U.S. Department of Health and Human Services. (2006). *Treatment, volume 1: Understanding evidence-based practices for co-occurring disorders.* www.samhsa.gov

Van Der Gaag, M., & Snijders, T. A. B. (2003). *A comparison of measures of individual social capital.* Unpublished manuscript, Amsterdam: University of Groningen.

Van Der Gaag, M., & Snijders, T. A. B. (2005). The resource generator: Social capital quantification with concrete items. *Social Networks, 27,* 1–29.

Vaughn, M. G., & Howard, M. O. (2004). Adolescent substance abuse treatment: A synthesis of controlled evaluations. *Research on Social Work Practice, 14,* 325–335.

Walker, J., & Bruns, E. (2006). Building on practice-based evidence: Using expert perspectives to define the wraparound process. *Psychiatric Services, 57,* 1579–1585

Watson, J., & Torgerson, D. (2006). Increasing recruitment to randomised trials: A review of randomised controlled trials. *BMC Medical Research Methodology,* doi:10.1 186/1471–2288–6–34.

Weinberger, M., Oddone, E., Henderson, W., Smith, D., Huey, J., Giobbie-Hurder, A., & Feussner, J. (2001). Multisite randomized controlled trials in health services research: Scientific challenges and operational issues. *Medical Care, 39,* 627–634.

Weisbrod, B., Test, M., & Stein, L. (1980). Alternative to mental hospital treatment II. Economic benefit-cost analysis. *Archives of General Psychiatry, 37,* 400–405.

Wingood, G., & DiClemente, R. (2008). The ADAPT-ITT Model a novel method of adapting evidence-based HIV Interventions. *Journal of Acquired Immune Deficiency Syndrome, 47,* Supplement 1, S40–S46.

Witte, G., & Wilber, C. (1997). A case study in clinical supervision: Experience from Project MATCH. In Carroll, K. (ed.) *Improving compliance with alcoholism treatment.* Bethesda, MD: U.S. Dept. of Health and Human Services, National Institute on Alcohol Abuse and Alcoholism.

Witte, S., El-Bassel, N., Gilbert, L., Wu, E., Chang, M., & Steinglass, P. (2004). Recruitment of minority women and their main sexual partners in an HIV/STI prevention trial. *Journal of Women's Health, 13,* 1137–1147.

Yin, R. K. (2003). *Case study research: Design and methods* (3rd ed.). Thousand Oaks, CA: Sage Publications, Inc.

Index

ACT. *See* Assertive Community
    Treatment (ACT)
ADAPT-ITT, 65–66
Advertising of RCTs, 148
Age factors, 125
Annie E. Casey Foundation, 183
Approvals, 34–35, 40, 50
Assertive Community Treatment (ACT)
    contamination, 106
    control condition, 89
    design, 69, 83, 97–98
    fidelity assessment, 106, 165
    flow chart, 182*f*
    outcomes, generalizability of, 179
    randomization procedure,
        97–98, 101
Assignment of study participants.
    See Randomization
Attrition, 111–14
Autonomy, 22

Belmont Report, 21–23
Beneficence, 21–23

Blinding, 10, 11, 119–20
Blocked randomization, 118–19
Bond, G., 61, 73–74
Boruch, R. E., 54
Brief Problem-Solving Therapy
    in Home Care, 120
Bruns, E., 70, 73

Calibration, 104
Care standards, 62
Carroll, K., 61
Case managers as RCT participants,
    32–33
Case study method, 173
Cavanaugh, M. M., 66, 184
Checklists, 77–78
Child abuse, 162
Children in RCTs, 31–32
Client–provider relationship, 62
Cluster randomization, 118
Coercion, 37–38
Communication skills,
    improvement of, 68

Community-Based Outreach Model
    (CBOM), 66
Community-based psychosocial
    interventions, 6–7, 16–17
    context, 90–91
    culturally responsive strategies, 53,
        55–56
    EBP in, 14
    ethics in, 22–23
    fidelity assessment, 73, 167 (*See also*
        Fidelity assessment)
    generalizability of, 171
    practice guidelines, 67
    provider participation, consent,
        32–34
    sample selection diversity, 38–39,
        126
    setting (*See* Settings)
    treatment manuals (*See* Treatment
        manuals)
Concept mapping, 68–69, 166
Conceptualization development,
        80–81, 83, 94–95
    hypothesis formulation, 90–94
    mediators/moderators, 83–87, 85*f*,
        86*f*, 92–93, 93*f*, 130–31
    outcome measurement, 130–33
    research question/control
        condition, 87–90
    theory in, 80–82
Condom use, 68
Confidentiality, 35–37, 43
Connections, importance of, 49–50
Consolidated Standards of Reporting
        Trials (CONSORT), 178–81,
        180*f*, 181*f*
Consumer case management study,
        88–89
Consumer-run drop-in centers
        (CRDIs), 74–77, 165

Contamination, 105–7, 109–11
Control conditions, 20, 25–27
    attrition and, 112
    contamination in, 105–7
    design components, 98–100
    ethics of, 20, 25–30
    informed consent, 27–30
    preparation, 140, 141
    randomization, 118–19
    research question and, 87–90
    staff training, 161
Cook, T., 138
Corcoran, J., 14
Cosden, M., 101, 103
Cost effectiveness of RCTs, 184–85
Critical Time Intervention (CTI) trial
    design of, 105–6, 113–14
    mediators, 85–87, 86*f*
    moderators, 92–93, 93*f*
    outcome measurement, 130–32
    poverty as moderating factor,
        86–87, 86*f*, 93, 93*f*
    preparation, 144–45
    randomization in, 117
    sampling criteria, 127*f*
Culturally responsive strategies, 53,
        55–59

Data analysis, 133–34
Databases, 150–51
Data collection
    design, 104–5
    fidelity assessments, 163–66
    participant tracking, 148–51,
        150*t*–151*t*
    provider characteristics, 168
    retention monitoring, 153–57
Data points, 130–33
Data safety, 39–40
Delphi method, 68, 75, 166

Dennis, M. L., 110
Design of RCTs, 18, 96, 136–37
    adaptive, 136
    components, 98–100
    confounds, 102–14
        attrition, 111–14
        contamination control, 105–7
        intervention drift, 107–9
        intervention environmental
            change, 109–11
    CTI trial, 105–6, 113–14 (See also
        Critical Time Intervention
        (CTI) trial)
    data analysis, 133–34
    data collection, 104–5
    efficacy vs. effectiveness studies,
        9–12
    encouragement/randomized
        consent, 27, 29, 30, 136
    ethical issues in, 15 (See also
        Ethics)
    evidence hierarchy, 13t
    interventions, complex, 100–102
    multifactorial, 101–2
    operationalization, 129–30
    outcome measurement, 130–33
    quasi vs. pre-experimental, 8–9
    randomization (See Randomization)
    randomized preference, 136
    reliability, 131–32
    sampling, 122–29
    service context and, 97–98
    Solomon four-group, 103–4
Desmond, D., 154
Diagnoses specificity, 125
Dialectical Behavior Therapy
    (DBT), 66
Dixon, L., 177
Dobson, D., 138
Dosage effects, 134

Draft implementation resource kits,
    64–65
Draine, J., 24, 88–89, 152

EBP. See Evidence-based practice (EBP)
Effectiveness studies, 10–12
    ethics, 19–20
    generalizability of, 171
    payment, 37
    recruitment strategies, 53
    treatment manuals in, 60
Efficacy studies, 9–10, 22–23, 60, 64
Eligibility
    determination of, 54, 55, 153
    factors affecting, 177
    informed consent, 31–32, 153
        (See also Informed consent)
    sampling criteria, 124–26, 127f, 135
    staff training, 161
Environmental context assessment,
    166–68
Equipoise, 21, 47, 148
Error measurement, 138, 163
Ethics, 17, 19, 44
    approvals, 34–35, 40, 50
    coercion, 37–38
    confidentiality, 35–37
    control conditions, 20, 25–30
    data safety, 39–40
    effectiveness studies, 19–20
    efficacy studies, 22–23
    informed consent (See Informed
        consent)
    Internet RCTs, 40–43
    interventions, untested, 24–25
    monitoring, 39–40, 43
    payment, 37–38, 53
    practice/research integration, 23–24
    randomization, 19–21, 158
    research personnel, 34–35

Ethics (*continued*)
  respect/beneficence/justice, 21–23
  sampling, 38–39, 126
  social worker evaluation, 15
  termination responsibilities, 38, 63
  waiting list controls, 25–26, 28
Evidence-based practice (EBP), 12–14
  draft implementation resource kits, 64–65
  generalizability of, 171
  hierarchy, 13*t*
  RCT contribution to, 97, 184
  training, 159
  treatment manuals, 69–71
  validity, external, 176
Experimental study, 7–8

Family education RCTs, 24, 26
Family-to-Family, 177
Federal-wide Assurance (FWA), 34–35
Festinger, D., 37, 114
Fidelity assessments, 71–78, 74*t*, 108, 134, 163–66, 173. *See also* Validity
Fidelity criteria, 73
Fidelity forms, 160, 161
Fidelity measures, 72–74, 74*t*, 134
Fidelity Rating Instrument for Consumer-Run Drop-In Centers (FRI-CRDI), 74–77
Focus groups, 67–68, 166
Follow-up procedures, 154–56
Funding
  cost effectiveness, 184–85
  as design confound, 109
  ethics of payment, 37–38, 53
  factors affecting, 123, 177
  planning, 48–49
  preparation, 141

Gellis, Z., 89–90, 120
Generalizability of outcomes, 116, 170–71, 185–86. *See also* Outcomes; Validity
Generalized estimating equations (GEE) models, 134
Geographic considerations, 126
Glisson, C., 166

Health Insurance Portability and Accountability Act (HIPAA), 35–36
Helper therapy principle, 83
Herbst, J. H., 84–85, 85*f*
HIPAA, 35–36
History, 109
HIV/AIDS risk reduction trial, 84–85, 85*f*, 118, 147, 167, 168
HIV/STI prevention RCT, 24, 55, 57–59, 68
Housing/employment RCTs, 46–47, 69, 113. *See also* Critical Time Intervention (CTI) trial
Human subject protection training, 34, 157
Hypothesis formulation, 90–94

Ideal circumstances, 9–10
Implementation, 5, 18, 138–39, 169
  changes, 146
  computer technology in, 147–57
    recruitment, 147–48
    recruitment monitoring, 151–53
    retention monitoring, 153–57
    tracking, 148–51, 150*t*–151*t*, 155, 156
  cooperation in, 145–47
  efficacy studies, 10
  environmental context assessment, 166–68

evidence-based practice, 159
factors affecting, 122–23
fidelity assessments, 71–78, 74*t*,
    108, 134, 163–66, 173
fidelity forms, 160, 161
follow-up procedures, 154–56
integrity, maintaining, 159–60,
    163–66
setting preparation, 139–45
standardized, 10
training (*See* Training)
treatment manuals, 62 (*See also*
    Treatment manuals)
In-depth interviews, 67–68
Index cards, 149
Informed consent, 22, 27–34, 44
attrition and, 111–12
blinding and, 120
eligibility, 31–32, 153
forms, 27–32, 41
HIPAA, 35–36
as inclusion criterion, 127*f*
Internet RCTs, 40–43
from providers, 32–34
randomization, 27, 29, 30, 136
timing, 31
Institutional Review Board (IRB)
    authorization, 34–35, 40, 50
Instrumentation, 104
Integrity, maintaining, 159–60,
    163–66
Intent-to-treat, 133–34
Internet RCTs, 40–43
Interpretation of data, 5
Intervention drift, 107–9
Interventions
complex, 100–102
environmental change, 109–11
implementation (*See*
    Implementation)

specifications, 62
untested, ethics of, 24–25

Justice, 21–23

Kaufman, C., 16
Kraemer, H., 52–53, 174

Language considerations, 126
Leakage forms, 160, 161
Leakage scale, 72
Liability, 51
Linehan, M. M., 66
Littell, J., 14, 183, 186
Locator forms, 151, 155
Locator information, 113

McDonald, A., 53
McKay, M., 12, 32, 73
McNeece, C., 17
Mediators/moderators, 83–87, 85*f*,
    86*f*, 92–93, 93*f*, 130–31
Medicaid, 67
Mental illness
consumer case management study
    (Solomon/Draine), 88–89
Critical Time Intervention (CTI)
    trial (*See* Critical Time
    Intervention (CTI) trial)
draft implementation resource kits,
    64–65
housing/employment RCTs, 46–47,
    69, 113 (*See also* Critical Time
    Intervention (CTI) trial)
hypotheses in RCTs, 91
research questions, 89
Meta-analyses, 14, 183
Minors in RCTs, 31–32
Moderators, 83–87, 85*f*, 86*f*, 92–93,
    93*f*, 130–31

Moher, D., 178–79
Monitoring ethics, 39–40, 43
Mowbray, C., 73–77, 165
Mueser, K. T., 113
Multilevel modeling, 134
Multi-site RCT, 123, 174–75
Multisystemic therapy (MST)
    RCTs, 183–84

Narrative summaries, 182
National Association of Social Work
    (NASW) Code of Ethics, 15,
    20, 23
National Institute of Mental Health
    (NIMH), 183
Nazi concentration camp
    experiments, 22
No-service controls, ethics, 25

Operationalization of, 129–30
Orwin, R., 72, 164
Outcomes, 90, 93
    administrative data set
        measurement, 100
    critique of, 178
    factors affecting, 167–68
    generalizability, 116, 170–71, 185–86
    interventions, complex, 101
    measurement, design, 130–33
    reporting criteria, 154, 178–81,
        180*f*, 181*f*

Participant diaries, 165
Participant retention, pilot studies,
    56–59
Participant tracking, 148–51,
    150*t*–151*t*, 155, 156
Patient selection, 3–4
    diversity, 38–39
    factors affecting, 177–78

pilot studies, 53–55
quasi *vs.* pre-experimental designs,
    8–9
Paulson, R., 165
Payment
    attrition and, 113–14
    ethics, 37–38, 53
Pillai, V., 14
Pilot studies, 52–53
    benefits of, 108
    culturally responsive strategies,
        53, 55–59
    participant retention, 56–59
    payment, 53
    recruitment assessment, 53–55
Pipeline study, 53–55
Placebo effects, 88
Planning, 17–18, 45–46, 78–79
    agency demands, 50–51
    authority issues, 49–50
    checklists, 77–78
    expectations, establishment of,
        51–52
    funding, 48–49
    negotiation, 49–52, 52*t*
    pilot studies (*See* Pilot studies)
    plausibility, 46–52
    site selection, 47–49, 54
    treatment manuals (*See* Treatment
        manuals)
Policy, research and, 46–47
Policy-level confounds, 109–10
Poverty as moderating factor, CTI
    trial, 86–87, 86*f*, 93, 93*f*
Practice, 23
Practice-based evidence, building,
    69–71
Practice guidelines, 67
Preventing AIDS Through Health
    (PATH), 66–67, 89, 91

Prevention intervention RCTs, 26–27
Principle of equipoise, 21, 47, 148
Privacy, 35–37, 43
Problem-solving educational
    intervention study, 89–90
Proctor, E., 67
Program evaluation *vs.* research, 7–8
Program/practice manuals, 60, 61.
    See also Treatment manuals
Providers
    client relationships with, 62
    environmental context influence
        on, 166–68
    informed consent from, 32–34
    research personnel, 34–35, 161–63
    selection/training/supervision, 63,
        77, 158–60
Psychosocial intervention, 7.
    See also Community-based
    psychosocial interventions
Psychotherapy efficacy studies
    design, 10

Qualitative syntheses, 182–83
Quality of life (QOL)
    measurement, 132
Quality of Reporting of Meta-
    Analyses (QUOROM), 183
Quantitative reviews, 14, 183

Random generators, 115–16
Randomization, 5, 97–98
    attrition and, 113
    control conditions, 118–19
    ethics of, 19–21, 158
    informed consent, 27, 29, 30, 136
    multifactorial designs, 102
    as objection, 3, 4
    procedures, 115–22
        ACT trial, 97–98, 101

    application, 120–22
    blinding, 10, 11, 119–20
    blocked, 118–19
    cluster, 118
    CTI trial, 117
    stratification, 117–18
    training in, 158
Randomized controlled trial (RCT),
    5–6, 11, 16–17
    advertising of, 148
    benefits of, 45–46
    cost effectiveness, 184–85
    criticisms of, 135
    design (*See* Design of RCTs)
    EBP and, 184
    ethics (*See* Ethics)
    failure/problem areas, 175–76
    focus of, 6–7
    as gold standard, 6, 15, 170
    hypotheses in, 91
    Internet RCTs, 40–43
    minors in, 31–32
    multi-site, 123, 174–75
    multisystemic therapy, 183–84
    prevention intervention, 26–27
    purpose/utility, 15, 186
    systematic reviews and, 181–84, 186
    theory as foundation for, 80–82
Randomized field trial, 7–8
RCT. *See* Randomized controlled
    trial (RCT)
REAL SCORE, 52, 52t
Recruitment
    assessment, 53–55
    computer technology in, 147–48
    culturally responsive strategies, 53,
        55–56
    factors affecting, 124, 135, 177–78
    integrity and, 163
    methods, 58–59, 152

Recruitment (*continued*)
  monitoring, 151–53
  referrals, 98, 127–28, 152–54
  sampling methods, 127–28
  staff training, 161
  strategies, 57–58
Referrals, 98, 127–28, 152–54. *See also*
  Recruitment
Regression models, 133
Reimbursement issues, 67. *See also*
  Payment
Release-of-information forms, 140,
  149, 153
Reliability, 131–32
Repeatability. *See* Validity
Replicability. *See* Validity
Reporting criteria, validity, 178–81,
  180*f*, 181*f*
Research, 23
Research personnel, 34–35, 161–63.
  See also Providers
Research question/control condition,
  87–90
Research *vs.* program evaluation, 7–8
RESPECT, 66
Respect, 21–23
Retention monitoring, 153–57
Ribisl, K. M., 114, 148, 149
Rosen, A., 67
Rothbard, A., 185

Sampling, 122–23
  capacity/fully-powered RCT,
    123–24
  challenges in, 135
  ethics, 38–39, 126
  inclusion/exclusion criteria,
    124–26, 127*f*, 135
  method/recruitment, 127–28
  quota, 128

size/power, 128–29
  snowball, 128
Scared Straight intervention, 22
Scope, 4–5
Scouting research, 53–55
Service system, 110–11, 123
Settings, 46
  cooperation in, 145–47
  negotiations, 49–52, 52*t*, 97
  preparation, 139–45
  in retention, 157
  selection, 47–49, 54
  validity measures, 177
Shadowing, 165
Site selection, 47–49, 54. *See also*
  Settings
Site visits, 165
Snijders, T.A.B., 85–87, 86*f*
Social capital formulation, 86–87, 86*f*
Social Enhancement Workbooks,
  67–68
Solomon, P., 24, 88–89, 152
Solomon four-group design, 103–4
Speaker-Listener Technique, 68
Statistical analysis, 134
Stratification randomization, 117–18
Substance abuse, 37, 125, 167
Substance Abuse and Mental Health
  Services Administration
  (SAMHSA), 64, 183
Suicidal ideation, 41–43, 185
Systematic reviews, 13–14,
  181–84, 186

TAU (treatment-as-usual), 25, 47, 87,
  108, 130, 185
Termination responsibilities, 38, 63
Testing, 103
Theory as foundation for RCTs, 80–82
Thyer, B., 17

Time-limited/control conditions in, 88
Tracking of participants, 148–51, 150*t*–151*t*, 155, 156
Training, 157–63
  control-condition staff, 161
  evidence-based practice, 159
  human subject protection, 34, 157
  manuals, 158
  of providers, 63, 77, 158–60
  in randomization, 158
  research staff, 161–63
Treatment access, factors affecting, 3–4
Treatment-as-usual (TAU), 25, 47, 87, 108, 130, 185
Treatment manuals
  applications of, 61–63
  care standards, 62
  client–provider relationship, 62
  criticisms of, 63–64
  definitions, 60–61
  development of, 65–71, 79
  evidence-based practice, 69–71
  fidelity assessment, 71–78
  focus groups/in-depth interviews, 67–68
  identification of, 64–65
  intervention specifications, 62
  practice guidelines, 67
  provider selection/training/supervision, 63, 77, 158–60
  special issue protocols, 62
  support/resource relationships, 63
  transitions/terminations, 63
Tuskegee Syphilis Study, 22, 39

Untested interventions, ethics of, 24–25

Validity
  attrition and, 112, 113
  construct, 172
  contamination control, 105–7
  ecological, 172
  efficacy *vs.* effectiveness studies, 9, 11
  external, 170–71
    defined, 171–72
    factors affecting, 152, 176–78
    neglect of, 176
    procedures, 172–76
    reporting criteria, 178–81, 180*f*, 181*f*
  fidelity assessment, 71–78, 108, 134, 163–66, 173
  gold standards for, 122
  inclusion/exclusion criteria in, 124–26, 127*f*
  internal, 109–11, 135, 173, 178–81
  measures, 177, 178
  multi-site RCTs, 174–75
  outcome measurement, 133
  restrictions in, 10
Van Der Gaag, M., 85–87, 86*f*
Variables, 90–91
  contamination of, 109–11
  operationalization of, 129–30

Waiting list controls, 25–26, 28
Walker, J., 70
Wilber, C., 160
Witte, G., 24, 160
Working Alliance Inventory, 168